It is not I who seek
the horse,

the
horse
seeks
me

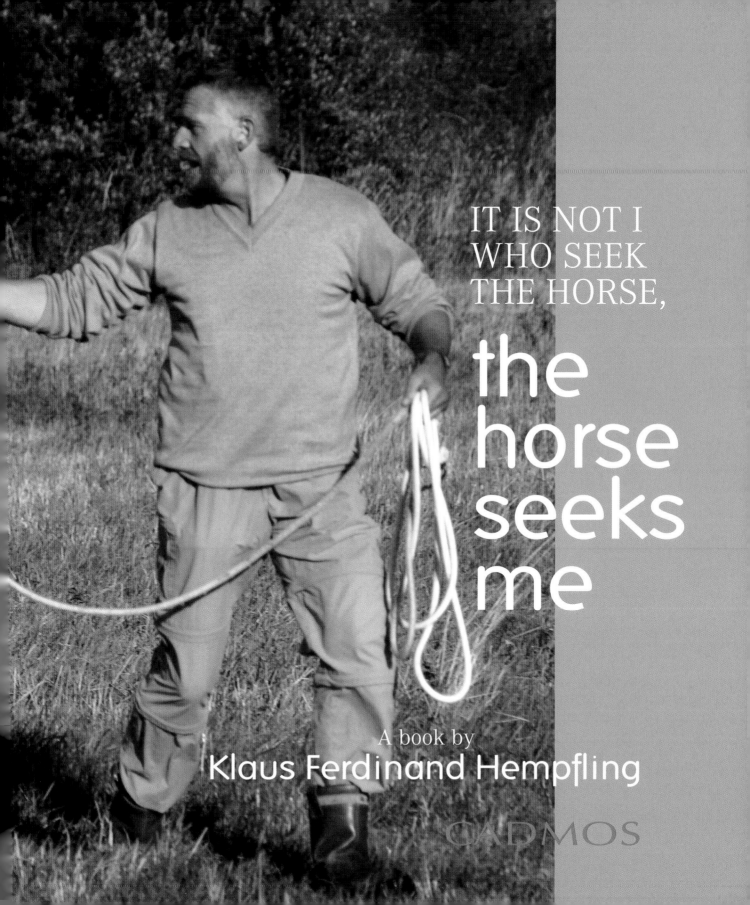

IT IS NOT I
WHO SEEK
THE HORSE,

the horse seeks me

A book by
Klaus Ferdinand Hempfling

CADMOS

Imprint

Copyright © 2010 by Uitgeverij Rozhanitsa, Kampen, The Netherlands

Copyright of this edition © 2010 by Cadmos Publishing Ltd., London

English translation: Helen McKinnon

Title photograph: KFH Archive

Cover design: Ravenstein + Partner, Verden, Germany

Design and Layout: Bert van het Ende, Uitgeverij Rozhanitsa, Kampen, The Netherlands

Photographs: KFH Archive, unless otherwise stated

Illustrations: Malene Lütken

Original graphics on pages 303, 304 and 305 by Klaus Ferdinand Hempfling

The photos on the following pages are by Margriet Markerink: P. 49 (both pictures), P. 172 (three bottom pictures), P. 173 (two bottom pictures), P. 174 (middle picture), P. 218, P. 219, P. 229

The photos on the following pages are by Wieke Wijnalda: P. 162/163, P. 172 (top picture), P. 174 (top picture), P. 175

Editorial: Christopher Long

Printed by: Grafisches Cetrum Cuno, Calbe

British Library Cataloguing in Publication Data catalogue record of this book is available from the British Library.

Printed in Germany

ISBN 978-3-86127-975-4

www.cadmos.co.uk

'KLAUS FERDINAND HEMPFLING is widely regarded as a master of equine body language. This book is the long-awaited follow up to the author's international bestseller, *Dancing with Horses*, now regarded as a classic all over the world. In this long-awaited new groundbreaking book, he shares the foundation of his profound insights into his unique art.

Here, Klaus Ferdinand Hempfling takes the reader to the very heart of his world of understanding horses. Using detailed, step-by-step illustrations and photographs, he shows us the basics and the first moments of togetherness with a horse, as well as the various types of development that leads up to the very highest levels of riding.

The development of different horses has been captured in minutely detailed photo-graphs, commissioned especially for this book. The result is a unique and intimate documentation of the work of this exceptional horseman'. (Horses for Life)

In his own words, Hempfling says: 'I've ventured forward in many different respects with this book. In it, I write about lots of methods, emotions, states and practical experiences, for the first time. On a one-to-one basis, I describe how I come close to horses, how I lead them to themselves and persuade them to break out of their inner and outer shells, so that they may finally dance freely. It has really got it all.'

The book is a remarkably rich work, filled with practical, theoretical and spiritual references – a must for any rider or horse lover, whatever their discipline.

WORKING WITH HORSES USING KLAUS' METHODS not only offers us the potential for a close relationship with the horse, it also offers us the key to unlock our inner depths, our intuition and our spirituality, to find our purpose, our peace.

'The Organic Equine', New Zealand

I HAVE NEVER SEEN A NATURAL HORSEMAN LIKE HIM. Whether you appreciate or not what this man does with horses, you will leave his workshops with an incredible amount of food for thought and you will never approach horses in quite the same way again.

'Horses for LIFE'

Contents

PART 2

The complete compendium for the natural handling of horses, based
on authentic personality development and development of awareness.

Like a cloud falling from the sky

Shortly after I finished writing this book, 12-year-old PRE stallion Harmón came into my life.

A course participant brought him to one of my compact schoolings. This impressive being had grown apart from his owner and she subsequently handed him over to various professional trainers, leading to his psychological and spiritual death. The video clip *Breeding Stallion Harmón Reborn* tells us this story, but also about the horse that he became after I had worked with him for around 2 weeks. No more depression, no more sadness - but trust, happiness and exuberance instead. In that course I described the stallion as Pegasus, saying "This kind of horse is like a cloud that floats between heaven and earth, full of gentleness. There is power within him, strength and the potential to amass violently, but also the ability to simply disappear". In my book, *What horses reveal*, I write that this kind of horse may simply evaporate if you do not understand how to live with the lightness of a cloud, with its freedom. The stallion came back to his owner. She tried and then she let the young horse cover a mare. Seconds later he fell down in front of her – dead. Like a cloud falling from the sky. It keeps appearing in my book – splendid, powerful, gentle. What does it tell us?

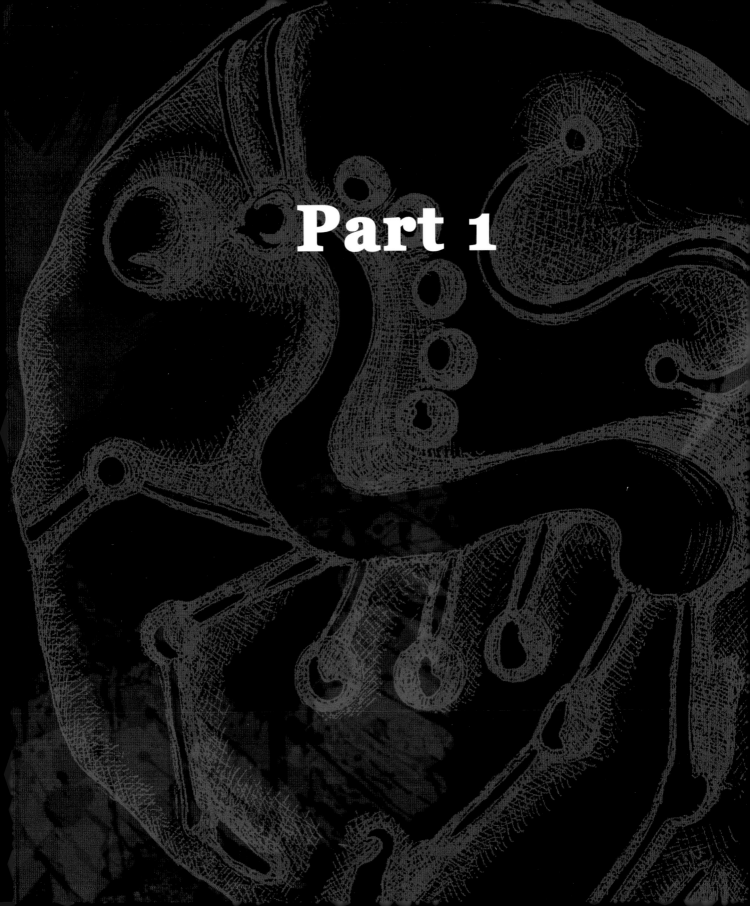

Part 1

Closeness to a horse
never comes
from the desire
for closeness.

Closeness to a horse
comes only
from closeness
to one's inner self.

Klaus Ferdinand Hempfling

The practical
and spiritual
foundations of
life with horses

About the structure of this book

Two recent events form the practical backbone of this book. Both were captured in detailed photographs, to document and describe the essence of my work with horses more explicitly than ever before. Together, both events essentially form the entire foundations of my practical work with horses. The first event was the arrival of an Arab stallion, Marouk. He arrived exactly three days late, primarily because of one of his 'problems': he was difficult to load. This 'problem' was supposed to be, indeed had to be, solved urgently. After I had worked with the stallion six times for around 15–20 minutes each time over a period of three days, he followed me happily and confidently into the trailer with a rope loosely around his neck.

This story is essentially very short, but it is interesting because the horse actually had an abundance of behavioural patterns that all had to be resolved first. The result is an account of a short, yet long journey that takes us from discovery to solution, then to the next discovery and again on to the next solution. The dynamic that lies within these processes and that fundamentally characterises my work will become very clear in this example. The documentation of this process shows the basic path that I take to get closer and closer to horses precisely looking directly at their problems or injuries, one after the other, in their interests and in terms of their healing and growth, to 'clean and heal' them. Horses are considerably less complicated than people, so it is a very easy process, providing the conditions are right, namely the conditions within ourselves. I explain all of the practical and theoretical details in relation to this first key story, to further draw out the essentials in detail.

A second event forms the next important pillar as the book progresses: the arrival of the Lusitano stallion, Queijo. Naturally, I started off by getting to know him, in the same way as with Marouk. The photographs and illustrations in this book explain clearly the fundamental principle involved, and show how Queijo learnt to 'dance', his long journey to physical liberation and 'rediscovery' of himself.

In essence, this is the foundation of my practical work with horses, from the ground up.

Part of the problem or part of the solution?

If you consider the whole, you are clearly not yet considering everything. I have included a brief chapter at the beginning of this book that describes the humans' relationship to animals and the environment from two fundamentally different perspectives. I only added this chapter later on, and I have to admit I deliberated for a long time as to whether to include it at all. In the end, the balance was tipped by the era in which we currently live.

It's spring 2009, the world is staggering under a global crisis, the like of which we have never experienced before, but what does this have to do with horses? A great deal, strangely enough, because, like no other important mythological figure, horses have always simultaneously represented man's two paths: namely the path where man is part of the problem, and the path where man smoothly and simply becomes part of the solution, and then feels at home both with himself and in himself. In fact, that is the essence of the situation that occurs every time a person is confronted with a real live horse.

The rider is either part of the problem, or part of the solution. I have had to learn to be cautious with descriptions like this and wait carefully for the right moment. I hope that this is it.

Calling a spade a spade

This is also new. I will explicitly compare the three possible ways of being with horses in a later chapter. There are many variations, but fundamentally, three basic principles can be attributed to each of the ways. It seems to me that the time has come where I can no longer put off highlighting misunderstandings and mistakes that have caused a great deal of confusion, especially in recent years.

In the end, togetherness with horses is always a question of trust and dominance. In the book *Dancing with Horses*, I explicitly introduced this concept into the horse world and described the inner relationship between the two. But what is often the reality? Instead of dominance and trust, we often find different types of training that actually 'bypass' each of these qualities, creating a kind of pretence. And after all, pretence is how many a wolf has worn sheep's clothing.

Focus on practical work with horses

In my practical work, I now stick very closely to a didactic path which leads from 'spiritual, holistic perception' to the 'physical' consideration of the distinct authentic experience. Finally this leads to the question of how that can be expressed and used in encounters with horses. This book breathes that spirit, but it is still primarily focused on practical work with horses.

More books are expected to follow that will explain the other areas in more detail.

Riding a horse has been presented as a very global quantity in this book. I did not want to go into things I have already written about, but having said that, I wanted to re-present the phenomenon of riding as an authentic, holistic experience. It is an attempt to bring a superordinate concept full circle and to go into the practical details in greater depth, at the same time.

Scarcely perceptible traces

The title of this book is obviously risky. For one thing, it is far too long, and it also runs the risk of appearing to depart from actual practical experience. Yet the complete opposite is true. It is practical experience, and being with these large, fast, powerful and potentially dangerous creatures, which means that this sentence is entirely born out of practice. Two or three books could be written about this sentence alone, but I will spare my readers that and stick to two or three pages, safe in the knowledge that we will agree about so many things at the end. In particular, I am sure we will agree about those scarcely perceptible traces that have not been covered by this book, but that can hopefully be read between the lines.

All that remains to be said is that this book can be understood as such and on its own. However, many of the technical principles about working in a Picadero, with and without ropes, and about the aids used in riding and communicating with the horse from the ground, are described in my first book, *Dancing with Horses*. You can find the basic principles for recognising the nature of a horse in the book, *What Horses Reveal*.

Looking back over nearly 20 years of teaching experience, I am doing what I can to pass on what I believe I know in this book. I do not hesitate to speak my mind, and on that note ...

Klaus Ferdinand Hempfling
Lyoe, Denmark, April 2010

We will meet Queijo (a ten-year-old Lusitano stallion) frequently throughout this book. He came to me for four weeks of training. I would like to use his example to illustrate the change that horses undergo when you give them both freedom and stability, then every horse will begin to dance – in his own unique way.

When the eight-year-old Arab stallion Marouk arrived at the training farm, he was very wild. His owner had had problems leading him, he had become aggressive and he was difficult to load. This book describes in detail the path that the author and the stallion travelled during their first three days together.

We are concerned with the horse

But the horse is concerned with the world and what goes on in it

Make a change?

A few days ago a man from Austria sent me an e-mail in which he wrote 'not losing optimism in the face of the realities of this world and all of the enormous global threats seems to me to be virtually impossible'. His letter continued, 'You obviously seem to manage it, but if people no longer know who they really are, how can they possibly be in a position to change anything?'

When I talk about horses, I cannot ignore the world and the life that goes on in it. It is related to the actual behaviour of the horses, and at the same time, to their significance as an ancient symbol. To get a better understanding and to grasp the immediate and general world around me, I turned to horses, on the trail of myths and mythology, traditions and those dreams that once drew me as a child to the legends of our fathers and their heroes.

Today I know that really positive, authentic togetherness with a horse is always based on a positive, authentic approach to life. A horse can see through any mask. He can recognise sadness, despondency, fear and despair, but also inner strength, calmness and happiness, and he reacts accordingly.

If I am faced with a personal problem, I start by trying to find a structure, a kind of order. That is also of fundamental importance when dealing with horses. Working with horses really forces us to achieve the greatest possible clarity, otherwise things rapidly become problematic, annoying and frustrating, not to mention dangerous. The magic is lost. Working with horses forces us to look very closely. Every illusion, every deceptive facade and every falsification of reality has direct consequences that are reflected to us ad hoc. That is what is unique about working with horses, that you cannot hide anything from them. The precision with which they can reflect what is hidden in us, through their behaviour, in their own unique way, is unsur-

passed. With horses, there is a very distinct line between illusion and reality.

Does it make sense to transfer these authentic qualities required by horses to life in general? Does it help us to separate things, which only reveal their true essence when they are separated and distinguished from each other, so that we can finally make them manageable? I am convinced that it does. To me, it seems that learning to differentiate personal states from historical and societal ones is particularly helpful. This is so important to me for the basic understanding of my work that I would like to go into it at least briefly in these first pages. That still leaves lots of space for purely practical experiences.

As a rule, a problem or a challenge represents a kind of overlap. Relating to existence itself, the overlap usually comes when personal perception, experience, hope and desire meet our communal, social, historical and political reality. However, how do you differentiate them today? Or, in the words of my correspondent, 'Not losing optimism in the face of the realities of this world and all of the enormous global threats seems to me to be virtually impossible.'

Without basic trust in life, without optimism and without great joy in life, I could not go to the horses that I am called to. In order to achieve these things I first have to make some very precise differentiations. What is the world of horses or animals anyway? What is the modern world? What is the world of myths? What is my world? Using simple structures, I would like to illustrate how looking at conditions in an organising and relativising way opens up new approaches and new opportunities, however hopeless the endeavour may seem at first. If horses have taught me one thing, it is that there is always a way, always a solution – always. For as long as I live, there will also be an authentic place for me. That much is certain. The challenge is finding it.

About how we deal with animals, plants and the environment
A statement for the beginning

This is my opinion. It is based entirely on practical experiences with horses, on life in general and on concurrent traditions from a wide variety of cultures and their eras.

For the description, I am taking the concept of the so-called modern, 'Western' world. This Western world, in particular, forms a simple structure (diagram 1 p. 29).

Humans are on the first level, and everything else – animals, plants and our environment as a whole – is on the level below. This model appears only too natural, if you simply take as its basis all of the skills that humans appear to possess and master, in contrast to animals or plants. However, if I follow this model myself, I cannot come up with a result that satisfies me, or horses.

Ancient cultures give a completely different picture (diagram 2 p. 29).

Here, there are also two levels. However, the relationships are now the other way around. Here, humans are subordinate to everything else. At first glance it does seem quite strange, but our culture also contains references to this kind of view, for example in the Bible's Creation story, when God says to the animals:, 'Let us make man.'

Ancient cultures differentiate the picture in another very interesting way (diagram 3 p. 29).

According to this view, people are on the first level, along with animals and plants, at the moment of their birth and during their childhood. Is that why children generally get along so well with animals and seem to enjoy a more direct and intuitive approach to horses? This view pushes humans down to the lower levels almost automatically during their socialisation and maturation. They then lose their original, authentic connection with the natural world.

We can now complete the first level with the concept of authenticity (diagram 4 p. 29).

Here, another concept is allocated to the second level: unconsciousness. We can now clearly illustrate what happens if human beings, or rather, archetypal, Western human beings, interact with animals, plants and the environment generally and fundamentally as the result of this view (diagram 5 p. 29).

The 'modern human' as an archetype does indeed experience and feel himself consciously and unconsciously on the 'first level'. Dealing with animals, plants and the environment means to him that he raises those structures to his level that, in his perception, are situated 'below' him. Consciously and subconsciously, he creates and 'shapes' a 'new', 'higher', 'better' order according to his own understanding. He imposes 'order' on the (original) world, 'regulates' the behavior and 'sorts' those natural structures that he perceives as little more than chaotic. We can still marvel at some of the excesses of the human mania for organisation and control, for example at the Palace of Versailles, residence of the Sun King, Louis XIV, where no blade of grass or tree branch would dare to grow out of place. Even ancient forms of human life were and are still this regimented today.

If we continue to follow the traditional archetypes, the exact opposite happens in reality. Man, having outgrown his childhood and thus been robbed of his authentic life form, believes that he is reorganising on a higher level, whereas in reality he is forcing the natural elements of his environment down to his own 'lower level'. In the consequent belief that he is organising, refining and perfecting, he destroys the natural structures of order that he simply cannot comprehend and that, indeed, frighten him. The result is always and inevitably destruction, disorder and reduction of energy. Applied on a global scale, it will inevitably lead to global catastrophe. It is only a matter of time.

At least two different things happen on an individual level:

People feel greater or lesser degrees of alienation from all environments. They long for authenticity, for closeness to themselves and to their environment. However, the more effort people make, by using purely cognitive, human and uninspired principles as a basis, i.e. 'organising' in their limited sense, the more despairing they become, until resignation takes over. Even if this human principle of organisation is used 'successfully', the inner void, the inner loneliness, will come ever closer as a result. A vicious circle is created, socially, politically and individually.

If we believe these traditions, and all of my experiences confirm them to be correct, then there is a kind of order on the second level, i.e. on the level of the (unconscious) human, which is supported in two ways. On the one hand, the understanding of use and benefit, i.e. one thing is done so that the other results from it. These benefits are shaped by a kind of cognitive/logical sequence. As a result, the available elements and natural resources are also consistently subject to this principle of use and benefits. Now everything has a purpose, a benefit, and will also be used.

On the other hand, this thinking always follows a timeline. This person's experience is orientated towards a benefit in terms of time, i.e. I do something today so that I can benefit from it tomorrow or next year.

Humans	———————————————— 1
Animals, plants, environment	———————————— 2

1

Animals, plants, environment	———————————— 1
Humans	———————————————— 2

2

Children, animals, plants, environment	———————— 1
(adult) Humans	———————————————— 2

3

Level of authenticity, children, animals, plants, environment	———————— 1
(adult - unconscious) Humans	———————— 2

4

Level of authenticity, animals, plants	———————— 1
Modern (unconscious) humans, animals, plants	———————— 2

5

Level of authenticity

Level of authenticity, level of conscious authentic humans, children, animals, plants, environment	———————— 1
Level of unconscious humans	———————— 2

6

Children do the exact opposite. They do not live and experience on a timeline, but in the present, and they do not see the benefit of things, but their holistic synergy, their interaction and the power and the magic, the mystic and the fairytale that are hidden inside – precisely the superordinate natural order that, in reality, connects everything. That is why they innately move in the natural world of animals and horses.

Now we have the opportunity to complete our 'original diagram' (diagram 6).

Now a meaning can be recognised in the long journey through life of any person, because they have the opportunity 'to be like a child again'. If they become conscious of their true state and condition, they stop their 'ordering' activities and instead orientate themselves to their inner authentic roots. They can then become aware of another, much larger order structure and experience it directly. They experience inner growth, develop their very own meaning and, as a result, enter the level of the beings with which they now feel directly connected, instead of fighting and destroying them.

This has been the way of humans since time immemorial. They then become an authentic part of the whole. Meaning is no longer a question of benefit and logic, but of immediate experience. In our Western culture, this way was embodied and symbolised by the process of consciousness and nobility. The fusion of the spiritual in humans with the bestial in animals formed the image of St George on his horse,

conqueror of the 'dragon as a symbol of chaos', patron saint of all knights and still a potent symbol and emblem in many parts of Europe today. The fact that the noble concepts of knight and knighthood were lost with the passage of time changes nothing about their origins in terms of history and content.

This 'cycle' has always been a firmly anchored part of human meaning. The path of man has been described in this way in all cultures. However, what differentiates us as modern people from our ancestors is a very simple fact. Nowadays, human life and experience on the 'second level' is desired, encouraged and the universally accepted norm. Our daily existence is based on this now socially legitimate fallacy. This has never happened before in the history of humanity. The outsider is not the person on the 'second level', who believes themselves to be enduring it. Instead, it's the person who wants to develop inside. The person who destroys the rainforest does not have to justify himself, while the people who want to protect it arouse suspicion. People who torture scores of animals for breeding and slaughter do not have to justify themselves, but those who denounce these practices do. The person who tortures horses with bridle, spurs and whip is not the one who is chased through the village streets like a rabid dog, but it is the one who is able and willing to do without these things.

I have invested a great deal of time in examining the question of how our social structure and image of humanity could have developed historically in this way. The answers I found were surprising, but to describe and formulate them would require another book.

Nearly 20 years after the publication of my first book, the world looks different. It is in danger of breaking down. Nobody can ignore it any longer, not even the very ignorant. That may sound profane, but what happens on a small scale often happens on a large scale too. As long as somebody tries to dominate a horse on the 'second level', progressive alienation will keep happening. Now humans really are the problem itself. It is the same with the world as a whole. We try to meddle everywhere, whole or half-heartedly, but the more we try to fiddle on this 'low' level, the more of a mess we get into globally. On the whole, recognition of the modern world's fundamental misconception would be the only way out. But that is not what we are concerned with at the moment.

Regarding our subject, we could say the following – when should we open up as individuals, in order to finally accept the gift of life, i.e. authenticity and closeness, if not when together with the horse, that ancient symbol of human, inner elevation and growth? In an authentic way of life, where feeling, thinking, acting and dreaming merge into a related experience, we do not need to worry about not being able to solve the problems that arise, because most of them will not occur at all.

Of skippers and knights

The early human communities had surprisingly consistent structures and comparatively similar forms, despite existing in different times and regions. As an individual, each person experienced themselves firstly through the social structures in which they lived. The different coloured circles in diagram I represent people in this way of life, with varying skills, qualities and opportunities.

In this way of life, skills, talents and characteristics were exchanged and combined together. Depending on their personal situation, a person occupied either a prominent or a more background position. The bottom line was that the individual qualities were not judged, but merely noted. Threats from outside the community, disturbances or even attacks of any kind were faced by the community as a collective of individuals that manifested the true nature of their life's reality only through their togetherness.

The reality of life in our modern world shows a picture that has mutated over the centuries, from extended family to nuclear family, and finally to singledom. As a pure fact we can establish that the development away from community has led to its endpoint today – the phenomenon of more and more people living alone. Now it is almost exclusively our own skin alone that forms the boundary against the outside, against external threats, disorder or attacks. To continue to

31

Long before the author was interested in the nature of horses, he followed the traces of our ancestors. In the end, they led him not just to horses themselves, but straight to the kind of interaction with them to which he is dedicated today.

The author at one of his 'Borderline' events with horses that strongly resist human influence and are considered to be extremely difficult. His motto is: 'In an authentic way of life, we don't need to worry about not being able to solve problems that arise, because most of them won't even occur at all.'

survive successfully as a 'closed organism', many skills, indicated by the coloured circles, must more or less be combined in one single person (diagram 2). How's that for a challenge?

The associations above allow us to transfer this second component to the previous diagram showing the two levels (diagram 3).

For this diagram, I have selected terms relatively non-specifically and arranged them to show that, by way of an example, a fulfilled and happy farmer or craftsman 'in an authentically harmonised way of life' does not essentially require the awareness of a samurai or a medicine man or a knight, or the human reliability of a ship's captain or a skipper etc. (which, of course, does not mean that he cannot develop them, and which is not supposed to mean that countless farmers, craftsmen and traders have not done so). All in all, however, the samurai would happily enjoy the farmer's products, and by the same token, the farmer would be happy to live under the protection of the samurai, and both would be thankful to hear the advice of the elders, the medicine men and the shamans. In brief, people have never been required to follow this steep and laborious path to consciousness to its greatest heights alone. It was only important that one knew the significance and the meaning contained, as an individual. Within an intact, authentic community and culture, each individual could add the energies and strengths particular to themselves, and automatically participate in

the rewards. The group as a whole, and therefore to a certain extent each individual in it, was also connected on traditional spiritual levels and integrated into a natural cycle, through the sum of its members and their varied experiences.

These structures have widely broken down and, where they still exist, they are mostly already in the process of collapse. I believe that being essentially connected with what I have described on these pages as the 'first authentic

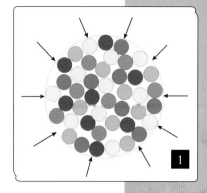

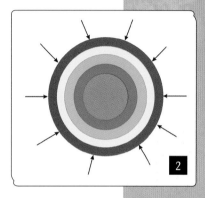

Ways of life from ancient cultures, authentically harmonised with each other.

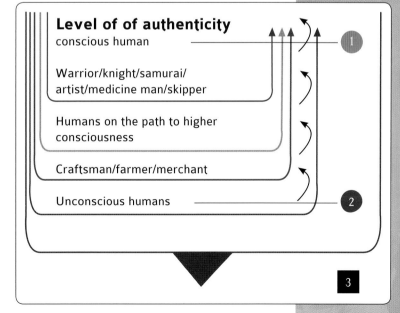

level' is crucial to being able to live and experience authentically. I have therefore come to the conclusion that each individual person would have to combine a great many of these qualities in themselves, especially within the structure of existence that we most commonly find today. As we know, this is not the case in the reality of our lives – quite the opposite. The consequence is a cultural and societal reality that is primarily characterised by the loss of consciousness, sensuality, naturalness, authenticity, basic sense of trust and relativised self-perception, on the broadest level. The horse world, as a relatively small part of current events, reflects this to the same extent as other areas. The shortcomings have now become so obvious that awareness of them has already reached many levels of society; indeed, fundamental knowledge about them has now reached almost everywhere.

A conclusion

All of this brings me to this very personal temporary conclusion. We live in a world that demands the absolute maximum from each individual. The external protective structures that have formed, with, rather than against, the principles of nature, over an inconceivably long period of time, have been largely destroyed and replaced by a system of use and benefits, of reduction and apparent order, that is now visibly collapsing for everyone. It may recover itself again, or its collapse may slow down, but the global impotence of these resource-devouring structures, at the expense of our own foundations for life and the sensitive structures of all natural processes, is becoming clear to everyone as never before.

The individual is no longer preserved and protected in an authentic, connected and natural-law structure. Each individual can now only connect to themselves and/or try to experience the appropriate exchange, support, contact and involvement by building a personal network structure of very superior quality. But that requires people to use their own initiative! The original structures and foundations for doing so, which had evolved culturally and historically, the expression of individual, ethnic peculiarities and formerly generally accessible knowledge about nature, have been almost completely destroyed.

We are concerned with the horse, but as a symbol the horse is concerned with the world and what goes on in it. In practical terms, the intrinsic training and moulding of a horse requires this inner resolution, this 'consciousness'.

That is my view of the situation and the enormously exciting task facing people today, sketched out in a few words. Fundamentally, it is no different from the demands placed on our ancestors. People have always fought this crucial battle in and against themselves and followed the path to consciousness in their own way, but never before have they been so isolated and never before have they had to try so hard just to reach the start of the path, because the gate that leads to this path has never been as hidden as it is now. Yet the balance is within creation. But what could be in the tiny pan on the other side of the scales? What could possibly weigh so heavily? Us! Each individual who sets out in life.

GUIDING PRINCIPLES – HERE ARE A FEW MORE OF MY VERY PERSONAL GUIDING PRINCIPLES:

• Trust and belief can cross a boundary, beyond which they change into knowledge.

• Personal, inner development and the resulting inner enrichment and peace are always accompanied by stabilisation of external social contacts and structures. A friendship develops over years, but it can be destroyed in a single, careless moment.

• Fate can teach you or be your mentor. Solitude can teach you, togetherness and coexistence with people as well. Any moment can teach you and any person can be your teacher. People who ignore that tend to be one-sided and miss out on the richness of life, but we need this abundance and all of the facets of this world.

• Authentic experience is like hearing a beautiful melody that rings out deep inside you, but this melody is so quiet that you have to consciously listen for it all of the time. You should always be thinking of it.

• Spiritual and physical wellbeing is the basis of every authentic experience. You have to devote all of your attention to it – everything else should take second place.

• Our body is like a vast meeting place. We can only encounter nature, our spirituality, our fate and the powers of creation, through and within our bodies. It is essential that you know your body, so that you can trust it and be at home in it. Take lots of time to do this.

• The past is not static. The future is now. The past is what the present makes of it, so present is everything. That is why the times of human maturity and old age are so significant. It is only in old age that the past appears in its final meaning, it becomes clear and it is only in old age that fate reveals to us its plan. Do not allow early success to blind you – early failure and hardship should only make you stronger. Success that comes too early often turns out to be false, while apparent failure can turn into victory.

• People who judge and assess believe that they know everything, while people who do not judge at all do not worry about what they know or don't know. They confine themselves to differentiating and discovering what belongs with what, so that everything can be allocated to its pre-determined place. Harmony can be created in this way. That is why judgement and assessment are always at

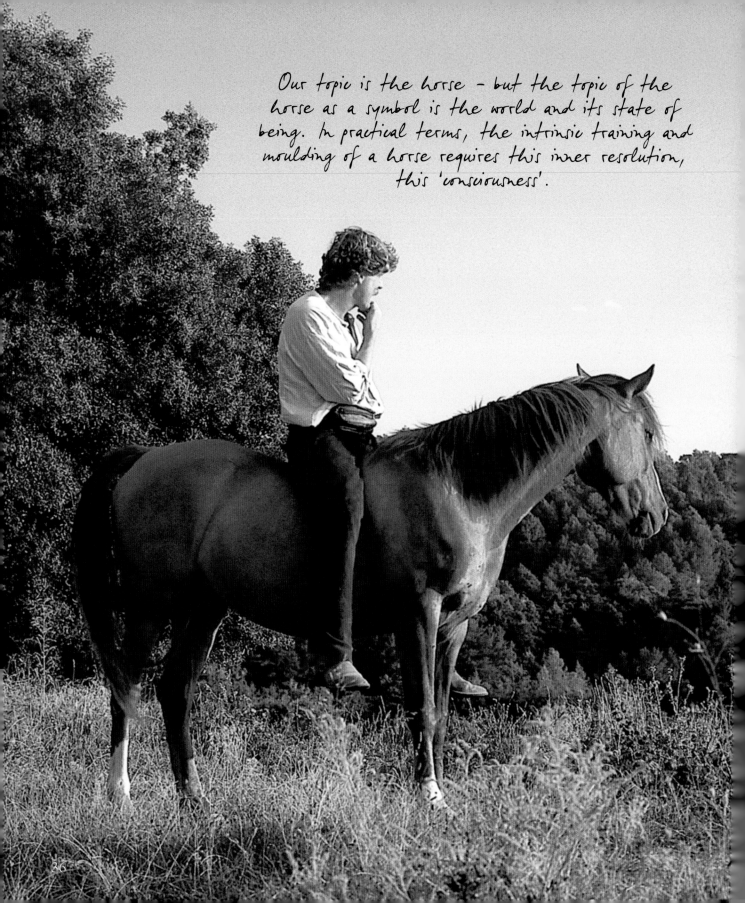

Our topic is the horse — but the topic of the horse as a symbol is the world and its state of being. In practical terms, the intrinsic training and moulding of a horse requires this inner resolution, this 'consciousness'.

Each individual can now only connect to themselves and/or try to experience the appropriate exchange, support, contact and involvement by building a personal network structure of very superior quality. But that requires people to use their own initiative!

When I write about my togetherness with horses
today, I am writing about authenticity,
about the home within myself and about
the path that I have had to travel so far
and that I must continue to travel.

My togetherness with horses can scarcely be
understood and classified without fundamental
understanding of the existence of this path.

the start of chaos and ignorance, while the ability to differentiate is always at the start of harmony and fulfilment.

It is not I who seek the horse, the horse seeks me . . .

… on which of the two levels? One is the superficial desire to act; the other is being ready, acting as a result of inspiration. One pursues the implementation of one's own structures, one's own will. The other rests in the devotion and in the deeper significance that one bestows upon oneself through inner dignity. One is the worry and the frenzy; the other one is the faith, the calmness and the knowledge that what is meant to come together will come together. If not today, then tomorrow. It is the unconditional respect for the inner and outer dignity of all beings, the recognition of a secret path in the existence of all creatures and the faith that these paths may intersect. Not following an order that appears absolutely stringent and logical to us humans, but following an order that teaches insight and wisdom.

One wants to be seen. The other one remains hidden, renounces external appearances, yet knows the inner forces that communicate with each other and attract each other even at great distances.

One seeks salvation in the detail. The other one sees the whole, the unifying qualities in even the smallest details. One rather wants to seduce, to manipulate, to control and to stack the odds in its favor, whenever possible. The other wants to run its course, wants to be a malleable material in the process of constant creation, of becoming and passing away.

One seeks stasis and mourns that which is transient; the other joins the forces of constant change and consequently becomes more and more a part of a perfect order. One wants power to cover up its own fears. The other wants strength in order to overcome its own fears. One seeks the development of superficial appearances in the world. The other develops itself. One observes external things. The other becomes a sensitive observer of its own life …

… One seeks the horse; the other lets the horse find them, because they:

are credible,

set an example,

radiate inner confidence,

are trustworthy,

clear and unambiguous,

relaxed and quiet,

peaceful,

positive,

hopeful,

balanced and controlled.

And because they keep on testing themselves and find much that they do not like, but still remain cheerful and confident. Possibly because they never doubt that they 'will fulfil the fateful meaning of their life.'

Riding as a holistic experience

*Summary and moving on to a slightly
different way of being with horses*

Like the eagle, the bear, or contrastingly, the
snake, the horse is one of the most important
symbolic animals in all ancient cultures – surprisingly even in those in which there were
no horses.

Upon closer consideration, you could even
describe the horse as the king of all symbols.
Horses symbolise qualities of being, that in
many respects, are directly opposed to those
of our modern world, although according to
anthropologists, our culture could never have
existed without horses.

We can choose to look beyond the evolu-
tion of the horse as a partner for leisure and
sport to discover a quite different, and indeed
virtually boundless world. If we follow the trails
of myths and the words of our ancestors, then
authentic, natural handling of horses has never
been a kind of sporting skill, but primarily a
mental exercise whose aim is a form of spiritual
meeting or encounter. This aspect gains a whole
new significance, in all areas of the human being,
especially in this time when violent threat is all
around us.

That is my opinion. Yet if togetherness with
a horse is supposed to be a unique meeting, it
can only happen if you strive to comprehend
the whole event in the simplest essential terms.

The horse then becomes a partner for meditation and a unique, objective reference to reality.
Personal development and the meeting with the
authentic self, resting within itself, are the goals
and no longer a superficial benefit, vanity or
profit.

This all requires a certain mental attitude
that everyone must either bring with them or
make their own. This mental attitude protects
people from constantly believing that they are
losing something, or that they have to hold on
to something with great strength. It allows people to dip into the simplest and most natural
event, with the certainty that they are protected
and supported by the creative forces that are far
more powerful than us humans.

The mental attitude that I am talking about
has much to do with becoming spiritually and
physically aware, and the ability to constantly
relativise one's own appearance. I do everything
I can to make sure that I always maintain and
experience a very direct reference to reality. That
is why I hold in such high regard methods of
meditation that have a practical connection, for
example, archery, sword fighting, hunting for
food or being with horses. Handling horses,
in particular, requires this direct reference to
reality. It protects us against losing the ground
beneath our feet as we try to meet our authentic
selves.

Progress on this path is naturally completely
different from progress that only follows technical skill and principles. Progress may not come

What could possibly
weigh so heavily?

Us!
Each individual who sets out in life

for a long time, and then may appear suddenly and surprisingly, like an unexpected meeting or like an event that you had stopped believing could happen.

On all sides, and in the most diverse areas, people are remembering to bring together each authentic quality of being, feeling and acting, believing and thinking.

I have developed and continue to develop my work with horses with this in mind.

Assembly, expression, balance –
Riding as a holistic experience

Authentic, natural handling of horses has
never been a kind of sporting skill, but primarily
a mental exercise whose aim is a form of
spiritual meeting or encounter

Body language in detail 1

An initial approach
with practical examples

What is body language?

What does a bird know about the size of the world
when he flies?
What does a horse know about his strength
when the wind plays in his mane?

When the soul dances with my body
there is no 'why', 'what for' and 'where to?'
All of the answers can be found immediately
in the movements themselves.

I don't do, I experience.
I don't try, I perceive.
I don't worry, I'm astounded.

That is how the invisible shapes the visible,
moves, renews and changes it.
The body becomes the authentic and
diverse instrument of the self-aware person;
a sensitive way of expressing their individual personality.
That is my understanding of body language.

Klaus Ferdinand Hempfling

Form is determined by precise, pared-down simplicity

What I experience with horses is, above all, a question of very practical, clearly formulated communication: a certain gesture, for example, or a sequence of different gestures and energetic information. Feelings and emotions become a clear expression, as precise as possible. I experience emotions, feelings and non-verbal exchanges as something very exact, which is then conveyed clearly and unambiguously to the horse. That is a very important factor for me, because experience involving emotions and feelings is commonly described as being 'wishy-washy'. For me, however, precision and clarity are the foundations of the emotional experience and the communication that builds upon it. When we adults disturb a child at play, the child can justifiably feel very annoyed, because what adults may thoughtlessly consider to be a trivial juxtaposition, is in all likelihood a very precise sequence of play elements for the child, and any disruption can upset it. I have found many adults to be considerably less exact and precise than most children. In a way, I seem child-like when I am working with horses through play. That is why it is so important for me to expose the accuracy with which play actually happens, right at the beginning.

For example, let us look at my body language in picture I. Everything looks light and playful, and yet must be immensely focused and precise. The left hand holding the rope around the stallion's neck is firm and decisive. This firm determination is only in the left, leading hand. Everything else seems almost naive, surprised and almost as if this person were doing what they are doing for the first time. From this picture, the observer cannot see that this stallion was hugely difficult and extremely dominant,

with enormous power and stallion tendencies. You can see lightness and naivety. The form is determined here by the lack of sophistication and precisely pared-down simplicity. My knees appear relaxed and slightly bent. Only the tips of my toes are touching the ground, but there is still a feeling of stability.

Above all, and this is the second most important thing for me, this person really seems to be happy with what the horse is doing. The scene is determined not by routine and training, but by a constantly changing experience. The man in the picture looks like he could float with happiness. This joy is quiet, directed inward and constant. Man and horse are with each other and you can see in both of them: they are truly doing together what they are doing. And that is what causes the stallion to elevate the way he is doing it here. And that is also what makes him still follow my tiny gestures even there is a mare in heat right in front of him (picture 2).

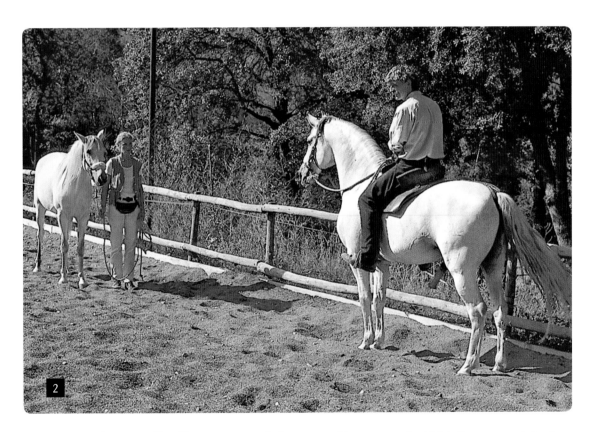

2

Here I am with the PRE stallion, Yunque at a so-called stallion training. Feelings and emotions become a clear expression, as precise as possible. I experience emotions, feelings and non-verbal exchange as something very exact, which is then conveyed clearly and unambiguously to the horse.
(See video clip: Rearing Breeding Stallion at Ease.)

Divorced from reality?

After a demonstration in Holland in the spring of 2008 somebody showed me the photo top right, with a smile. At first I had to smile, too. But then, when I took a closer look at the picture, I realized that it showed something like an important cornerstone of my work. In the moment when the photograph was taken, I am showing the participants how you can jump with a certain lightness. It sounds quite easy, but it is not. Unlike most of the participants, I seem to be floating in the picture, and that is the humorous aspect to this photograph. To lift up with a small jump, you need a certain amount of muscular effort and tension, but look at this 'floating' person a little more closely! He is relaxed and still talking in the process, without showing the slightest tension or anything unusual in his face. Even in mid 'flight', his shoulders are quiet and low and his feet hang in a relaxed way, almost dangling. In short, the photograph is so surprising, precisely because the man seems to be floating, as if he is hanging on something invisible.

Now imagine yourself in one of your riding lessons. The instructor asks one of the students to tense a very specific part of their body, in order to convey selective information to the horse.

What often happens in real life? The student tenses not one, but thousands of muscles, and the horse does not know what to make of it.

In the bottom right image, you can see how I am crouching to show the group how it is possible to do anything in a relaxed and simple way; for example, sitting in an armchair, reading or playing with your children. How is this useful? To show the simplicity that is always required if you want to get back to the roots, in any sphere, and if you want to experience the simplicity of nature and naturalness in itself.

There is not enough space in this book to show body exercises, but what I am concerned with here is fundamental understanding. I want to write again and again about the simplicity and relaxation that can be found before any really astounding natural event. Without it, the event simply would not happen, and the most beautiful thing about it is that if we devote ourselves to it seriously and, in the end, successfully, then the positive effects extend far beyond what we actually wanted to achieve, and into general life. We become richer and more fulfilled, both inside and out.

The floating man demonstrates how to activate a very specific part of your body for a brief second, in order to return immediately to complete relaxation and normality. Conscious and targeted tension and then complete relaxation a moment later — that is a very important basis for using our bodies as an authentic means of communication, and not just with horses. Yet is this a question of physical training, more than anything else? No! It is primarily a question of mental attitude. The body then tries to find the right way. And it will find it.

Imagine yourself in one of your riding lessons. The instructor asks one of the students to tense a very specific part of their body in order to convey selective information to the horse. What often happens in real life? The student tenses not one, but thousands of muscles, and the horse does not know what to make of it.

I want to write again and again about
the simplicity and relaxation that can be found
before any really astounding natural event.

. . . a mystery?

The five-year-old Lusitano stallion Xingu that you can see looking so peaceful together with me, in the photograph below had been a real 'problem horse' just shortly before. You can see that clearly in the short video clip *Aggressive Stallion Tamed*. Correcting this horse was definitely a real job for me.

How did I manage it? This is one of my surprisingly simple secrets, rooted in the places where there is apparently nothing and where apparently nothing happens. Many horse people hardly give it any thought, if indeed they think about it at all. Leading, an action that appears so simple, actually involves constant correction of the horse and constant, precise communication. I would like to make you aware of these 'unspectacular details' and unremarkable mysteries, without which I could not convey the slightest thing.

Many people who come to my demonstrations look fruitlessly for big gestures, but I do not have any. At first glance, I essentially appear to have nothing, as you can see in the pictures at the bottom. However, if you look more closely, a hidden world opens up behind this 'nothing'. This series of pictures show two beings calmly

moving in a field. It looks like a game. The observer scarcely senses the enormous vigilance, great caution and awareness of the man throughout this entire process together with this ever-ticking time bomb.

The man, strolling along in such an apparently relaxed manner, knows that it would only take a moment's inattention to trigger new eruptions that could quickly lead to a new, total collapse. At this point, I would like to introduce you to my world. As you can see, when I am standing in front of an unknown horse that often nobody else trusts any more, it is not a game. The human world has seen many horses become genuine killers. I often feel like a classic Japanese warrior, a samurai, before a battle, where out of necessity, intense quiet and relaxation must pervade everything and yet each of the players knows about the importance of the moment, the importance even for their own survival.

My readers do not want to stand in the way of extremely aggressive horses or spin skilfully with a flashing sword like a samurai. Both are for the specialists. Materials that are high quality and long-lasting enough to carry astronauts to the moon can also be used successfully in normal cars. Something that has proven itself under extreme conditions is unlikely to go wrong in normal, everyday life. That is what I want to offer you.

Leading, an action that appears so simple, actually involves constant correction of the horse and constant, precise communication. I would like to make you aware of these 'unspectacular details' and unremarkable mysteries, without which I could not pass on the slightest thing.

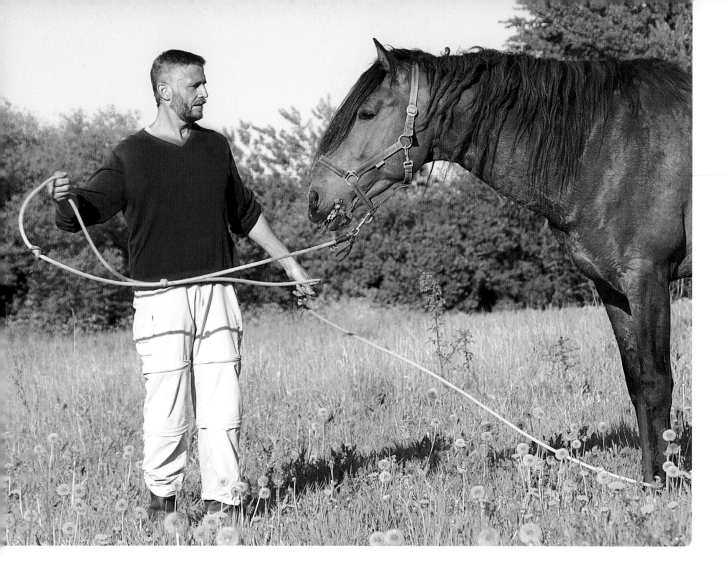

The surprise is that it is much simpler than you think, that is, if you still believe in simplicity.

Beginning, journey and destination –
the human personality

Everyday existence, the everyday care, the normal, everyday contact, leading and going for walks with a horse are, and will always be, the foundations of the relationship. This is where the wonder or the drama begins, all depending on your preferences and personal attitude.

Let us look at the left picture. The man is standing looking peaceful, obviously stable and grounded in himself. His shoulders are relaxed and low. He is doing something with the rope, but it does not appear to be having the slightest negative effect on the horse. Quite the opposite in fact, the horse's ears are pricked forwards in a friendly way. The horse reacts amicably, because the person in these pictures presents an example for him in all of his forms and gestures.

The horse is constantly testing him, but the man remains obviously unperturbed. The man's personality is actually the defining, changing and quietening factor here. Nothing can replace that in the long term, not if you want willing achievement, satisfaction, fulfilment and authentic contact in the end, for both horse and human.

A person's personality is actually the defining, changing and quietening factor here. Nothing can replace that in the long term.

At the end, the two beings meet in complete serenity, as can be clearly seen from our pictures. The human will no longer notice his constant awareness – it is simply there and life flows like a quiet river, but the awareness, the constant attentiveness and consciousness, flow with it.

Routine is a flat, distant, boring grey that has no place in what is happening here. Each moment is new. That is the only way that reliability and wonderful peace can be created together.

After this initial, careful introduction to the subject of body language, it is time to take up our positions and set clear boundaries.

The first decision

look,
look through,
decide and
distinguish

3

Please judge for yourself

In this chapter, I will compare, in detail, the three possible ways of being with horses. There are many variations, but fundamentally, three basic principles can be attributed to all of the ways.

Henceforth I cannot help calling a spade a spade, and to point out mistakes and errors, because it seems to me that the time for it has simply come.

In the end, togetherness with horses is always a question of trust and dominance. In Dancing with Horses I explicitly introduced this pair of concepts into the horse world and described the inner relationship of them both.

57

What often happens in real life, in my opinion? Instead of dominance and trust, we often find different types of training that actually bypass the qualities of dominance and trust, creating a kind of pretence. Without the appearance of trust and dominance, much of what we do with horses in the public eye will be ignored or even impossible. These two levels often become very clear at my Borderline events, because usually the horses that are brought to me have broken free from the world of training and can no longer be handled.

Horse training is the attempt to present horses (and riders too) in movements and actions that they are not actually able or ready to perform. A horse will willingly show himself off and present himself by doing just that, if he is offered the platform to do so. Within the context of training, I am talking about patterns and sequences of movements that horses would not show entirely freely and willingly. For example, in the video clip *Collecting a Stallion at Liberty*, anybody can see that the horse actually only needs the person so that he can present himself. The person is the mirror for the horse, for his very own need to display himself, to grow and surpass himself in play and happiness. The joy leaps out at the viewer with every second. That is why it is an example of being with horses authentically, as I understand it.

A few days ago, I received a phone call from the Netherlands, from the owner of the stallion. She told me in surprise that she kept seeing Queijo going through the exercises that we had developed together, in his field by himself. I have experienced this again and again.

An overview of the three ways of being with horses

1. External violence (drawings 1 and 2) I do not need to say much about it any more, because even the non-riding public keep hearing about scandals. However, far too little is known about the enormously painful effect of bits, even including jaw bone fractures, which happen even at the highest levels of sport. Genuine dominance through inner strength and trust, through an inner relationship, can naturally never be achieved in this way. Let us leave it at that. You can find relevant pictures and descriptions anywhere (also about 'rollkur').

2. Complete spiritual/mental submission. On the following pages, drawings 3–5 describe another fundamental difference between what I am trying to do and what has, and I say this with great sorrow, become fashionable today. We see a pen, a horse on the track, a person in the middle and a horse trailer. Let us stay with drawing 3. The horse is moving more or less on the track, because he wants to get to his friends in the field or to his feed, so they have two plus signs. The track has a plus sign because the horse has relative peace here, to begin with.

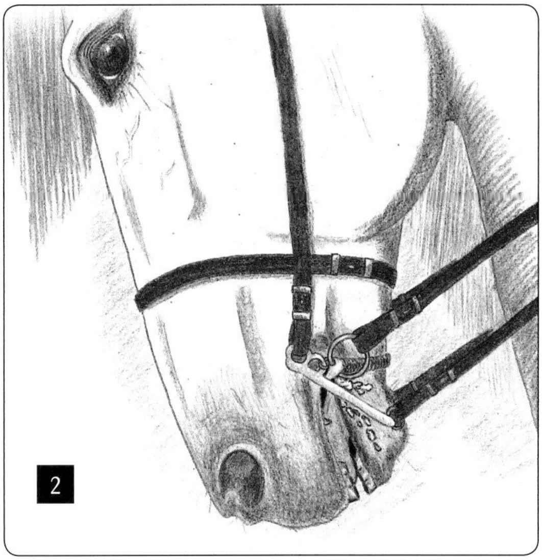

The person in the middle is comparatively uninteresting for the horse and so is insignificant at the moment, meaning that he now has a neutral zero symbol. The horse trailer has a minus sign because of its daunting effect on the horse.

However, the person in the middle wants to get closer to the horse. Whether this is to abuse it or to make it useful or for some other higher purpose remains to be seen. If possible, he wants to know that the horse is always near him, because he wants to control it. He also wants to be able to dominate it quickly, for example so that he can load it into a trailer, and if possible, safely handle it everywhere. What unfortunately happens so often today? Let us look at drawing 4.

The handler imitates a predator and chases the horse, and the outside area, the track, becomes very negative. Sometimes the horse is chased until it is exhausted and gives up completely, which is exactly what is prescribed in the relevant literature and what is unfortunately also carried out in practice, often under the delighted gaze of thousands of spectators. Now the formerly safe area has become very negative, which is why there are two minus signs on the track right next to the horse (drawing 4).

The human becomes a being that chases, an enemy, a predator. That is why he gets a minus sign too. At this point, the time of the chase, the horse does not know that he will not die at the end. A real hunt, with the aim of killing and eating, would follow exactly the same procedure and the process would be the same for the horse's inner life. The area with just one minus sign, i.e. the area that the person represents, is now always better than the one that used to be positive (i.e. the track), because the track now only means hunting and exhaustion.

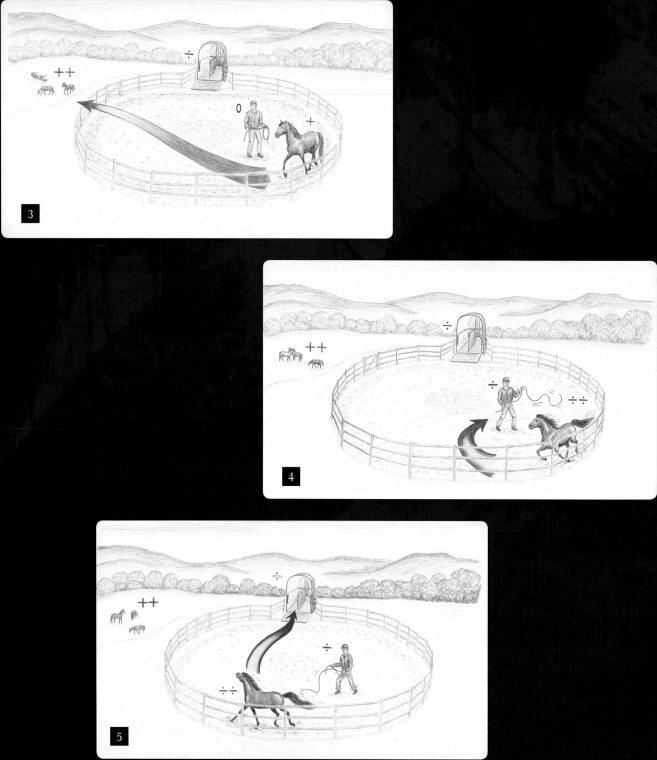

For the horse, the person becomes a predator – you can read that in many books. At last, the horse comes to the person, as a last resort and as the only escape from hunting and exhaustion, not because he suddenly likes him or because he has suddenly become a trustworthy entity. Instead, it is precisely because everything else has become more intolerable, more painful and more negative. That is how to get a horse into a trailer very quickly (drawing 5), because chasing and predator behaviour themselves have made all other paths and alternatives more threatening. In the trailer, there is finally peace for the now extremely distressed and spiritually lifeless animal. It all works so well that this simple method has made it around the whole world. Obviously, it does not have anything to do with understanding horses, but it is unfortunately just presented as such, and believed to be so by a large and ignorant public. Even in apparently heroic Hollywood film productions, the horse is robbed of his freedom, flung to the ground and forced to give up in the most brutal way, without any dignity and without any feeling.

What we have just described is the archetype, so to speak. Many variations of forcing and oppression have developed from it. In many cases today, we see a fatal mix of forms of suppression, the external and the inner, spiritual submission. A wide variety of forms exists in between, but the principle is always the same – make the path of the free will and environment of the horse more unpleasant than the path or gate, along or through which you would like to ride or direct the horse. That is the whole trick. In this process, horses are not only chased and thrown over, but pitchforked, beaten or have their desire for freedom inhibited in some other way. This is genuine torture for the horse that lasts until their soul is completely dead. The terrible paradox is that proximity to the oppressor is, in the end, the most peaceful place for the spiritually lifeless horse.

My prognosis is as follows – over the next decade, we will be able to uncover and re-evaluate what has greatly damaged horses, riders and riding during the past ten years, and which has been supported by an enthusiastic but misguided public. When this book was written, we had reached a point where the mood seemed to tip. The signs of deception have now become too obvious and the completely jaded and 'spiritually abandoned' horses too numerous. Unimaginable damage has occurred, the full extent of which is not completely known.

3. The way of the knight : Being and Trust. We now come to drawings 6 and 7 and to what I consider to be the only right and worthy thing, to which I have devoted myself. The person gets three plus signs here, because he works on his own unique qualities as a helper, mentor and healer and on his exemplary leadership qualities, his body language and his coming to awareness, until the horse really wants to come to him, not because everything else has been spoiled for him

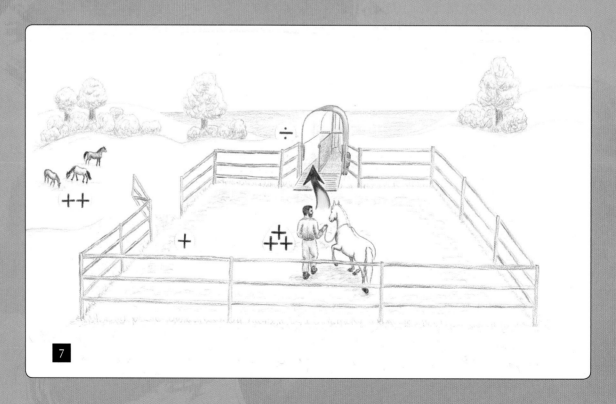

and he simply gives up and gives in. No, simply because he really wants to build closeness to this person. The horse wants to follow this person, because he believes and genuinely trusts in him. (View also video clips *Breeding Stallion Harmon Reborn*, *Horse Dream* and *Bonding With Beautiful Horse*.) A person who acts in this way will lead the horse through all obstacles and apparent dangers, obviously including into a trailer, because the horse thinks there can be no danger where this worthy and graceful person is.

Where there is trust, there is trust all around. In the end, the horse can even be worked freely in any field, even right next to other horses, because in the perfect scenario, the person becomes the central support for the free development of the horse. That is the fundamental principle. Everything revolves around the inner qualities of the person. In days gone by, that was the (ideal and idealised) path of the knight.

The way of life of our ancestors was based on this principle, and on its legitimacies of energy and authentic approach to the world as a creation.

What I have just described is my world with horses. All of what happens in the first pictures happens quickly and requires nothing from people other than a total lack of consideration, or even lack of humanity. My path is seemingly stonier, but you can choose for yourself the path you want to take.

When the soul dies. Rico's day
Record of a very specific complex of symptoms

The range of symptoms that I see in the horses that are brought to me at my events has changed, and not for the better. In the past, there were essentially two groups. One group consisted of those horses that were pressured more or less intensely because they were expected to perform, and had to perform. They had been worked and trained through the system of punishment and reward, with punishment playing a significant role. Surprising as many may find it, these horses were the easiest to correct and to return to their natural state, unless they were extreme cases. This is essentially because, although the experiences that they had undergone were far from natural or pleasant, the basic treatment was essentially predictable for the horse and comparatively stable, even in its harshness and unfairness. The suffering, the suppression and the pain were constant and consistent.

The second group consisted of horses that were confronted with people who only wanted to do their best for their animals. Such horses are very often overbearing and dominant. Depending on the degree of anthropomorphism in the general treatment and day-to-day contact, these horses are a little more difficult to bring back into balance. I mainly attribute this to the general lack of clarity in their handling, something which creates an enormous amount

The loss of the soul is the saddest thing that can happen to a being, a horse. Sometimes it seems to me as if the horse is in a kind of waking coma. I really have to pull myself together to maintain my inner happiness and balance. That helps the horse too – my personal example and my ever-strong inner belief in healing. That was how it was with Rico.

of insecurity in the animals themselves, as well as a unique kind of isolation. It is very hard for an animal to compensate for the confusion that results. Someone who only ever tries not to do anything wrong, hesitantly and without enough basic sense of trust, is actually getting it wrong, even if they are doing something right in principle. This is because they are not used to taking clear steps as a consequence of clear decisions, and even the correct steps are only half-hearted and hesitant, which makes them damaging. To the animal, such a person will seem confused or even insane. I find that this kind of behaviour is then reflected in the horse. With horses like this, I usually work with great spatial distance and with the greatest clarity imaginable, and very small steps. That gives them back a notion of precision, clarity, reliability and predictability.

Naturally, horses belonging to these two groups are still found, but they have been pushed into the background by a third. I get more and more horses that are, quite simply, dead inside – their soul has been murdered, and these are among the saddest. They function up to a certain extent, but some of them, such as Rico, are extreme cases. When he came to me, his eyes were completely lifeless and dead. Several horse whisperers had tried their hand with him. As we have already seen, Rico had also been through an impersonal and wildly put together muddle of pushing, pressurising, chasing, 'playing', clicking, shooing, moving backwards, sacking, confinement and whatever else features in this programme, and in the end, his soul had fled, dead. The horse had resigned himself under all the pressure. Until ...

... Until the moment, when he saw the last gateway into the light. A system of suppression and manipulation like this has to be watertight, so to speak. If there is a loophole anywhere, then the horse has nothing left to lose, having already resigned himself to his fate. That is the moment of real danger, because now the horse no longer knows anybody and the person near him is actually the subtle oppressor – public enemy no. 1.

Rico had succumbed to the pressure and was functioning, but without any sparkle in his eye, and without any relationship. That was what troubled the owner the most, and she was very unhappy about it. In fact, a steep, unbridgeable chasm had actually opened up between owner and horse. If I emphasise the pictures on this page, it is to illustrate how the horse changed back again, but only after a whole day, when normally I only need minutes! However, the next day almost all of the sparkle had gone from his eyes again.

With horses like this, I virtually have to start from the beginning again, because the soul is floating over the horse and is no longer anchored in him.

To date, Rico had only found one 'loophole' for escaping from the pressure he had experienced. After being 'treated' by trainers, he could no longer be ridden. Believe me, I have seen a lot of horses buck – but nothing like this! It was different, in that Rico waited until the exact moment when he could be sure that he was going to get through the tiny hole out of the prison of death. For example, you could put a saddle on him and nothing happened. You could lead him for half an hour, or ride him for a while, and nothing happened. At the precise moment, when success on Rico's side seemed entirely possible, the horse started to buck as if his life depended on it, and then nothing else could get through to him.

I have only seen this kind of extreme reaction in horses like this. It can be aggression that occurs quite suddenly, or total apathy. It can be out-and-out refusal to cooperate, sudden panic, refusal of food and many other symptoms of an almost autistic kind that always have one thing as a cause or trigger: the light of life, and the refusal to let it flicker and die, at the exact place where it is still possible. This is the new form of horse autism, the consequence of the most advanced expression of the unconditional, human desire to use.

Of course, this circle is being completed everywhere. The fact that this unpleasant and extreme way of dealing with horses has, until now, been sold to the public as its exact opposite, precisely corresponds to our present reality, to our world today. But this too is only a matter of time.

When a horse seeks me – as Rico does – then every inner contradiction falls silent. We have only known each other for a few hours, but it seems like human and animal grew up together.

I hope that you experience this – let's look forward together to see how it can happen.

The first decision

These pictures show Janosch, who at first anxiously and hesitantly approaches some barrels that he finds terrifying.

Everything is happening in a large field, so Janosch could just choose to wander off and graze, for example, but he does not. I use gestures to ask him to follow me and he does, even into the perceived danger. He slowly moves nearer, takes a closer look and then jumps over the barrels, completely free.

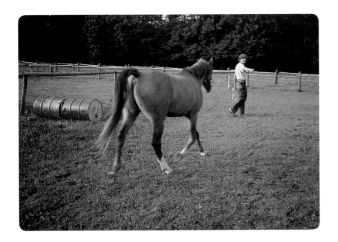

My principle is that with the right appearance, consciousness and clear communication, with compassion, leading, instructing and lungeing, always keeping the horse in mind, and following his nature, foundations are established whose solid structures can achieve much more than you could imagine. Time invested in this way creates the quickest and most astonishing progress in so many other spheres.

Using the example of Marouk, I will explain in detail how all of this can be integrated into everyday work.

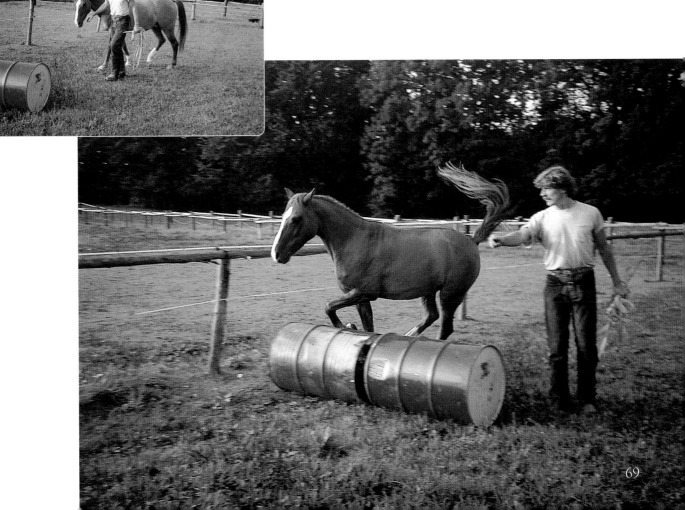

If the foundations are right, then little or no further training is required

Here is another example. What amazed the course participants at this event in Norway was not so much the fact that the horse stood so calmly opposite the machines and sounds, but the fact that it needed no further work.

The story is that the participant had brought me the horse because he went into an extreme panic whenever he came within sight or sound of agricultural machinery or other equipment. The rider was powerless and at a loss. The essential point is that I did not do anything special with the horse in the arena during the course and when working with him. I worked with and encountered this horse in the arena naturally, according to his individual personality, but I did not work specifically on his symptoms. I simply did what I always do. I did my normal

leading and lungeing exercises with the horse, building on the animal's individual qualities, character and rhythm, but I did not go through any particular habituation with him. However, I was able to promise the participants that I could walk past a tractor with this horse straight away – and that is what happened. The owner then repeated it, because the horse's trust in me transferred to the rider herself.

Please have a quiet look at the gestures and the expression of the horse. There is no panic, no pressure. That is what I mean when I say that the horse is no longer alone. He has found a home, complete trust, and with it, new security. That is the beginning of my entire path. You should also look at the picture bottom left. Here, the horse still is hesitating a little, but what is he actually doing? He is just taking on the woman's body language, and both look a little bewildered and tense. That is why I had to 'work' a little more with the woman and give her the security that she could then transfer to the horse. It is quite simple in principle. The pictures document some everlasting experiences for people and animals, i.e. authenticity and genuine understanding in a new world of experiences, trust, new security, new quiet and new relaxation. But now let us look at the whole in context and in detail.

We should always remember: our horses always mirror our inner and outer behaviour precisely. Understood in the right way, this is an incredible opportunity for us.

Marouk's long,
yet short journey

A 'royal child' finds his dignity

Marouk loses his fear of loading

A basic example

At this point I would like to move straight to practical experience. Using the example of the Arab stallion Marouk and his fear of loading, I shall describe in great detail how you can basically approach and overcome all obstacles, problems and difficulties.

This chapter is also about the specific problem as such, but that is not the main issue. It is more about presenting a basic path. Among others, the following things are crucial:

73

- Try to recognise what kind of horse you have in front of you, even if you think you know him and have been with him for a long time. Follow your intuition. Another helpful way is to try all kinds of comparisons, for example, what kind of house would this horse be, what colour best expresses his being, which time of year, music, landscape and so on. Short 'symbolic journeys' like this are generally very beneficial for the outset and for training intuition, and they will definitely bring you a little closer to your horse.

- Try to recognise your horse's state of mind. What inner qualities, and if any, problems does it reveal? Using this basis and this preparation, you should briefly check your own mood, if possible, each time you are with your horse. You cannot change it by snapping your fingers, but even brief conscious access to your inner world opens up the gates for harmonisation and relativisation. At the end it becomes almost automatic and a natural part of your day. In terms of how the work is structured, particular attention during leading work follows at this point, and that basically means every step that you take with your horse.

- Then try to find the next step of the path, relating to the current situation and the changes in the horse. The longest journey starts with the first step, and that applies here too. Nobody, including your horse, is expecting perfection and mastership from you. You just need to be heading in that general direction.

- You should then try to walk this path with clarity and consistency, in close cooperation and constant communication with the horse, with the greatest possible relaxation, quietness and understanding of what is necessary. It is about clarity in simultaneous deliberation, it is about thoroughness, determination and decisiveness, in simultaneous equilibrium, inner balance and the ability to prepare contemplatively and centre yourself in advance.

I would like to ask you again to take a moment to look at this whole series of pictures. They already show everything, the entire way, and above all, they convey the basic mood and the atmosphere in which everything is happening and growing. Look at my posture and the reaction of the horse. Look at the horse's expression from moment to moment, and his increasing relaxation and familiarity.

Let us begin: Taking away a horse's fear of loading is easy. When doing so, we not only bypass all of the unpleasantness, and above all, the dangers that arise when a horse hasn't mastered loading perfectly. This kind of exercise, in particular, is wonderful for profoundly establishing and shaping our relationship with the horse.

We approach everything quietly. There is nothing to fear. We have a path and a clear form.

Marouk's essence and character

First, let us look at the little stallion more closely to find out where the problem is based. That is what I did a few days before the stallion arrived, because the owner asked me for a characterisation by telephone. Basically, three different parts of Marouk's head are striking. One is the position of his eyes and the shape of his forehead, another is the shape of the line of his nose, and the third is the way the nose leads down to the nostrils and the mouth. In this case, we can use this and many other details to very precisely determine the horse's nature. Marouk's nostrils, mouth and eyes show a great sensitivity, intelligence, alertness and curiosity. The ears show that too. They indicate lots of energy and temperament with their relatively small size and inwardly curving shape. The position of the eyes and the shape of the forehead indicate a high-ranking, on the whole inwardly strong and assertive being. In this case, the eyes themselves, the shape of the forehead and the position of the eyes determine the horse's character, based on the 26 basic characteristics that I have developed (read *What Horses Reveal*).

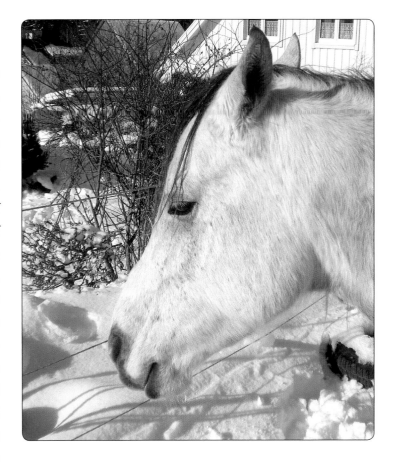

Marouk is a mixture of 'King' and 'Child'. This means playful exuberance, a constant child-like radiance, even in old age, coupled with the strength and energy of a king, and with his will to rule, decide and dominate. However, it also means that there is a certain inner turmoil in the horse that must be overcome, and that is the challenge for the people on his side, to help him to overcome it and to negotiate the pitfalls along his path.

For the people around him, Marouk is not an easy horse, and definitely not a novice or child's horse.

The lower part of the line of this stallion's nose shows a convex, outward-curving shape and if we now look at the relative width of his head from the side, this too indicates dominant behaviour. Between the forehead and this 'bump' above the nostrils is a concave dent that indicates a certain insecurity and anxiety.

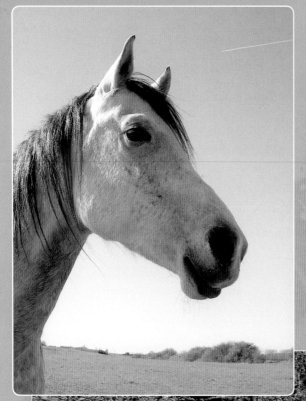

The very knowledge of the inner being of the horse will automatically trigger reactions in us that lead to greater closeness – it is already unconsciously taking place within. The wonderful power of (inner) pictures.

Now we come to a special feature. The child-like, playful, sensitive behaviour of the horse, together with the 'coolness' of the king and the characteristics of the nose line, indicates, in this particular case, a certain quality of reserve or guardedness that says:

'If you don't want anything from me, then I basically won't hurt you either, but you had better not want anything from me. If you start telling me how things should be for both of us then I'll show you who's in charge.'

So you have to be prepared when you start with the actual forming and the actual work. That was confirmed to me by the owner, and that was precisely his greatest problem. Marouk had become almost impossible to lead. He was aggressive, and loading was also a problem. And so he finally arrived at my farm for training.

Marouk finds his expression . . .

. . . for seconds. I only want to mention this first part of work with Marouk briefly, for the sake of completeness, because later on in the book we will go into it in more detail, along with the experiences of the Lusitano stallion, Queijo, but back to Marouk.

What we see in the following three pictures here is basically almost always the beginning of every relationship and the beginning of my work. It always turns out differently in terms of details, depending on the horse, but the principle remains essentially the same. It is about showing the horse its own inner and outer 'space' as directly as possible. That happens very quickly with horses. Marouk, this agile boy suddenly begins to build up his posture, he starts to show himself off and we can clearly see how he accepts me as an opposite, as a mirror. We can clearly see how the stallion is already rounded, how he begins to collect from 'back to front' and so reacts to my position and my gestures.

The horse directly experiences an 'expansion' and an 'inner and outer push'. Animated by me, he fills and experiences his entire body and becomes greater and more dignified. All of this can be seen very clearly in these pictures, as well as the joy that can be found in the movements and expression of the horse. Details of everything else can be found in the next few chapters.

This part of the work with Marouk lasted around 15 minutes. Other steps then became important. We should now take a moment to consider the other steps that lead to loading. Obviously there were moments and phases of work like this one in between time, but they only lasted for seconds.

Once the most serious problems had been solved, after around eight sequences of exercises, we picked up here again. It was now a question of awakening the 'dance' in the horse and bringing 'fire and water' into balance.

It is about showing the horse its own inner and outer 'space' as directly as possible. It happens very quickly with horses. We can see clearly in the pictures how this agile boy suddenly begins to build up his posture, how he starts to show himself off and how he accepts me as an opposite, a mirror.
We can also clearly see how the stallion is already rounded, how he begins to collect from 'back to front' and so reacts to my position and my gestures.

During the initial minutes of togetherness, the following still applies — understanding the horse's general mood is crucial at this point, in order to approach him in a targeted way and to achieve a general change, metamorphosis and connection. People who have been observing my work for years know that this initial approach is hardly ever repeated. This first phase in particular is completely free from any thought of following only one specific method, a routine action. So what happens?

After having sorted out the horse's personality, I wait for the right moment to act until I know without a doubt, through a clear and unmistakable intuition (I cannot describe it any other way) how I can get through to the animal's soul in the most direct and immediate way. The moments of 'inaction' are sometimes only seconds but can last for minutes. During a demonstration I then usually stand silently and immobile, but I never act without this clear 'start signal'. I can only thank all of my past spectators, because there has never been a murmur or any impatient restlessness. I think people can feel what is happening here.

Can you also learn what I have just described? I do not know. However, I honestly have to say that I have yet to meet somebody who has experienced it in this deep sense or who could demonstrate or imitate it. That is a fact. However, experience has shown me that people have always been able to develop greater sensitivity in this respect. It is not necessary for you to successfully work with three to five horses a day. There is one thing I would like to mention,

which is if somebody really wants to experience being in complete harmony with a horse, then I believe that in the end, they really have to feel. Until then, they will definitely keep on getting closer to this experience, but they will not actually achieve it. I would really like to, but I am unable to put it any other way.

The first parallelism

Here is something else very special that follows on from the previous section. I have never described it in words at any of my events before, but at the end of the next section I will say something about how useful this procedure is for you in practice. In any case, I think it is appropriate that you take in the following description in peace and quiet.

First, our stallion was given the opportunity to show off and present himself, which always happens in the form of free work. As I have said, it certainly is not always the first step, but for Marouk it was important to give him this opportunity straight away. Right at the start he wanted to come out of himself and fill his inner space. Basic trust is created after just a few moments. From there, horses follow me very precisely with a natural consistency and at a slight distance. They stand when I stand, and walk when I walk. The 'first parallelism', as I call it, is different from the leading, following, coming and going exercises. I will describe this important difference here for the first time and I will try to explain what goes before it, although it is not easy. To illustrate the first parallelism during demonstrations, I often count down three steps and then stand still, at exactly the same time as the horse. We then fall in step together and continue. Over the years, this process happens more and more quickly. Now I often do not need to do anything else first. For me, first parallelism is the basis and prerequisite for the next steps.

Only the day before yesterday, I was called to a mare in the neighbourhood, who simply did not want to be led, or even touched or caught. A television team from Germany was there and we did not have a lot of time. The only thing that I could do was demonstrate the first parallelism. The mare instantly became my partner in this 'pas de deux'. The next day we got a call. They told us that the horse had undergone a magical change.

The effect of this process has an amazing force. Throughout this book, I will examine these things from various sides. I would now like to introduce you directly to the magic of the first parallelism.

First, have a look at the pictures that go with this paragraph (pictures 1−7). Please try to explore the impression in the pictures of unquestioning concentration on the part of the person in himself, and likewise, the certain apparent 'indifference' towards the horse. The horse seems to be pulled into this implosion of energy. At this moment, I am fully in my physical centre below my belly button. Nothing matters, I think of nothing, I let nothing distract me. I hope and believe that you can see this from the pictures. When we later come to the topic of leading in more detail, the basic idea will naturally be the same, but I then also have a goal, a task, a path, an exercise in mind, a test or challenge for the horse or something similar. Leading therefore has a different form and is guided by different rules. We have already talked a little about it in previous chapters. With the stallion Xingu, everything was about leading, and the enormous attentiveness involved. The first parallelism does not involve any of that, or at least not in this form. It is pure being, and if possible, complete togetherness. The awareness is channelled to flow into direct perception. I have no tasks for the horse and no tasks for myself. I am simply being, and the horse wants to be near me. Naturally, the boundaries between first parallelism and normal leading are fluid − that is also shown in the pictures here − yet you can very finely differentiate between one and the other. In any case, first parallelism draws spectators along in its wake and often shows them the great gulf that lies between it and their own experiences.

I am obviously aware that I am writing about things here that may compel you, the reader, to look far beyond the boundaries of your experience. I hope this will not keep you from continuing to follow me, because I can assure you that in all this I am talking about something that really requires absolutely nothing of you. In fact, that is the mystery. For me, the 'first parallelism' is the main focus of meditating with horses.

Metaphorically speaking, it is as if there is a kind of 'dip' in the ground beneath me, and everything – including the horse – aspires to this 'natural deepening'. Scents, sounds, wind, sensations on the skin, cold, heat, the heaviness of my weight on the ground, all of my limbs, my heartbeat, there is space for all of that in my perception and also for the whole appearance of the horse. There is nothing else. It is crucial that everything is very light, especially for the horse. It is different from leading, in terms of learning and experiencing, because when we are leading, we not only advance further along the physical path, we are also moving on the axis of experiencing, learning, trying and maturing. That does not happen in the 'first parallelism'.

Let us look at the pictures in detail:

1. Right after the first meeting, I went for a stroll around the farm with Marouk. There is no goal. Everything is like on a warm summer's evening. We are all familiar with this: there is music coming from a distant speaker, life is passing by in the distance, detached yet close at the same time. The warmth that had been resting on the ground and is now rising, bringing with it the moist, fresh, earthy scent of the evening, is precisely adjusted. It is neither a tiny bit too cool, nor a fwhisper too warm. Time has found its own calmness with which it accompanies the events. It is gentle, full of peace and in harmony with the rhythm of the beings around us. And the horse remains under this spell – there is nothing I want to change now.

2. At a Borderline event in the UK, a gelding was presented to me as the last of three horses. He was apparently extremely shy and nervous, and if he panicked, he would run through fences or even stable walls. Here, we see him in the 'first parallelism' with me, after around 15 seconds. I went to the animal and he followed me. He then let me lunge him, as if he had been doing it all his life. Afterwards I asked the public to applaud and make a noise – the

1

2

horse stood near me like a statue and did not move from the spot. Take a look at the horse's expression – it looks like he is in a trance and is magically drawn to me. The horse's eyes (which previously had been panic-filled) now radiate absolute peace, relaxation and even a certain languor in the completely strange arena. It is as if the horse has been transformed. He is in the first parallelism. In these moments, horses are simply completely at home.

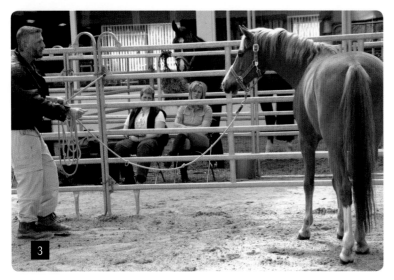

3

3. and 4. These are pictures from a Borderline event in the Netherlands. This horse simply could not be separated from the others without reacting with extreme panic. He did not show this behaviour with me from the first second on. The owner later wrote that the horse's being had fundamentally changed for the better, after meeting me. It was the 'first parallelism' more than anything that brought about this 'miracle'. This picture shows the exact moment when the horse opts for me. It had previously reacted in a very dismissive way. I only walked next to the horse at a certain distance for a few minutes. Then he approached me and the 'first parallelism' happened.

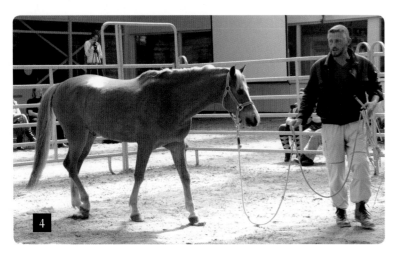

4

In picture 4 we can also see very clearly how much the horse is trying to follow me and to seek me out. This is because of my body language and the expression of my inner state. Everything about me tells the horse that I am able to guide him, to protect him from danger, to support and strengthen him, but also that I do not want the slightest thing from him. My body language promises the horse that I will never use him. This promise and security for the horse can be seen in my expression.

5.-7. After I had been with Rico for several hours, he reconnected with his soul. This moment was so dramatic and significant that we both wanted to enjoy and savour it for a good while. That is why I went over half the island with Rico and then down to the sea. Yet we had no goal and no task. None of the images of Rico show a leading situation, because they are evidence of the 'first parallelism'.

If you look closely, you can also read that from my posture and body language. It can also be seen in the horse's expression, because he appears to be in a trance in all of the pictures.

Everything that I describe in this book concerning inner and outer presence and authenticity serves the first parallelism. That is where everything comes together. Even if it happens when I first meet a horse, it is always a kind of recurring highlight for me. Each meeting with a horse should always be like a completely new one, and that is why the first parallelism can happen again and again.

Over time, the transitions to actual leading and riding keep blurring more and more. You can see this particularly well in the video clip *Collecting a Stallion at Liberty*. Here, the horse has reached a high level of his own body experience together with me on the one hand, but on

5

the other, he is in the first parallelism in many moments and in many scenes. That is what makes the difference, the magic.

So what is the 'first parallelism'? If you do nothing more than just appear, if you want no more and do not have to prove anything else, if you want to be neither good nor bad, if you simply trust that what has to happen will happen, and if you know the horse by your side so well and understand him almost better than yourself, then you have reached the 'first parallelism'.

Do you need this? I would definitely like you to experience it! All of the exercises and all of the forms that I describe in this book point towards it in the end. We all have the chance of

getting closer to this way of being with horses. That is all I can say about it at this point.

The magic of the moment in time and space

If we move on an appropriate, i.e. authentic level, if we rest in the feeling that we can perceive reality with factual distance, yet full of compassion, then we have the tools in our hands to react to everything appropriately. Let us have a look in detail, because Marouk's example is still interesting. Quite early on in the work he showed a particular problem. He tossed his head if you

7

tried to put a halter on him, and sometimes stood with his head turned away in the corner of the box or ring. He seemed to be 'testing' the people around him. After all, he is a king.

Unless I find a solution to such problems immediately, or if I ignore signs of this kind, then not only will this problem persist, but the following will also happen:

- Each problem that occurs is always an external sign of inner processes – often something like a 'test'. Our horses usually start out at a low grade and then escalate slowly but surely. If I do not solve a problem that arises immediately, or at least soon, then I would be willing to bet that the horse will come back to me with a second problem, a third problem and so on, in the near future.

- The problems that the horse presents can never be considered in isolation. They usually indicate that there are other related problems. If we do not react to them in an effective and targeted way, then we are saying to the horse that we do not want to deal with his problems. Conversely, the horse knows that it is being taken very seriously when we immediately deal with his signs and problems. Problem-solving becomes the point of entry for real understanding and real trust. The horse looks for us because he gets direct and targeted attention, closeness and trust.

- Horses often use these 'tests' to check our strengths, because they depend on our strengths as a leader. In the wild, a horse could only survive with us as a leader if we

Solving a small problem is one thing; the effect and the praise from the horse is a hundred thousand times as much.

Back to the scene. In the meantime, Marouk and I had become quite close. By this point, I had worked with him twice. His whole posture shows that he is already very well-balanced and has been able to develop new self-confidence, but at the same time he still follows the signals of the person at his side very attentively. The time had now come to turn to and sort out the first issue in his behaviour. As I have said, he had learned to escape people as fast as lightning if they tried to put a headcollar on him, for example. Behaviour like this often means that the trust and dominance relationship between human and horse is still out of balance.

This kind of action by a horse usually shows itself by the horse turning his rear end to people, rather than his head. Picture 1 shows that clearly. Admittedly the horse is in very high spirits and well balanced, but he is 'playing' with the person. I then maintain my complete calmness – I have all the time in the world (picture 2). Here I have chosen a path that initially requires a special kind of attentiveness from the horse. With low shoulders, and completely relaxed both inside and out, I throw the rope straight past the horse a few times. Under no circumstances may I touch the horse with the rope. I do not want the stallion to move now. I make this clear with my firm stance. If the stallion moves, I simply take a step to the side and 'stop' him in the corner, remaining

were strong; otherwise it would have to look for another leader or even take over leadership itself, and the horse would then begin to fight with, or rather, against us. That is why he immediately transfers each positive attempt at a solution that comes from our inner centre to our appearance as a whole.

at the same distance. If the relationship between human and horse is correct, then I am able to – and I have to – ask the horse to stand unfazed in a corner while allowing me to play around with a rope. The horse accepts all of this very calmly.

Now look at the pictures in detail. Both the moment and the form are right. Finally the stallion looks at me very trustingly, but also curiously (picture 3). The horse quietly turns to me at last (picture 4). I can now go to him to touch and halter him in a confident and clear way. The stallion stands calmly and solidly. I can put the bridle or halter on him without danger of him withdrawing from this gentle handling – the problem has been solved, but that is not all.

The pictures clearly show the quietness and trust with which everything is accepted. I have not just treated a symptom. Instead we have moved further along the path together towards ever greater trust and understanding. Why have these kinds of actions solved all of the problems so effectively? You may have to repeat this kind of action a couple of times, but the intensity of the effect is created by the preparation, the logical consistency of the path and the 'distinct clarity' of the person. That makes a powerful impression on the horse, and he also realises that he no longer 'needs' this problem. The problem belongs to a different time that is now past.

I occasionally use this kind of process in different situations. It is not really possible for me to go into everything that goes hand-in-hand with it at this point, so I can only ask the reader

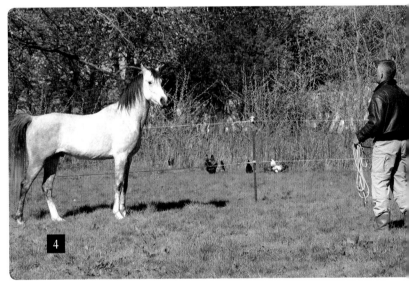

to understand the magic in these moments, the quiet and the moderation, to feel the spirit behind them, so they can understand the principle and put it into practice. It is important that this example is used as just that, one gentle form among many others that follows sufficient preparation together with the horse. I will give

The first problem has been solved for ever, but that is not all. The pictures clearly show the quietness and trust with which the horse accepts everything. I have not just treated a symptom. Instead, we have moved further along the path together.

First the horse
seeks the person,
then he finds them
and everything else
happens almost by itself

you the tools you need in the pages of this book. You can use them to create works of art or to wreak havoc. You do not need lots of different bricks to build a palace – it is the way they are joined together that creates the radiance and the magic.

Can this example help you progress in your own experience? Do you recognise the clarity and the confidence, yet at the same time, the gentleness that must form the basis of each individual action? In any event, the stallion was now ready to take the next step with me.

The backbone of togetherness with horses
Become sensitive, come, go, follow

The process of each new meeting always involves these qualities and forms of communication – becoming sensitive, the possibility of coming, going and following, and the flexibility that can and will result from it. Again I am writing straight from practical experience. Most riders usually do too much in all phases and unfortunately too much of the wrong thing. I manage to get contact with horses in a visible and surprising way and overcome problems very quickly, because I am concerned with putting something simple into action in the simplest way. More demands equals more complications.

To begin with, I have to recognise and acknowledge what I, as a person, can and cannot do. Unless I can clearly understand this difference, I am wasting my efforts on futile activities and I will not have enough energy left to use where I could achieve something.

In short, I am not responsible for the development of the horse, because this responsibility belongs to the horse and fate alone.

I am only responsible for providing the basis for this development to happen. How do I prepare the basis? Mainly by using the simplest lungeing exercises and leading. In this book, both will be examined from different angles. At this point, we want to concentrate on the picture commentaries that let us continue to follow Marouk's 'long, yet short journey'.

Let us take a moment to look at the next eleven pictures:

1. Marouk is being led from his stable to the field. The 'first parallelism' is no longer there. You can see that clearly in the horse and in the man. There is a clear purpose here. The man in the picture has a clear aim in mind, and if he said it aloud, it would be something like: 'We're going down to the field together. No two ways about it and no discussion. We won't have any stopping, eating, leaping about, overtaking or pulling on the rope, because you know what we want and that it's good for you and I know that too. End of message.'

Would you agree that the body language of the man in the picture expresses exactly that and nothing else? Do you also think that the horse's expression shows firstly that he sees it in exactly the same way, and secondly, that he is completely happy with it?

2. The horse is playing happily in the picture. His nostrils are flared and he is approaching the man in a mischievous way, but what you could describe as 'sweet' or 'nice' is actually a test by the stallion. Hence the raised finger of the man and the clear expression on his face. This reaction is clear, but not overbearing. It just says what is what, and nothing else. It is direct and unambiguous.

3. Marouk learns to go free and then to come back again. I emphasise this by walking backwards. The clear, upright posture of the man becomes clear again. A seven-year-old stallion

comes racing up. He is still supposed to be 'nice' when he comes to a halt – a good metre from the man and not right on top of him.

4. I have chosen this picture because it clearly shows how carefully the stallion takes his last steps.

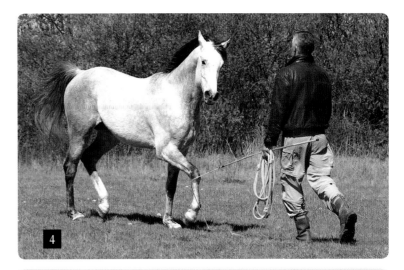

5. The best way to lead a horse. The distance is right, the stallion's head is slightly lowered to show, in his own language, that he feels good and has transferred general responsibility to me. The horse has a relaxed and very contented expression. Can you see the difference in expression during leading, compared with the 'first parallelism' pictures? This difference becomes very clear in the next picture.

6. Let us look at the man first. He has his hands full – looking at the horse, he moves to the right in a concentrated and focused way. Because the horse goes too far to the left. The normal reaction would be to move a little to the left too, but then the horse would be leading the man, and not the other way around. That is why the man goes against the pressure from the horse, instead of yielding to it. That causes the horse to return to the correct position to the side of, and behind the person. In the beginning, however, this has to be adjusted constantly through the signals from the human, because now he is leading, and now it's work.

the rope, and even his shoulders. His expression is very stern, because this is not a game, it is work and requires the highest concentration. It says a lot to the horse when the man holds the whip and his hands this high. It is enough to make him remember about the reality, even with his tail raised, the most foolhardy thoughts beneath his flowing mane and the fresh Danish island wind in his flared nostrils. The stallion's status is greatly influenced by my claims to rank. I make these very clear, using gestures. It is now also apparent why you have to be so careful with your body language. If it is used in an inflationary and constantly exaggerated way, this kind of sign will no longer have any effect on the horse, and an argument could result. But here the stallion knows – 'This guy means what he says. I'll just slow down.'

7. Here we have another situation that could be described as 'play'. The horse is frolicking around and running up to the person. It is a lovely picture and it could be fun too, if it did not involve an animal that weighs around 500 kilograms, so the man holds up the whip,

8. I think this picture is very beautiful, but not just in terms of photography. The stallion's ears are pointing forward and he and the man are looking in the same direction. Both are feeling good. They are together and yet separate. The horse has a clear expression in his eyes. He is visibly content. He has found his leader, but he is not a minion. On the contrary, they are partners, and both radiate a certain dignity. Yes, it is a beautiful picture.

9., 10., 11. Three more beautiful pictures. Man and horse are together, they are enjoying themselves, they have a relationship together and they speak the same language. This is the

picture after leading. The work is done and progress has been made. Look how satisfied the horse in picture 11 is, and how proud! Now the 'next round' can begin. The trailer, at last? No! It is still much too early.

Why I value fearfulness in horses
Marouk becomes bombproof

Hardly any horses are entirely confident about meeting the everyday objects that clutter the human world. As everyone knows, spooking can become a real problem and can be very dangerous. It is a risk that we need to eliminate. This is the next step that we will take with Marouk. Why does this step come before loading? You might think it is obvious, because a trailer also represents an object that the horse is afraid of, but that is not the real reason. Rather, it is about the following.

I absolutely do not want to take away a horse's fear of strange things, because this wariness has many benefits. It means that the horse is or can become sensitive, and usually indicates a certain level of intelligence. I prefer, instead, that the horse keeps his awareness. Obviously, a very alert, sensitive and intelligent horse will spook at boundary tape, for example, or at least back away from it warily. That is only too understandable. I initially see this behaviour as being something positive. That is important.

Secondly, I want to preserve this basic behaviour, so I do not want to do what many riders aim for, namely to get the horse used to all and sundry, in order to desensitise him. If I do that, I may end up with a deadened 'dope' beside me who is fazed by nothing, but who in the end, does not care about himself, me, or his development.

So what do I do? In a very short time, I decisively and irrevocably lead the horse into a relationship with me, where the horse will think: 'I am a bit scared of this thing, but Klaus is not, so I can now disregard any fear and put my trust in him'. From my point of view, that has many advantages, some of which are:

• It would be practically impossible to desensitise a horse to every strange thing there is in the world. If I get him used to blue bags, we will meet a red bag on our next ride. What happens if a helicopter lands next to me (which happened to me in Spain, when I was sitting on Janosch with no reins and no bridle)? How do I train for that?

• I am happy to have an attentive horse, especially when I am riding somewhere I am not familiar with, because he can warn me in time of the unexpected and any possible dangers. I need the horse's sensitivity for that too.

• It takes a lot of time to get the horse used to so many things, and the procedure is anything but pleasant for the horse. Friction quickly builds between the horse and rider. General trust tends to suffer during tedious procedures like this.

• Instead, I quite quickly try to show the horse using my body language that he can simply go everywhere with me, however threatening it may seem, even into a trailer, for example. It all happens unbelievably quickly and the effect of dominance and trust in general is enormous.

- A sequence of exercises like this often works wonders with dominant horses, in particular. The horse is amazed by the human's courage as they surround themselves with so many 'dangerous' things.

How do I do it?

Path I

It is crucial that you have won the horse's trust first, and you should at least have mastered the steps described above. Do not start with this procedure too soon. When you do start, take plenty of time, preferably the whole day. Not so that you can work with the horse for ages – please do not – it can be done in just a few minutes – but so that you can have all the peace in the world to stop at any time and take long breaks. You have to be solid as a rock and convincing as a person. If you can do that in this kind of exercise, then you will be rewarded in many ways. Now let us look at the pictures:

1. I have attached a metre of boundary tape to a whip. I know that the horse will be scared of it. Try to use something that makes the horse nervous, but that does not send it into a blind panic. Now forget about absolutely everything, but especially about the fact that you are holding something that the horse could spook at. You do not have anything in your hand – at all. Control your horse's first shying reaction using the trust that you have

already gained. Here, Marouk takes one or two steps backwards. I give him some rope and then the most important thing about this exercise happens fairly quickly.

2. Marouk becomes curious! So will every other horse, because he wants to be as cool and strong as you are! Especially a stallion. Quite quickly, Marouk puts his head down and starts to sniff. He is snorting through flared nostrils, but he is coming to me.

3. I take a few steps backwards, so the now quiet horse follows me, but he is actually following the object he was afraid of. That is the essence of the whole thing. The horse overcomes it himself, so the problem has actually already been solved.

4. and 5. Now the reinforcement comes again. It requires a lot of patience and vision. I now start to wave the object around in front of the horse, moving the tape gently and then

wildly. I keep walking backwards, inviting the horse to follow what he is afraid of.

6. Now I hand over control for what happens next to the horse. He will sniff the tape curiously, get to know it and think: 'Okay, I understand. If this person is not endangered by something, then I am not either. I can trust him.'

7. I now touch his hooves and then his belly with the tape.

8. Finally, the horse stands calmly beside me, and the exercise is complete.

9. The spookiest horse by far was Don Carlos. The photograph just shows him at the moment where he enters my arena through an enormous gate. Even that causes him to panic.

10. and 11. Soon this giant was a quiet as an old Zen master. Marouk's anxiousness was of a completely normal extent. Don Carlos was the ultimate extreme, but the principle is always the same. Can that help you?

I have something else to add here. Please never go too far. It does not matter in the slightest whether you can touch the horse with the tape straight away, for example. You can spend an entire day repeating the whole thing and then do it again. The following principle is important – the horse follows you, and so follows the object that it perceives to be dangerous, at the same time. You should always reach a point where the horse is visibly relaxed and feeling good, a point where he clearly shows that he trusts you, and then finish the exercise with lots of praise and kind words. It goes without saying that this kind of verbal praise is especially important in these types of exercises, but that should already be obvious. For me, this kind of exercise takes between two and a maximum of five minutes.

Being with horses means always
being open to wandering
on the ridge
in order to rediscover its boundaries.
Here, it is crucial that you always
stay on familiar ground and do not
take the slightest risk.
The steps you take can, in fact,
never be too small.

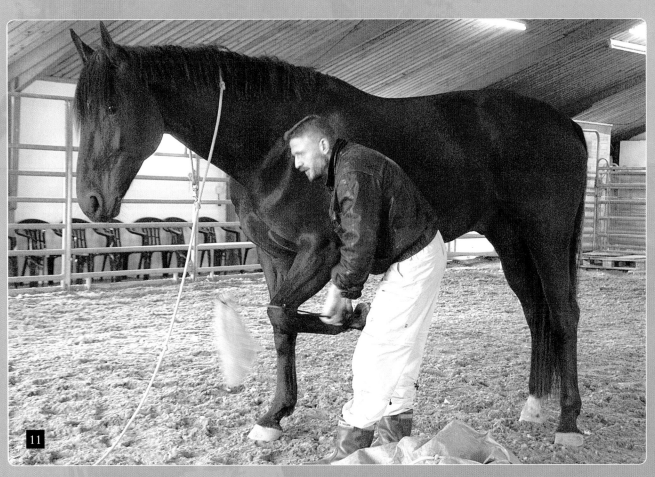

Marouk becomes bombproof

Path 2

In principle, this second path follows the same procedure. However, another essential element has been added. If we look at the pictures in this section, it becomes clear that the individual steps mostly represent a very precise improvement. For me, it is important to always reach a point where I am actually challenging and supporting the horse, without running the slightest risk of asking too much. In case of doubt, it is always better to set the bar too low, rather than too high. Again, it is of fundamental importance that the person completely 'forgets' that he is handling something that makes the horse anxious or nervous.

Let us look at the pictures in detail:

1. Marouk is clearly hesitant and nervous when he sees me handling this terrifying tarpaulin. Important: the horse is already very used to the fundamental approach, because of everything that we have done before. Even though the horse is anxious, he stays with me and next to me, and does not run away or against the rope that I have also been holding in my hand for the entire lesson. I am using my body language to express that I am completely 'at home' and that it is absolutely no problem for me to handle this tarpaulin. I do not reflect the horse's nervous reaction, or if I do, I do it by becoming even calmer.

2. and 3. The tarpaulin is now fully unfolded, but the horse quietens down after just a short time and becomes more of an observer. The man is engrossed in his activity and hardly seems to notice the horse. Naturally, he is completely 'with' the horse and he will match the speed and type of his actions exactly to the horse's actions – but the horse thinks that the man is not bothered by anything and simply knows what he is doing.

4. We see the active reaction of the horse again on this picture – now he is visibly quieter and willingly makes contact with the 'monster'. Everything is going well, very quietly.

5. Now here is what is really special about the second path. The man leads the horse through the narrow passage formed by the fence and tarpaulin. What this achieves is getting the horse to follow the person through the supposed danger on a loose rope. Important: the man does not appear to be concerned with the horse. It is completely clear to him that the stallion will follow. This security and self-evidence is clear at every point. You can wander through the lane a few times, making it a little narrower each time.

6. to 9. Finally, the horse follows the man onto the tarpaulin, still a little hesitantly. Once all four feet are on the tarpaulin, the horse gets praise. The horse quietly enjoys his 'success', because he knows exactly what he has

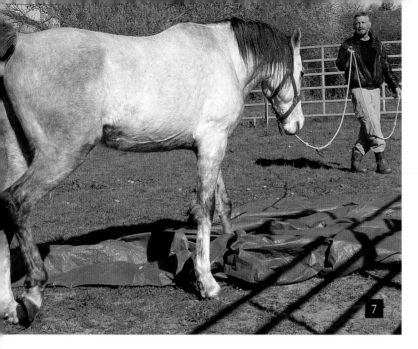

achieved. This is immensely important for his self-confidence. Neither the person nor the horse could ever have this experience taken from them. That is a real asset.

I would like to add a further point. The horse was never pushed, pulled or forced. Everything has built up on top of everything else organically. Everything is based on the pillars of correct leading, initial meeting and 'first parallelism'. All of the pictures clearly show how organically and self-evidently everything happens. That is why I always know that I am going to succeed. In the end, it is just a question of details and the final time frame. There is never any hint of punishment, the atmosphere never becomes loud and I never get annoyed. Not only is this unnecessary, it would also shake the foundations. See such an excercise also in the video clip *Connecting with shy Arabian Horse*. Now the trailer can finally come into play and you can easily imagine how we will travel the path just as safely and harmoniously.

When you undertake this kind of exercise with a horse, it is important that you have your goal clearly in mind but that you immediately forget it, at the same time. This leaves you free to respond to the slightest reaction from your horse, to allow him all the time in the world and to lead him to the goal in the best possible sense.

On the third day of the correction period, the trailer comes into play

The principle is now that the horse looks for and enters the trailer himself, out of pure curiosity on the one hand, and on the other, to follow the person exactly as we saw before in the leading and trust exercises. If we are well prepared, everything will continue organically. In the description, I will keep going into problems that you could run into along the way. We will stay with practical experience, and in particular, your practical experience, meaning that you should obviously try your best. Not everything will always work out this smoothly to begin with, but it will work out in the end. That is why I also want to give you a Plan B. Our aim is to be able to load the horse into the trailer at any time and place, straight away and with no hesitation, and we are going to do that by quietly following a clear path in the right order, from the beginning. The horse will learn to master loading and unloading slowly, safely and quietly.

Let us look at the pictures:

1. The best way to start is by building a small paddock in front of an open trailer using fence elements. If you do not have any fencing, just be creative and improvise, but always keep safety in mind. The paddock must be well constructed. We will load the horse into the left-hand side of the trailer. This is where the fence should also touch the side of the vehicle. If the horse is going to try to run out (Plan B),

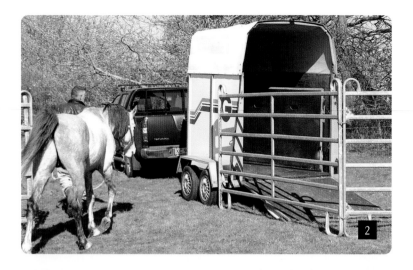

he will try to do so on this side. The way to the right side is open, but we have come from this direction so the horse would have to turn back, and he will not do that. In case of doubt, a patient and a well-briefed helper can stand at this point (Plan B).

2. The horse is now led very quietly around the fence into the paddock behind the trailer. The horse follows us on a loose rope because we have already worked on this. We keep coming back to that throughout the book.

3. I show the stallion the individual elements of the paddock and let him sniff the ramp. Everything is as if it were an established habit for the horse, because the stallion knows the basic process already – everything is familiar.

4. and 5. Marouk quickly shows curiosity and puts a foot on the ramp, but I have not asked for that at all yet, so I walk out again and praise my friend. Now and then I give lots of encouraging words, apples and carrots. Do it three or four times and then end this lesson. Continue after a break or on the next day.

6. and 7. Do the same thing again, but this time, go onto the trailer ramp. Do it confidently and without any hesitation – the horse will follow! Should the horse be a little hesitant, then (Plan B) the helper can touch the horse's croup

5

with the end of the whip very (!) gently in a steady rhythm, from behind the barricade. This may take a while. The consistency and peacefulness of everyone involved and the foreknowledge of success are crucial.

If the horse takes a step onto the ramp, praise him and finish the exercise. You will see that the horse steps on the ramp of his own volition the next day, and may even take a step into the trailer. The principle is so simple, as the pictures show. You have to remember that, just two days ago, Marouk would have reacted to nearly every situation with violent headshaking and panic. Now everything is easy and safe, even the sensitive issue of loading. It would now be easy to load the stallion completely, but I do not want to. I want to make sure that the horse gets a lot of security concerning this point.

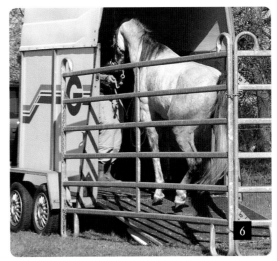

6

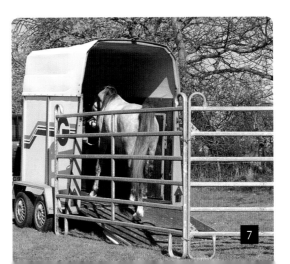

7

8

9

8., 9. and 10. Now the following point is important. When leaving the trailer, many horses are fast or even frenzied. We want to avoid this right from the very start. It might be necessary (Plan B) to let the horse tighten the rope slightly.

So, if the horse steps back without being asked, we hold the rope until it tightens and maintain a slight (!) traction. The helper can carefully touch the horse with the whip in a steady rhythm again. Tact is required throughout. The general idea is that the horse only goes backwards, carefully and calmly, when we give him a clear signal to do so.

I slowly and carefully guide the stallion back. Everything is done very quietly. I use his head to determine the direction of his hindquarters, to prevent him from slipping off the ramp. The horse should never charge out of the trailer – as so often happens – because this can be very dangerous.

10

Whatever happens during these exercises, you have everything under control. You can determine the speed and keep helping the horse to be quiet. Nothing can go wrong – everything has been well prepared. It is just a question of time. Stay calm, consistent, friendly, and follow the inner logic of this path, which is now yours as well. I completed the next steps quickly with Marouk. However, you can easily leave this set-up standing for a while and keep working on it until the next step. So the path continues …

Every outer success with our horse reflects the beauty of the inner maturation process.

Loading: we are almost there

After I had removed the fence, it was still possible to lead the stallion quietly into the trailer. I did it two or three times, without hesitating and the once so-anxious stallion now followed me with the quietest possible expression.

What has happened here will stay with the animal for ever. The pictures clearly show how the relationship of trust and the fundamental quietness in the horse grow with each individual exercise. You can achieve it in this way too. Maintain the rhythm, and if you have any doubts, give yourself a little more time. If things are going well with the fences, then dismantle them piece by piece.

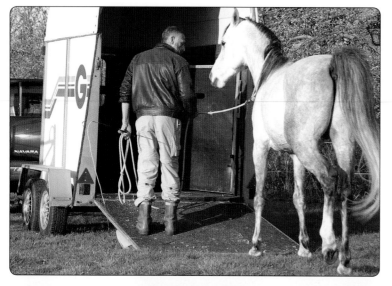

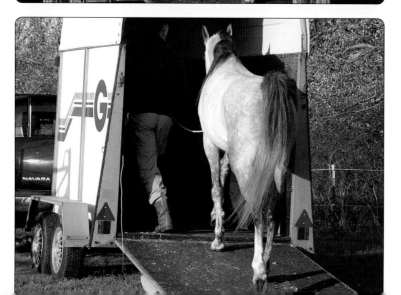

Loading: the last step

Marouk eventually learnt to follow me into the trailer with just a rope around his neck in one day, but it could have taken several. It is important that we keep moving forward consistently, and that we grow and know and recognise the path in front of us. If we have worked on the foundations, and if we devise a way at the right moment, let ourselves be inspired, then we are in paradise – nobody, except ourselves, can take away our quietness and our happiness. After all, we were not put on this earth to do that. A long journey, but a wonderful journey!

Obviously you should always load your horse with a halter, and tie him up in the trailer, but including this kind of exercise is useful for trust. The important thing is that you always judge your abilities well, because you should take care that it works. The horse should not learn to refuse you, simply because you have rushed ahead too fast.

This series of pictures also shows clearly how I carefully lead the horse out of the trailer again. Now it can only react to body language, because with the rope loosely around its neck, I can not give any other stimuli.

The horse has been 'corrected' or, to put it better, the conflicts and reactions that had developed in the stallion have been 'neutralised' as much as possible. In turn, he can now help his owner to improve his body language. Now the owner has to work on himself so that they can both continue on a harmonious path together.

Marouk was not and is not a terribly complicated horse. After a relatively short time, the stallion was himself again, but the problems that this horse had caused his owner would have quickly snowballed if things had been different and their paths had kept on dividing. Yet fundamentally, one path is so easy and the other is so risky. The change is so touching, but the consequences of continued misunderstanding are dramatic and shocking. The language of the soul is amazingly simple, and the logic in it may be surprising for many, because I have yet to meet a soul without logic and understanding.

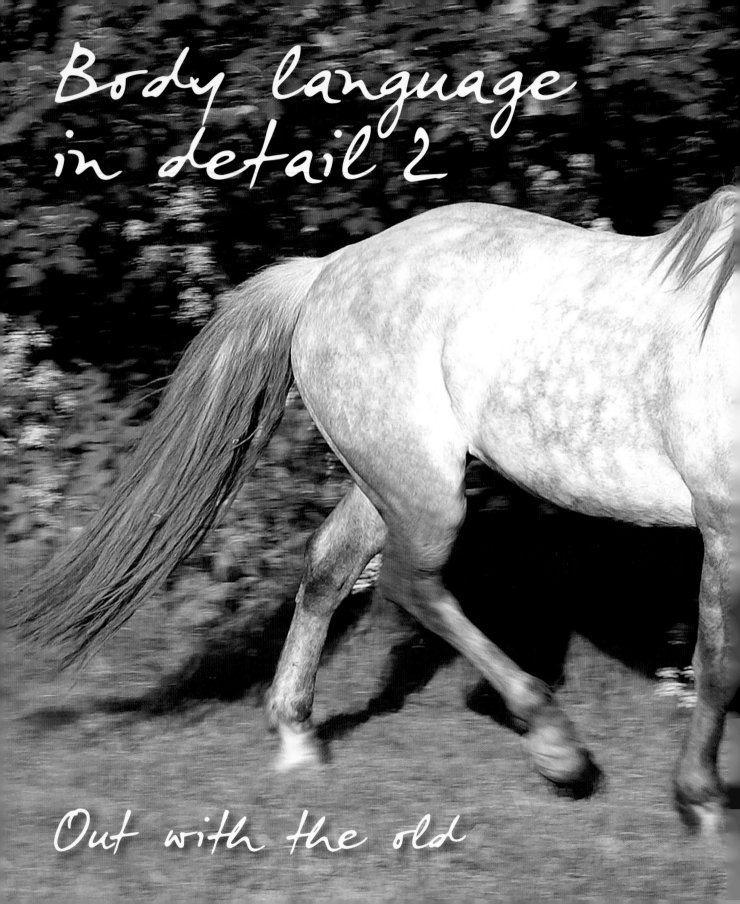

Body language
in detail 2

Out with the old

Opening up to reality

Let us take another extreme example, this time from my encounter with the Breton stallion, Phaeton, of the Spanish military stud. Weighing in at 1,000 kilograms, and having stood in his stable for months on end, this horse was considered extremely dangerous. If you look at the pictures and the man in them, you will certainly be able to see that his body and facial expressions remain basically the same. In one picture, the 'giant' is fighting him, but the other pictures show the horse after the fight, peaceful and obedient.

However, I always stay the same (see also the video clips *Borderline Demonstration* und *Wounded Horses Can't Cry*), because that is the only way to survive in this kind of exercise. One of my principles is that I always act 'normally', both inside and out, preferably wholly unconcerned by whatever is going on around me, however powerful it may be. This steady consistency is then communicated to the horse.

In situations like this, there can be no hint of 'fight' in me, or of anything special or unusual. If you look at the pictures again more closely, you might almost get the impression that I was presenting something quite ordinary. Indeed, in my experience I go even further – I do not feel sorry for the horse, and above all, I do not expect success. Compassion and expectation would simply restrict me in myself and in my thoughts; my preferred approach is to completely abandon myself to the events and the reality I am faced with.

Adjusting your heartbeat

I have prepared a little exercise. You will find two pictures on the next page, both of which are really menacing. Please look at the pictures for a moment and then answer the following questions:

- Have your breathing and your heart rate changed?
- Have your perception and your physical state changed?
- If yes, how, and in what way?

Now, please look as closely as possible and try to find out which feelings are aroused and located in which parts of your body. Examine these sensations. The essential question is this: if you were actually in this kind of situation, what would most likely help you? A spontaneous physical reaction, or the greatest possible composure and calmness? The latter, of course, because then you would have much freer access to all of the possible reactions – from de-escalation to flight, from smooth physical evasion to the last option, self-defence and active resistance. Either way, your chances of getting out of the situation in one piece are improved considerably, which could be the case many times over when handling horses.

If you like, you can now extend the exercise so that you prepare yourself for the situation almost meditatively. You remain in your inner tranquility, breathing calmly and deeply, certain that you have mastered all the dangers of life to date, and that you can trust in your fate completely. When you look at the pictures again, can you manage to stay familiar and composed? Give it a try.

Escaping everyday stress

These pictures illustrate minor, everyday chaos. Everyone has experienced this chaos in one situation or another. The Zen masters of archery say that a single shot, not fully consciously

triggered and therefore poor, will also have a negative effect on the shots that follow. These Oriental people have a reputation for being very strict, but horses are at least as strict. All the tiny, so-called trivialities of everyday life, 'the pervasive little chaos', really mark the relationship to us, to the horses, and they mark the horse's quality of life as well. In truth, the horse is actually often very alone, with scarcely a foothold in the human world and the feeling that he

lacks leadership and a framework of life. That is a real disaster for a horse.

Please note – there are no trivialities when it comes to horses, because nobody knows what might develop from some apparently minor event. Also view the video clip *Wounded Horses Can't Cry*. Big things are created by the accumulation of many small things, just as large-scale chaos is the result of the accumulation of many small incidents of carelessness. Many people who ask me for advice want to take one big step, believing that everything will then be better, but carefully taking each tiny individual step is a laborious process.

As far as the two horses in these pictures are concerned, the people are not present, at least not as dignified beings to be held in high regard. The little dappled grey simply runs over his owner. I would like to ask you to do one thing: do not look at the people in the photographs in detail, but rather as an 'overall quality'. Do you notice that they are actually only present in their head, shoulders and arms? Even in the pictures, where the horse has already pushed ahead of the woman so that you can no longer clearly see her, this energy can nevertheless be clearly perceived. Everything is deeply engraved in her body language. For horses and other creatures, it is as if these people simply are not 'present'. A horse's instincts will tell him to simply take no notice of a person like this, who scarcely seems able to safely and responsibly lead and support another.

1

The beginnings and the chaos

Let us look at picture I, and empathise with the two beings in it. The man, along with the same stallion that we saw earlier on in the book, is trying his best, but he fails in the end. Eventually, the horse could no longer be controlled and became vicious. Things have not yet become that bad in this case, but everything is well on the way towards it, and I would like to make you aware of that.

To begin with, this stallion's posture, with his eyes closed and his ears laid back close to his head, means: 'I am ready and everything in me is geared up to attack you at any moment.' That sounds dramatic, but I intend it to. This situation is extremely dangerous. A stallion has only one role in life – to win a herd and to reproduce. He just wants to win, to be the first, the most attractive, the strongest: he wants to lead.

However, we want to – or, rather, have to – lead as well. If a horse approaches me in this way, alarm bells start ringing – extreme caution is required.

2

However, nothing happens here. The man quite plainly does not notice the horse. His arm is well stretched out, which is good, but everything else is extremely dangerous. The posture does not indicate outer calm and inner vigilance, but rather a lack of awareness, a certain 'sleepiness' and indifference; in any case, that is how the horse will interpret it. The man is not really 'there', he is not really present in himself and in the situation and he is not really grounded.

His stance is bent forward, unstable, and at this moment, it even looks as if he is in danger of falling forward. Even a small stone could cause him to trip.

This man in picture 2 only wants the very best for the horse. He tries with all his might, and in so doing, makes another very serious mistake. He wants to liven up the horse by 'playing' with him. This has become very fashionable and I myself have made a contribution to this fashion, without pointing out more clearly that it can become very dangerous. You actually see many people apparently 'playing' with their horses, most of which have their ears back, or even bared teeth. 'Play' in the human sense does not exist for horses, not even for foals. Everything is preparation for life, and in that sense, everything is connected with surviving in the wild. Play, as we understand it, does not simultaneously contribute to concrete growth, and often triggers unwillingness in horses, and above all, a feeling of superiority. They can then quite quickly begin to displace people from their driving and therefore dominant position, and actually chase them. What could be interpreted as play in my films is actually a very precisely coordinated, 'timed' interplay that gives the horse plenty of opportunities for inner and outer growth. Rehearsing something and allowing it to become routine because it looks nice is one of the quickest paths to misunderstandings and problems. Trust and absolute dominance underpin the 'interplay' where you see me together with horses. For every horse-lover, that means taking a consistent path to the final recognition of how a horse can continue to grow constantly by 'playfully messing around'. Until you have reached that recognition, or if you are in any doubt, then please do not play any games!

In picture 3, you can see me making a clear gesture. Everything points to connection, amicability, respect and existence in the here and now. A horse is always 100 per cent, and we need to devote our undivided presence to him.

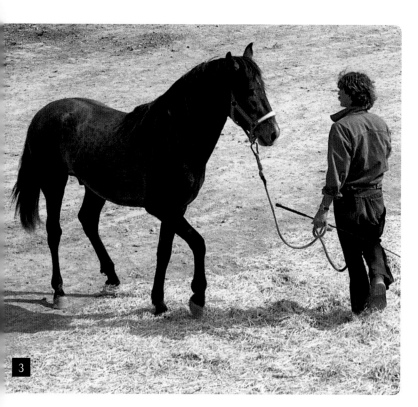

3

Composure as an expression of readiness to act at any time

This picture shows me standing quietly in front of an open stable door. The raised hand asks the horse to stay in the stable. It is a picture from a demonstration. The spectators are all standing a few metres away from me. What am I demonstrating? It is quite simple! The owner has barely managed to keep the horse in the stable for even a moment with the door open. Panicked and almost wild, the horse would then barge past anything and anyone to escape – extremely dangerous, and unfortunately not uncommon in many riding stables.

Unless you were aware of these circumstances, it would not be possible to infer them from this picture, because neither the horse nor the person shows any kind of anxiety. However, this composure can never come from the horse first. It can only be continually transferred to him. In any case, the horse is standing behind the open door in a very relaxed and friendly way, full of respect. Now let us look at the man a little more closely.

Here is his body language in detail. His facial expression is friendly, but very alert at the same time. He is very focused. His eyes are looking straight ahead, but it becomes clear how closely he is observing the horse in each of his movements. He is carrying a whip in his left hand, which looks as if it is in his hand by accident. It is important that it looks that way, although on closer inspection, the hand position indicates

that the man is ready to raise his whip hand with a jerk to mark the boundary as clearly as possible. The nonchalant right leg is also very relaxed, but at the same time forms a barrier and is ready to react in a second.

In brief, the man is well balanced and harmonious, but everything in him expresses that he is fully there and ready to react at any moment. Calmness without this constant inner readiness is not really calmness! Without it, 'calmness' would dissolve into absence and indifference. The calmness that I am talking about is always coupled with inner vigilance and a readiness to act at any time. This aspect of calmness is comparatively unknown in the Western world, where we tend to be familiar with the kind of relaxation that is a reaction to strain, and is usually associated with entertainment and distraction. Horses invite us to find a clear viewpoint here so that we can consciously deal with this topic.

Instant success guaranteed?

Let us look again at the gestures, the posture and the body language of the man in the pictures. It reminds us very much of the image from the previous photograph where I was standing in front of the open stable door. Again, one leg is relaxed and bent, the shoulders are low and heavy and my right arm is resting calmly on the back of an extremely nervous Arab mare. I am leaning my whole weight on this horse, as if the animal had known me for a long time. The whole thing is actually rather unusual, and on closer inspection, we can deduce and discern many things from it.

Firstly, it is important to know that deep inner contact is being made with this horse at this moment, and that this moment guarantees success, i.e. the horse's complete devotion to me. This 'strange' posture is preparation for the 'first parallelism', because, this first gesture actually encapsulates the entire secret of deep access to the horse, and for her profound change.

As you can clearly see in the video clip *Calming Spooky Arabian Horse*, the horse's problem was that she would not allow anyone to touch her. She simply ran away from under me and under my weight this time too, but after just a few moments, she followed me like a very close friend. What happened?

Again we can see that great attentiveness and presence are concealed beneath the complete unflappability of the man. This is clear from

At my events, I invite the spectators to mentally complete the exercises together with me – I then say to them: 'We all know that we will succeed today. Nature is always successful.'

his facial expression. Indeed, the man seems to be doing it quite consciously. He appears to be consciously putting his weight on the horse in a relaxed way. In this brief moment, I use my body language to tell this horse, with all her very individual experiences and qualities, roughly this:

- Feel my whole body and sense how relaxed it is, how at ease I am. Please do not confuse me with other people.

- Please be aware of how strong I am and recognise through my relaxation that this strength is as you know it from the horse world.

- Please sense that I recognise your problem – you are afraid of strain, of the insensitive actions of people and of the consequences of tension. Can you see that I am not like that?

- Please sense that I am not at all afraid of you. See how I move calmly with you. I am not afraid of your reactions – I understand everything – I already know you, I see how you are.

- Please realise that I am not holding you, and not pushing and pressuring you. You want to run away underneath me? Then do it, you are free, even if you see that I would have the strength to hold you.

- Please realise that people are able to support horses, yourself included, and to heal and to

lead in this natural sense. Please consider this and use your gestures to show me that you would like to accept this offer.

- Please see, through my gestures and my body language, that I will never do you harm, and that I want to be there for you, and that I do not expect anything from you in return.

Naturally, I do not go through all of this in detail before acting. My body and the moment do that for me. After a short time I then see the result – as in this case too. I can now even place the saddle cloth that she was so afraid of, gently over her head. We understand each other in spirit and our bodies communicate with each other. The horse is at ease. Yes, you can say that success is then guaranteed – it is simply nature and it always works reliably. At my events, I invite the spectators to mentally complete the exercises together with me – I then say to them:

'We all know that we will succeed today. Nature is always successful.'

Strengthen the foundations, examine the starting point

Again, we see two extremes of behaviour in one and the same horse, a young stallion. The owner had considerable problems with her horse – the situation escalated and everything became very dangerous. If we look at the gestures of the horse owner at this moment, then we can see

a certain stoop and a lot of tension. Of course, at this point, anyone would say the woman is tense because it is a tense situation – so what else could she do?

I say 'stop'. Her stooped and tense posture is actually just a continuation of the physical and spiritual action in relation to the dangerous behaviour of the horse. What I want to say is this: if a person gets into a tense or possibly even dangerous situation, for any reason, then their expression that follows is not always the consequence of what happens at this moment.

For example, three people are standing on diving boards with the water below them. For some reason, they feel compelled to jump at the same time. While they are still in the air, everyone watching can see the height from which they have jumped. It is just the same in real life.

The posture of the rider on foot in our pictures clearly shows that she has jumped from a very low height. These circumstances are very important for me, because many people are in the habit of explaining and justifying their behaviour and its consequences by reference to the circumstances of the event. However, they are not and do not become sufficiently aware that these circumstances only arise through their own actions and through their own position. Nor are they aware that the behaviour triggered is merely a direct continuation of their underlying behaviour.

The horse recognises this basic inner attitude and reacts to it. Horses are tough as nails in this respect. With this horse owner, I was able to approach the entire problem from the foundations in order to get to its roots. That means that it is not enough to just observe this one moment to find a quick remedy. Rather, the fundamental problem of considering the circumstances that led up to it, applies.

If a horse wants to run at me, I would never, even to a slight extent, adopt the bent posture of the rider in the pictures, especially under such dangerous circumstances. It is a question of the general starting point, not the current situation, because in a specific situation, I can only express what was in me already. This difference is very important.

The problem with this horse owner is not even so much the fact hat she is practically encouraging the horse through her stooped posture during the moment of danger to continue with his attacks.

The lesson that can be learned from these moments is that the body reflects a fundamental inner attitude in the moment of affective, spontaneous action.

Communication – the essentials

I would like to briefly draw your attention to the following observation.

In my work with horses, I try to reach a point, as quickly and directly as possible, where horses fall back into the flow of their own, original being. The 'first parallelism' is a sign of it. Another sign is complete peace, security, relaxation and contentment — they yawn with abandon. The pictures in this section illustrate this beautifully. When you see the first signs of this kind of behaviour in your horse, then you are on the right path.

We can never force this, or anything else. At best we can only encourage it. Like the spectators around me, I am touched by it again and again.

I have practised for many hours to make my body soft, sensitive, quick, powerful and mobile. It is a good instrument and it now begins to play. It communicates through my gestures, my hands. It flows — that is essential.

Like a lump of clay or butter in the sun

This inner softness, this inner implicitness and simplicity make the horse malleable, like a lump of soft clay. They completely let themselves go. In practical terms, I attend to the following areas of the horse with special consideration:

- Lifting the front hooves. I keep doing this every now and then, because this kind of treatment has an enormously calming effect that encourages trust. I do it very gently and I am especially careful when I put the hooves down. When I do it, I gently move the leg forwards and backwards with a gentle rhythm that the horse is happy with.

When you see the first signs of this kind of behaviour in your horse, then you are on the right path.
Please do not force anything - you will increasingly become an observer of events. Action as a consequence of inspiration.

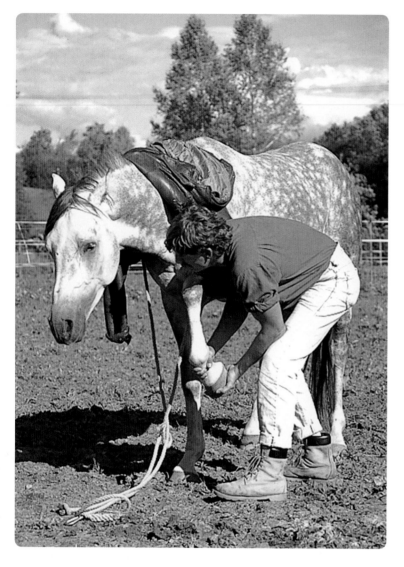

- As a rule, I only touch the nostrils and the mouth a little later. This area is very, very sensitive too and touching here also creates calm and greater trust.

- As a rule I touch the eyes last. I put the palm of my hand over one eye and rub very carefully and softly. With many horses this renews trust and creates wellbeing.

Self-evidence always?
Closeness always?

Here are some more illustrative studies, taken from practice, on the subject of body language.

If you do not want anything and are not after anything, then you have achieved your aim from the beginning.

The pictures on the right show scenes from a Borderline event in the Netherlands, in 2008. The sequence of pictures at the top and bottom show two different horses, which you can just about make out from their halters. The problems and characters of both horses were very different, yet look how similar their expressions are! Our horses simply want to come to us — we just have to let them.

- The part between the neck and the withers is also particularly important, because touching here has a calming effect that creates trust. Not every horse likes to be touched in the same way, so be sensitive and aware.

- The underbelly area is also very important. If a horse's expression is relaxed when he lets you touch him there, it is a sign of trust.

Through free
expression to
perfection

Part 1

A brief preview

*At this point, I would like to include a brief preview.
I have divided the topic of this chapter into two parts. In
this chapter I would like to give a kind of introduction
to the topic. We return to the topic in Chapter 8, where
I use the example of the stallion Queijo to learn, step-
by-step, how a horse can be led to his very own 'dance',
and change or even be perfected on the outside as a result.
In Chapter 8 we devote ourselves to the beginnings of
lungeing, again using a very practical example. Then we
come to Chapter 9, 'Practice from the beginning'. I have
positioned this chapter here because it was important
to me that I gave an overview of the entire path first,
because it is only after this that the individual practical steps can be better evaluated and understood. After
two more small chapters we come to the topic of riding.
So first I would like to ask you to follow me into the
'higher spheres'.*

The horse in the top illustration has drawn itself up from the back to the front. Even non-riders should be able to tell immediately which horse would be better to sit on and which horse, with which qualities and with which back and neck line, would carry a person better and more easily.

The perfected horse

Of the three pictures, there is no question about which one comes closest to the appearance of a perfect horse – both horse people and non-horse people would probably agree. Any adult or child would identify the horse shown at the top as the more beautiful one. Of course, it is the same horse, but in one picture, the Lusitano stallion is moving as he pleases in the field, while in the other, I am very close behind him, so that I can communicate with him to give him a special kind of help, using my body language. There is a lot going on here and it will be the subject of discussion in the following chapters.

Let us start with this. When I first got involved with horses – against the background of my experience as an artist, a communication researcher and a historian – people told me that you need to keep the horse between the seat and hands, to be able to give him a nice outline. That is a concept that I have disproved, hundreds of times, by my actions, confirming the view that I immediately formed during my very first encounters with horses.

I would now like to suggest that we formulate a clear understanding of how a really developed horse should look, and how it differs from others. First of all, we want to trace it back to its external form and appearance. The horse in our pictures is not any old animal. He is a high-quality Lusitano breeding stallion, but even the most valuable horses almost always have one thing in common – they do not really carry themselves. That is expressed differently from horse to horse, but in the end everything is roughly the same:

- The head of the untrained horse is carried more or less high, and the line of the nose is not almost vertical, but follows a more or less shallow angle. Please compare the two bottom pictures with the top one.

- The top line of the neck is more or less straight in comparison with the curved neckline of the perfected horse.

- In the bottom picture in particular, you can see the downward-pressed, largely immobile back, compared with the raised part of the back that now follows a more or less straight line.

- You can see that the croup is higher than the withers, especially in the bottom picture. In the top picture you can see that, in the extension of the now straight back, the croup has lowered and is therefore lower than the withers.

- The picture in the middle shows the horse galloping, as does the top picture. However, in the top picture the horse is reaching far underneath his weight with his hindlegs, far underneath his body. This frees up the forehand and you immediately get the impression that the horse can now move very nimbly on his hindquarters.

In brief, the horse in the top picture has drawn itself up from the back to the front. Even non-riders should be able to tell immediately which horse would be better to sit on, and which horse, with which qualities, and with which back and neck line, would carry a person better and more easily.

We should consider the following:

- It is one and the same horse, and in both cases it is free from the effects of any reins or lunge reins.

- Please note the neck musculature in the top picture, and for comparison, in both of the lower pictures. You can immediately see how differently the muscles are used. In the top picture, the horse is using its weight-bearing muscles in the neck area. Important: the muscles and tendons of the horse's entire topline are interrelated, from the dock to the ears. That is also why I say that the horse carries the rider with his neck muscles to a large extent.

- Please memorise these different equine postures very well – we have lots more examples in this chapter – because, using body language, using its all-round free action and play, your body has the task of 'chiselling out' this shape in the horse, just as a sculptor creates a statue out of raw material. This can be achieved with your hands, with all of your body's gestures and postures and without any external coercion, ropes, reins or straps. However, in order to do so, the image of the shape and movement patterns of a perfected horse must first be developed in your imagination.

The laughing horse

Apparently it is about external successes, about 'achieving' something with the horse, which can then be seen in the horse's appearance. However, the opposite can prove to be the case. There is a Confucian saying: 'Every plan for effect will only destroy this effect.'

With regard to horses, this is how it all seems to me. If I look at the world, then I see the wonder of nature, the spectacle of fauna and flora. I see nothing that is not perfect. However, when I look at horses, I see creatures that do not appear to be perfect in their natural form. Mythological traditions all over our world confirm the unique position of the horse in nature. The person at the horse's side has the possibility to 'finalise' this act of creation, to perfect it.

No person can create, but creation can happen through him.

132

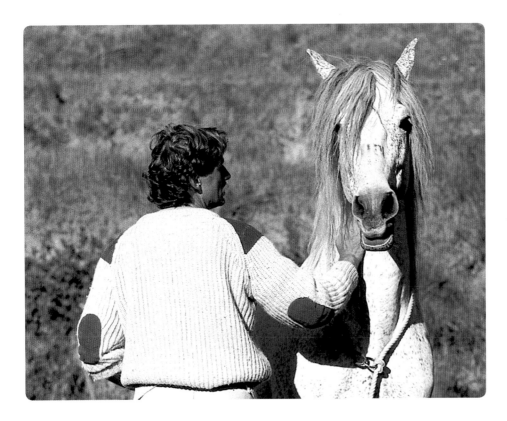

The laughing horse always carries an invisible rider on his back.

The horse has traditionally been considered to be a mythical messenger between heaven and earth, on account of its symbolism, in all of the ancient cultures of this world. In its visible manifestation, the horse represents the earthly, the material in its purest form. The horse can be completed and perfected by the hand of man.

A free horse that has been effectively and authentically trained by the human hand is always stronger, braver, more confident, more flexible, of higher status and simply more beautiful than a comparable one in the wild. This can only be achieved through the counterpart of the purely earthly – the spiritual. The human awakens the spiritual in the horse, and by doing this, he confirms and releases the spiritual being within himself.

The moments of absolute composure – symbol of perfection, shape and power

The following middle picture shows the stallion, Queijo, galloping again. We can recognise all of the features that we have already covered in detail. The horse has drawn himself up from the back to the front.

He has wonderfully free movement in the forehand and therefore appears to be infinitely more alert, mobile, powerful, impulsive and even friendlier and joyful. He has the shape that a woodcarver would give to a circus or carousel horse – quite simply a picture of natural aesthetic beauty.

133

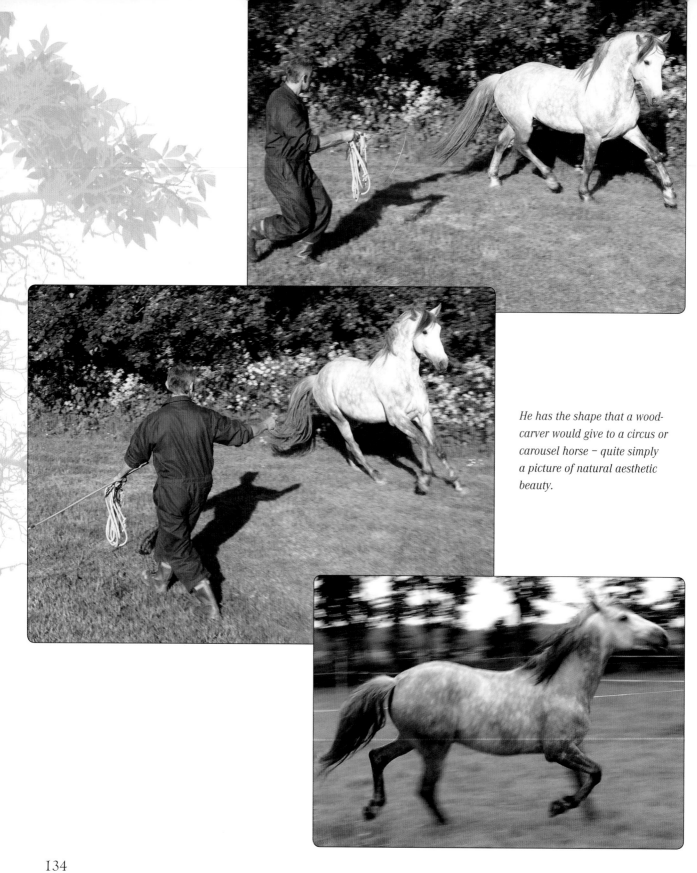

He has the shape that a wood-carver would give to a circus or carousel horse – quite simply a picture of natural aesthetic beauty.

> ## 'The rhythm must never be defied.
> ## Even the formless and invisible has rhythm.'
>
> *Musashi*
> ### Samurai master of the 17th century

In the picture at the top (opposite page), we can see the same horse in a wonderful trot. Here, the simple trot movement is already becoming passage to some extent. We can clearly see how the weight-bearing strength becomes effective in the horse, the wonderful submission, the raised back, the lowered hindquarters and the beautiful neck line.

For comparison, the picture at the bottom the same horse again, without my gestural support. It is like day and night – for the horse as well, because he immediately realises the immense benefits of treading the path of uninterrupted development with a supportive person.

What we perceive as an external shape and an image of beauty, balance and power, is experienced by the horse as an immense thrust of its entire, individual being. The horse changes to the same extent both inside and out, and with the change, comes the recognition of the cause of this enormous, positive development – which is the person at his side. The person now becomes a real mentor, more than just a friend, he becomes the most important supporter ever.

Important: you should never repeat an exercise with a horse just because it 'looks so nice'.

What happens, happens in the rhythm of the horse. I always try to sense it, to feel its state and its readiness for the next step.

The fundamental path

The further development of my work and my togetherness with horses can now be organised as follows:

I. Because we are now 'swinging' with the horse, following the first preparations that we have already discussed, and the horse is showing trust and respect for his mentor, we can now start opening up and making possible the framework within which he can move, develop and carry himself as well as possible. This starts from the beginning mainly through the individual rhythm of distancing and coming closer. This point is very important.

Right from the start, the horse learns that it can move and stop right next to the person, at a shorter or greater distance. People are always asking me why horses so quickly accept the lunge line around their neck as

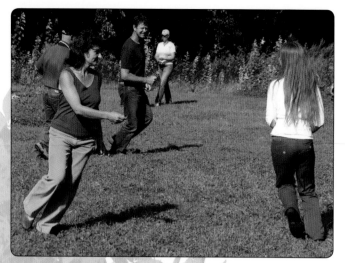

Horses have taught me to seek out
 boundaries without overstepping them,
which also applies from a
        physical point of view.
Only then our physical intelligence
can grow. Body awareness can mature in
us through play. We become stronger and
more flexible almost without noticing.

a limitation, and do not just fight against it (in particular see the video clip *Breeding Stallion Harmón Reborn*). They would certainly have the strength to run away from it. Eventually, I also do this with stallions in open fields. The answer is that if the horse recognises you as a mentor in the first place, then it will also quickly respect any free structures that you offer. Naturally, it also depends on the horse, but the principle remains the same. In the video clip, *Aggressive Stallion Tamed*, you can clearly see how I drive the stallion away from me and bring him back again, immediately after solving the stallion's first problems. This step, accompanied by very clear body language, is fundamentally important in my eyes. It is an essential part of the development to come. More about this later.

2. With my clear support, the horse then experiences how it feels to move completely freely in balance (see video clips *Dancing with Horses* and *Stallions in Authentic Horsemanship*). Naturally, the horse will only experience brief moments of this optimum shape, and the path to it should be trodden with all of a person's thoughtfulness and capacity for empathy. Here, it is important to keep this particular horse's optimum way of going very clear in your mind. The horse is usually surprised by this new way of moving, and shows it with a totally new revival of his spirit, becoming much livelier and happier. The connection to the mentor grows again considerably during this phase (see video clip *Collecting a Stallion at Liberty*).

3. In the weeks and months that follow, the horse will continue to grow into this optimum, but constantly free posture. The horse will present longer and longer periods in a perfectly balanced shape. In its movement, the horse will seek the proximity of the person more and more, so as to merge with the human in a solid unit of movement. A horse that has been freely developed like this from the ground has practically already been broken in, although nobody may have sat on his back yet.

Important: all of the patterns of movement should first be practised carefully alone without the horse, or with human partners.

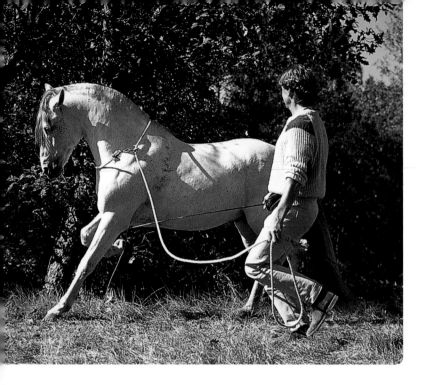

When you encourage a horse so much inside that its external expression seems to explode, if only for a moment, then a very special kind of connection takes place. A horse loves nothing more than the being who understands how to nurture him properly.

The basic position – the basic stance

These pictures show me with my PRE stallion, Yunque. Here, the state that I have just described has been achieved. You can see the wonderful shape of his stances and the distinctive power and strength of his expression as he moves right by my side. As we will see, this horse was not born with particularly high qualities. The requirements here were also below average. (See the video clips *Dancing with Horses, Stallions in Authentic Horsemanship* and, in particular, also *The Art of Lungeing*.)

We come to the most important moments of expressing body language in the work. As you can see in the video clip of the Lusitano stallion, Queijo, I always move behind, in front of, or next to the horse. The latter is a kind of

dance that requires a certain level of mastery. However, if my course participants leave, even to a minimal extent, the first basic position in relation to the horse, the horse will automatically stop. The basic positions are described in great detail in my other books, particularly in *Dancing with Horses*.

Here, the following is happening: in these pictures, you can see me exactly at the level of the horse's croup. This is the lungeing position, which, in the beginning, you should not leave under any circumstances, no matter what the horse does. It is the key to the art of lungeing! Everything else and all other positions result from this one, and I will keep on coming back to it. It is taken directly from the nature of horses and is not up for discussion. That is of fundamental importance. Maintaining this position is not easy and it requires some hours of practice, especially with friends and partners.

(See the photographs on page 136.) Please maintain this position strictly at the start, and keep coming back to it as soon as any communication problems arise later!

There are two basic ways of moving next to the horse or on the central lungeing circle. When lungeing, we move in a small circle. You can find the details in my other books, or by carefully watching the video clips on this topic that can be found on the Internet.

Next to the horse or on the circle I usually walk very quietly with accentuated steps. I only take on the trotting movement of the horse occasionally. I do that either to reinforce the horse in his rhythm or to change his rhythm and his action. By doing this, I can speed up or slow down the rhythm. Later on this will be very important for exercises in high collection. You can clearly see the synchronisation of the movements in the pictures.

Important: the posture of the upper body is basically very straight. Occasionally, you will also find me in a position where my knees are more bent. It then looks as if I am crouching down a little, and sometimes I also lower my head slightly. This is not necessary at the start, and is rather risky, because it immediately causes the horse to become subdued in all of his movements. He then becomes rather sleepy and unwilling to move. If I have channelled the horse to his optimum expression, I then do it quite consciously in order to bring him further into collection, but without flattening its expression in the slightest. However, this requires the body to be completely loose and relaxed, as a result of which full impulsion is maintained. Otherwise, the horse will just be inhibited. As it is, I observe this very frequently in my encounters with horse/human partnerships. Freshness and delight are often missing from the horse's 'big expression', and those are the qualities that we are looking for. So, to begin with, please maintain the basic position at croup level and ensure that the body is perfectly straight and the eyes are always on the horizon, i.e. looking straight ahead.

Keep working from the back to the front

I often work with loose horses, and that is precisely how I bring them to high collection, indeed genuine collection that then physically 'changes' the horse and re-shapes him – he becomes and remains more beautiful.

Riders and trainers who are fixated on the reins have to ride, or unfortunately force, their horse gradually into position each time. When the pressure is released, the horse collapses back into himself. I consider this kind of collection to be artificial and false. I believe that a horse needs basic collection that benefits him even before he is broken in. This collection must be genuine, and must also be shown in the field and in free movement.

I only achieve
this genuine collection when I
continually strengthen
the horse's spirit,
his psyche and physical aspects in
free work
through impulses almost exclusively from the hindquarters.

The pictures emphasise and clarify this impression again. In the picture above you can very clearly see the enormous effect of these gestures and support through body language. The horse is completely free at the front, and

140

his collection is genuine and natural and it is only caused by stepping further underneath and lowering the hindquarters.

These pictures show me in the central position in relation to the horse. As we have already said, the choice of position in relation to the horse must be made very consciously. Here I do this to very deliberately keep the horse in his forward movement, but without reducing his action and his expression. Now my body acts as a kind of brake, without any physical effect. This then leads to the increased collection of the loose horse.

At this point, I would like to refer to another important element, namely the inward position of the horse's head. Please take a look at nearly all of the pictures in this book. In them, the horse, at the most, has its head straight, but it is usually turned inwards, towards me. Only then can the horse rise up, and only then can the horse train the weight-bearing muscles that are so very important to us as riders. This is usually achieved using mechanical aids, by pulling on the lunge, with reins, martingales and so on.

However, in reality, this just means that the horse puts up a fight against the pressure applied, and develops and trains precisely those muscles that are not weight-bearing. As soon as the pressure is released, the horse falls apart again and reveals his real level of development. There will be more about this later in the book.

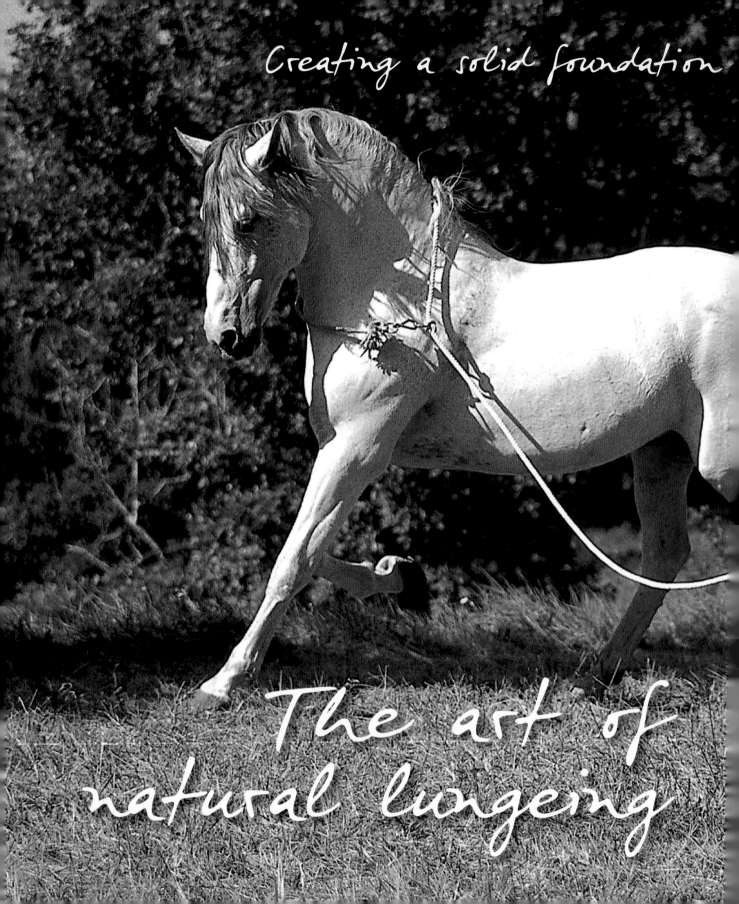

Creating a solid foundation

The art of
natural lungeing

Do little, but make it precise, gentle, careful and clear

At this point, it would be beneficial to clarify how the work is resumed and continued, and how the good relationship is strengthened, after the initial encounters where we get to know each other, using an example.

The following pictures show Maria, an assistant and long-term student, as she lunges a gelding for the first time in the grounds of our school. If we look at the horse we can see the calmness and the relaxation in his entire being. The horse feels well, and that he is understood. The position of the head is relaxed, although further relaxation, and later on, balanced self-carriage will soon come in the next lungeing sequences.

143

If we look at the horse, we can see the calmness and the relaxation in his entire being. The horse feels well and feels that he is understood. The position of the head is relaxed, although further relaxation, and later on, balanced self-carriage, will soon come in the next lungeing sequences.

You can already easily see the correct lateral bend of the horse, with correct inward flexion of the neck and head. That is a wonderful starting point for further work.

Open yourself to these pictures, the visible and palpable peace, balance and amicability. This fundamental composure and the basic understanding and trust make all of the next steps possible. Such pictures gladden my heart. In a moment like this, it is important that you do not do too much, and jeopardise these wonderful vibrations of initial harmony. You must constantly be on guard, monitoring yourself. You have to be more and more conscious, feel and observe more and more deeply, and communicate alertly and openly with the horse and your environment.

Now let us look at how Maria does it, because what we actually see is not calmness in the horse, but calmness in Maria that is transferred directly to the horse. To begin with, Maria calms the horse and gives him absolute security and trust, by going behind his quarters. That is always the best position to begin with. She is on the safe side where she cannot get too close to the centre of the horse. It is perfect! We can see that very clearly in all three pictures.

Maria's entire posture signals inner peace, of being rooted and grounded. It conveys peacefulness and gentleness, but at the same time is very clear, assertive and unambiguous in its expression. The upper body faces the horse's middle or his withers. This relaxed posture gives the horse all of the space and freedom needed

to move freely and to bend. The pictures show clearly that horse and handler understand each other very well, respect and listen to each other. That is a good basis for the next steps.

At this point, I cannot over-emphasise the fundamental importance of these initial clear and cautious lungeing steps.

A surprisingly different picture

These pictures show the horse's owner. She has known the animal for much longer than Maria has, so she should be more familiar with it. However, the pictures tell another story. The rider was very open to our help, and by the end of the course she had some excellent exercise sequences together with her horse, in perfect harmony. However, immediately after she had taken the horse from Maria, the gelding appeared very different from before. The head is considerably higher and the neck is tenser. The tail swishes back and forth agitatedly, and the back is tense and pressed down. Not only the left, but also the right ear is turned back to the rider, indicating that the horse is not remotely in agreement with what the person is doing. Absorb these pictures and compare them with the ones that show the horse with Maria. Also these differences mark the border between happiness or unhappiness, contentment or suffering, progress or stagnation.

Let us consider in detail what the rider is doing differently from Maria, and interpret the body language:

1. In this picture, we can clearly see that she is not standing at the quarters, or even better, behind them – she is already too far forward. The horse cannot understand this, because it is a braking, halting signal. At the same time however, her body and the whip in her right hand tell the horse that he should go forwards. This inconsistency immediately unsettles and annoys the horse. The reactions follow swiftly.

2. The rider's entire posture is neither grounded, peaceful, nor well balanced. In this picture in particular, we can see how challenging the woman's posture is at this moment. Her entire posture states: I want something from you. I want you to do this, that and the other. I am not really listening to you and I do not really see you either. I have my pictures in my head and my demands, and I now expect you to fulfil them too. Naturally, this also comes from the general uncertainty of a person who at this point wants to learn something new. For the horse however, these demands pierce the personality and the soul like a sharp knife. He is unhappy.

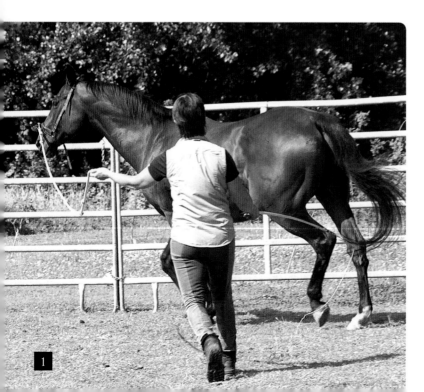

1

2

3. Like Maria before, this rider also has her hand raised. While Maria's hand was a little high and she had to correct it slightly after the session, this rider holds her hands almost threateningly high, and the horse reacts correspondingly. Just look at his body language. The handler's shoulders and hands are raised, and all of the energy is in the upper part of the upper body, and therefore cannot flow quietly throughout the whole person. The pictures are also particularly expressive, because of the horse's collection, because these pictures clearly show how the horse falls apart with his head raised and his back hollow. You can create collection and straightness, quietness and balance just as quickly as the opposite. It is a question of self-carriage and the example that the person represents and offers.

3

Those are the most important points for now. Let us return to the lungeing sequence with Maria, because we can learn a few more things from it.

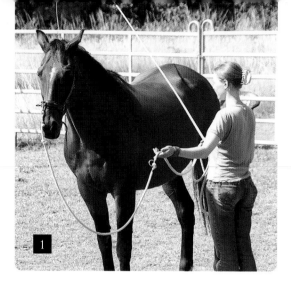

1

The start of harmony, from beginning to end

Let us look at the first picture. Maria gives clear signals to start lungeing. To do so, she stands firmly on the spot and does not move. This is very important, and it is done incorrectly over and over again. If you do not stand still, then you end up with a horse that just creeps around you, or pushes his hindquarters outward. The left hand shows the horse the way, clearly but gently and amicably. The whip is over the gelding's centre of gravity. That is exactly how we

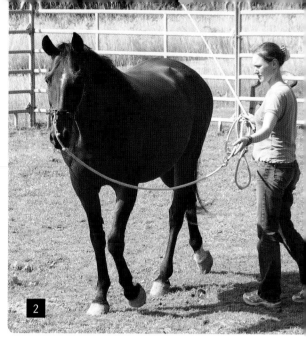

2

start the first lungeing sequence. She does this in exemplary fashion. We can give a very fine signal from this position. If the horse does not react (hardly any horses do, right at the beginning), then we slowly but constantly amplify the signal until the horse does at least a few steps. You can see this point in the second picture. Maria's body language is also exemplary here. She lets the horse pass by her quietly, putting her in the correct position behind the horse, takes the whip down and accompanies the horse into the lungeing sequence. Everything is wonderfully quiet, with the gently grounded expression of her body. The horse looks very contented and well balanced.

In the third picture, you can see that the horse is raising his head up. That is something that we really must eliminate in our work with horses. In principle, it is very easy and usually fairly quick. In the fourth picture, you can see how the horse

3

is bending nicely on the circle with a relaxed head carriage. The difference in the position that can clearly be seen in these two pictures is fundamental. I cannot emphasise enough how important this point is for everything else. Please consider the pictures very closely – I will come back to them in more detail later.

In the fifth picture, Maria is preparing for a change of rein through the circle. I describe how to do this in detail in my book, *Dancing with Horses*. For this picture, it is important to me that we can see how Maria continues to concentrate on the movement of the horse, how attentively she follows him, in order to observe each reaction. You can also clearly see that she remains in exactly the right position to the horse. All of these things are of fundamental importance. Once they have become conscious and ingrained, everything else seems relatively simple.

The events in the last picture seem rather ordinary – Maria is close to the contented animal and shows him in a familiar and friendly, but not overbearing way, that she has enjoyed her time with him and that she likes the work. That is enormously important. Breaks like this are essential, including between two repeats of the exercise. Everything therefore begins and ends in perfect harmony and in complete agreement. What more could we want? The horse will naturally begin to dance. He will decide that by himself, and we can only marvel.

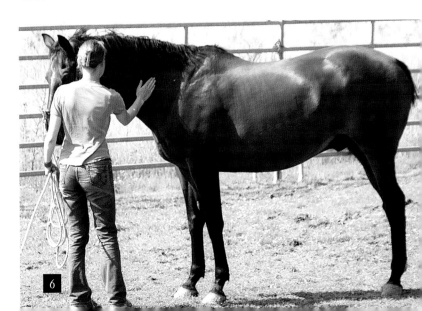

Practice makes perfect:

following tracks like a train

The following is a topic that I have also been emphasizing very much in my practical courses over the last few years – walking in an exact circle. It is really a matter of practice, but there are a few tricks too. It is actually very important that the person moves in the most precise circle possible, in order to maintain their position to the horse exactly. That is a basis for the exact, happy and expressive co-operation of the horse. We must pay particular attention to the following:

- The smaller the arc of your own circle, the more difficult it is to stay behind the horse. As a rule, the circle should have a diameter of around 1–3 metres. I very seldom move by just turning on the spot in the centre, as you see in the majority of riding schools. I do it to calm a very hectic horse and to bring it to a halt, for example, because turning on your own axis always slows the horse down.

- The person's chest should generally face the horse's withers.

- It is crucial that you walk in two circles, with the outside foot on the larger one. The diagrams illustrate this clearly. Here, the inner foot determines the diameter of the circular arc. You therefore have to place your inner foot very consciously, tending towards the inside, in order to really follow the inner arc.

- If you do not do that, then your legs will automatically cross over each other and your walk will become more and more unsteady and you will practically start wobbling. The circular arc will then mutate into an increasing elongated, irregular, elliptical shape. This is immediately transferred to the horse, who will respond with a lack of concentration and other possible reactions. Please never cross your legs as shown in the middle illustration.

- The feeling of being grounded is very important. The small pictures show me practising and demonstrating with course participants. The overall impression should be clear, assertive, steady, but also soft, friendly and sympathetic. Please look at my body language in the pictures. My shoulders are low, and the focus of energy and the starting point for all movements is in the area below the navel. Here I am demonstrating how you send the horse away quietly, but in a very determined way. When you do that with a horse, your attention is naturally no longer directed at your own circle and at its correct shape, but at the horse's signals. That is why it is so important to always practise these things with a partner first. It can also be helpful to place an object, a pole or a bucket, for example, in the middle, as an orientation aid to help keep the distance the same.

Of course, later we will want to 'float' over the field with the horse in advanced exercises, in a different place each time, and it is then

Here I am demonstrating how to send the horse away quietly, but in a very determined way. The overall impression should be clear, assertive and steady, yet also soft, friendly and sympathetic.

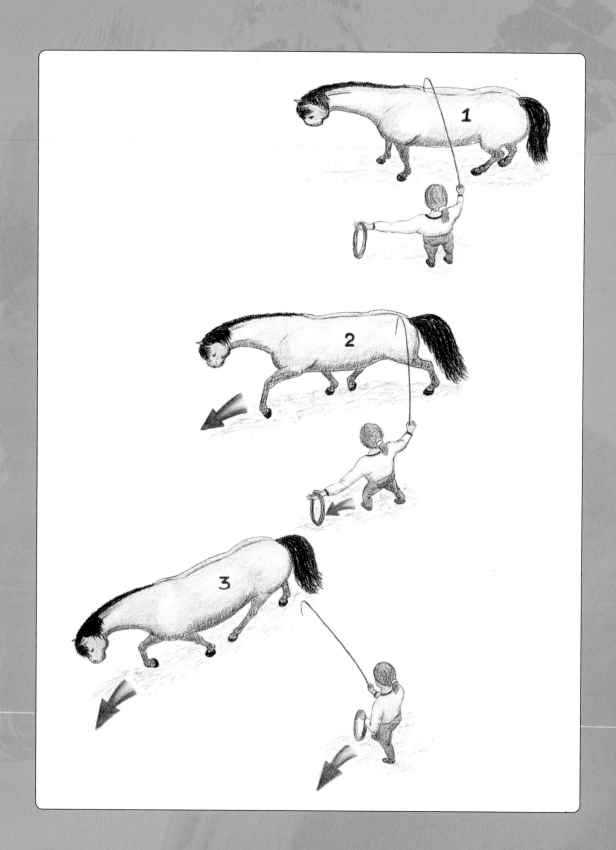

that we need to move very correctly around the centre point, even if it keeps on moving. This is an important key to success.

Turning the horse away, in detail

As already described in the example with Maria, you can easily see at point 1, how the person's clear posture, guiding hand and the whip over the withers guides the horse out on the circle. This basic gesture is very important, and I know that many people will have problems at precisely this first point, and sometimes will simply not get any further. If the first steps have been taken clearly, then progress to the next important points will also be made.

Important: to begin with, make sure that you remain on the spot until the horse has reached point 3 of the diagram. Only then(!) can you begin to walk on your small lungeing circle, in order to stay behind the horse or at the level of its quarters. This point is very important.

In the diagram right, we see a reaction that the horse will keep giving at the start of the exercises. Lots of people have problems with it, but the solution lies in just a small gesture. Namely, if the horse comes in again, point the end of the whip at the horse's withers quietly and without leaving your spot. The horse will react to it immediately and continue on his way to the track. Then withdraw the whip and point the end at the quarters as usual.

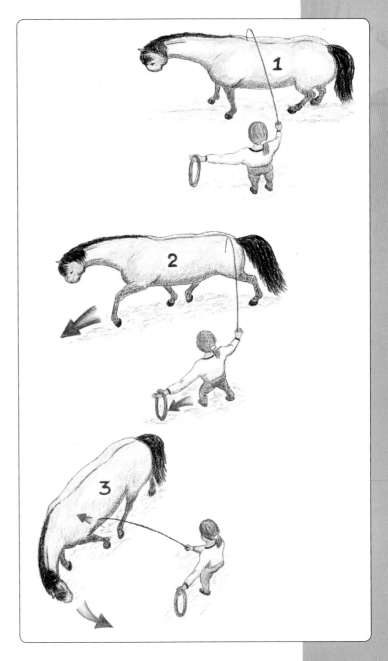

As the lungeing sequence progresses, you should always point the end of the whip at the quarters. Only when you are quite confident and very familiar with your horse can you point the end of the whip at other parts of the body to stimulate or

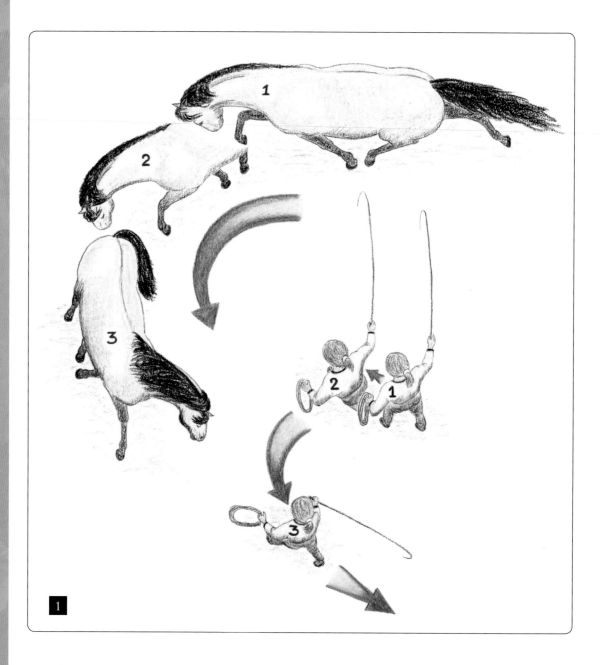

1

train them more. However, in normal cases, and especially at the beginning, always point the end of the whip in the direction of the quarters! When doing so, you should get used to holding the whip as still as possible. Again, I would like to point out that the person in the centre should appear to be as solid as a rock. You should only move if you can tell that it is beneficial for the horse. Get a friend to check you or record it all on camera. You will probably be amazed at how many unconscious movements you notice in yourself that you knew nothing about, but that will unsettle your horse.

Guiding the horse in, in detail
Three possibilities with different effects

The horse really wants to come to us. He feels safe and well when he is close to us. With the sequence of exercises that comprises directing away, remaining on the track and guiding in, we now have a comprehensive selection of possible actions. Combined with the various balance exercises for the horse, the exercises can be used to encourage new, individual ways to shape him. I have three fundamentally different ways of guiding a horse in to me. Each has a different background and a different meaning for the horse. The emphasis shifts between collecting, suppling, dominating, calming or primarily confidence-boosting effects.

The first way of bringing the horse in is the most composed (diagram 1). The suppling effect is comparatively small. The horse is guided in to the person in the centre in a very fluid and organic way. To do this, I move from a position behind the horse or at the level of the tail, quietly and steadily in the direction of the flank and withers. This automatically causes the horse to slow down and pause. In advanced work, I can use this deceleration to lead the horse back into collection on the spot by simultaneously using activating gestures and altogether more animated body language. However, if my body language remains generally neutral, then the horse will slowly turn to me and follow my backwards movement inwards, to get to

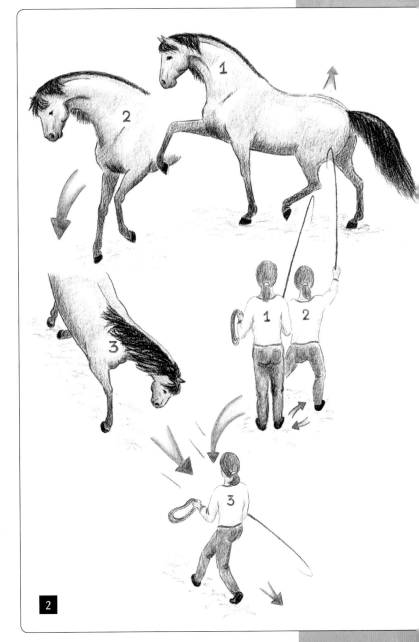

2

me quickly. The pictures in this book and the various video clips show examples of this procedure, which you can analyse and understand more clearly. I choose this kind of guiding in, for example:

- To stop a rather nervous horse quietly and make him calmer.

- To show a horse that he is in a quiet balanced posture inside and out and that I want to support him.

- To end a sequence of exercises very quietly.

- To relax the horse more, especially in the neck area or to intensify existing relaxation.

Some advice at this point: should the horse slow down or stop, for any reason, but not want to come in to you, please do not keep asking him. Instead, you should quietly continue with the general confidence-boosting work, in order to gradually build up closeness and trust in this way. Naturally, we should continue to observe and refine our body language.

The second form of guiding in (diagram 2) also has a calming effect, with the addition of a more powerful collecting effect. The move inwards towards the person is more precise and direct. This is the form of guiding in that I use by far the most frequently. As you can see in the diagram, I move away from the basic position to get behind the horse and closer to the croup through a type of lungeing step. Immediately after that I move back to my starting position to then reinforce the movement of the horse towards me, which has already begun, using a backwards arc. This kind of guiding in can

be seen very clearly in the video clips *Aggressive Stallion Tamed* and *Collecting a Stallion at Liberty*. Later on, the lungeing step is only hinted at in many cases, sometimes even with just a small movement of the hand. However, in the early phases, this action must be carried out clearly, using the support of the indicating whip.

With time, the horseman or woman's eye and their feel for rhythm become more and more precise, so that they can give this signal simultaneously, the very second the hindleg lifts from the ground. As a result, the horse steps sideways far under his weight to gather himself up forwards and to complete a tight inward turn from the hindquarters. This entire process not only has its own, very subtle beauty, but the gymnastic effect laterally and vertically is immense. The inner and outer growth process of the horse is much greater than you would think from the apparent small size of the exercises.

I have written a great deal about the third form of stopping and guiding in, in the book, *Dancing with Horses*. Here, the person comes out of their flowing movement to an abrupt halt, as can be seen in diagram 3. The horse will almost always stop immediately, with his hindquarters underneath him. The horse can then stay in place or be guided in with a corresponding, backwards gesture from the person. This kind of stop usually does not have a calming effect, but quite the opposite, with the horse becoming more alert and attentive, and prepared for higher levels of action and activity to come. This kind

3

of stop should not be performed too frequently. In addition to its collecting effect, this kind of halt has an enormously powerful dominating effect, that you should only use selectively. You can see this very clearly in the video clip *Aggressive Stallion Tamed*. Here, the issue of dominance is at the fore. It can also have a very calming effect, but only in such special, exceptional cases. In this clip, you can clearly see precisely how the person's body signals are used, and how immediate and pronounced the effect is. One can see very nicely how the stallion is even tossed upward with both front hoofs. However, you can also clearly recognise how minimal the person's gestures are. After stopping, I often allow the horse to stand quietly on the track for a while and then direct it forwards again, in walk, trot or straight into canter.

That describes three more important foundations for precise body language, which we can use in very different ways.

My entire system is based on just a few such foundations that are each of great importance with an immense effect.

For safety, you should start by limiting yourself to the first two variations described here. When you have mastered them confidently, you can try out the third.

The benefit of moderation and reservation

It is hard to believe that the stallion (Yunque) shown opposite is one and the same horse as on this page and on page 160. We can easily see how the weight-bearing muscles in the upper neck area and the stallion's back, chest and quarters have shaped themselves as a real feature of the horse's being and an expression of genuine development of the whole animal.

In the picture opposite, we can see how he started off – an extremely low and heavy forehand, a substantial lower neck, the top line of the neck is flat and relatively weak – the whole horse appears to be low at the front and quite long.

Before we look in detail at another example of how this great change can basically be achieved in a loose horse, using body language, I

would like to clarify once again that it can only be done with the right degree of moderation and restraint. Compared with the result, the work process as such is indescribably humble, minute and unobtrusive. Impatience and any kind of pressure will not only hinder success but actually prevent it.

Change in the horse is always holistic, and naturally, strengthening is too. That means that the horse not only appears more self-confident, stronger on the whole and therefore more

beautiful on the outside; he will also gain enormous inner strength. Let us look at the stallion's body language before and after the change brought about by the work. In the first picture, the horse appears comparatively weak, hunched and even sad, as if he wanted to hide away. He had enormous power inside, but it only found expression in the form of spontaneous rebelliousness, that the previous owner often could not explain.

You can see how differently the horse presents himself in the next two pictures. On the one

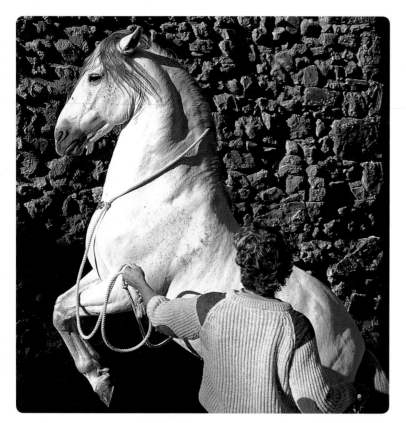

hand, he is very close to the person and very attentive, while, on the other, he is also enormously alert and self-confident. A horse like this, especially a stallion, will naturally use his increased self-awareness and stronger personality to keep questioning the person about their claims to leadership. Once a horse becomes aware of the full extent of his agility, and the spectrum of actions open to him, and thoroughly enjoys them, he can be a very big challenge. It is all the more important to keep refining and reinforcing our body language and our inner strengths. Person and horse then grow together, and there is no uncertainty about their roles within the relationship.

Part 2

The complete compendium
for the natural handling of
horses, based on
authentic personality development
and development of awareness.

Dancing the power

A drop of potassium permanganate
Summary, outlook and thoughts

You're bound to have heard of the stupid boyish prank of putting one tiny drop of the purple chemical potassium permanganate into a swimming pool, to make all of the water turn red. I've never dared to do anything like that, but working with horses has frequently reminded me of this not-so-funny prank. Why? Because just a tiny thing can be enough to create an enormous effect.

I have just come back from one of my Borderline events in the Netherlands. During the two days of this course, many points were made, naturally with the help of the horses. While I'm still full of impressions from this weekend, I would like to use its essential points as a summary introduction and preparation for the second part of our book.

The rearing stallion and three broken vertebrae

When I arrived home, I found a message on my desk, beneath printouts of the latest e-mails, informing me that a rider we know well had fallen off and broken three vertebrae. It appears from the e-mail that the woman had nevertheless been 'lucky', because the doctors were not anticipating paralysis. However, her freedom of movement might well remain impaired in the long term.

It is worth noting that I introduced the event in the Netherlands with the advice that the insurance statistics would reveal involvement with horses to be comparatively the greatest relative cause of accidents.

As the owner of a stallion led her horse into the arena on this Saturday morning, he seemed more rushed, wild, excited and even a little playful, than anything else. However, one thing stood out at me through all the chaos – the immense danger in which the woman constantly found herself. The stallion turned out to be an enormously strong 'King', and the work with him was a pure pleasure for me. I was quickly able to win the horse's trust with the smallest of steps in order to do precisely what he had waited so long for – to be supported with precise guidelines. He could be lunged as smoothly as if he had hardly ever done anything else. Without changing my posture, and only using conscious breathing and the play of inner energies, I could change him from one gait to the next, where he remained quietly or sought to join me. The surprise then

came shortly before the end of the event. When the owner returned to the work area during an exercise, the cogency of the warning concerning accidents, that I had given so emphatically at the very start, became clear to everyone. The stallion, now considerably more quiet and centred in himself, suddenly stood up on his hindlegs again, but the purely aggressive background was now blatantly obvious. The most astonishing thing for most spectators was the change from one second to the next. With me, the stallion showed no signs of aggression, but that changed the moment the owner took over the exercise.

What should be done?

Let's look at the following, to recapitulate:

- If the riders were prepared to take an equally great risk when driving their car, as they do with their horses much too frequently, they would probably have been removed from traffic a long time ago by law. For here the law watches with good reason that everything is done to ensure the greatest possible security for everyone. I consider interaction with horses to be like a constant, uncontrolled game with fire. Close calls are actually a constant occurrence, and it's just a question of time before it ends in an accident. That's saying nothing about the suffering of the horse, or the constant frustration of the rider caused by the latent or obvious threat that is present until the accident happens.

For the sake of my own safety, I would be reluctant to ride any of the hundreds of horses that are brought to me, without prior training.

Any fall from a horse could cost you your life, and even if it is only a minor fall, it still isn't fun. The 'rodeo mentality' and the imitation of stupid film scenes from budget westerns is only funny, if at all, until chronic disability marks a break with life as we know it.

From a mythological point of view, a fall from a horse describes death, or the loss of the soul. From an earthly point of view, almost every fall from a horse is either a kind of a declaration of bancruptcy regarding the trusting relationship or the result of exceeding reasonable boundaries, in other words, playing with risk. A really confident horse is very careful to keep carrying the rider even if they make a serious error.

I backed the stallion Xingu with his owner. The professional rider was really surprised when she was able to experience that the horse was as gentle from the very first second as an experienced horse that had been backed for a long time. I never allow myself to fight with a horse, especially not during backing. However, most accidents happen when leading and loading horses.

• Be aware of everything that can happen with horses and think about the situations in your life together with these large animals that could have turned out differently.

• Keep asking yourself whether you can clearly evaluate the relationship with your horse, especially with regard to safety. It is important to admit to oneself what will happen or what could happen if the trodden path, the routine, is left behind and something unusual happens. Do you still have your animal completely under control, whether in hand or under saddle? Your level of genuine control over the horse is revealed in these very exceptional situations. To be affected once by an accident is once too many. Being with a horse is a little different from playing tennis, music or painting; being with horses means being constantly exposed to a risk that is almost always underestimated.

• These emphatic warnings may make me sound like a killjoy, and they don't fit into the glossy image of the horse world, where hardly anything is said about accident statistics or the often drastic consequences of accidents. The aim of this book is to put forward my point of view, and I am almost always shocked by the recklessness and carelessness of many riders, especially when we consider that it is so easy to make a horse really safe, to the benefit of everyone.

• With regard to safety, these aspects should also be taken into consideration – the risk increases greatly with a stallion, because stallions are genetically programmed to be number one and to keep putting this fact across.

A horse that is unsuited to a person, for whatever reason, also poses a more general risk to safety.

Please do not underestimate the enormous effect of correct work with the horse in everything regarding reliability and safety. Good, communicative work always makes the horse considerably safer.

Lots of noise, or subtle signs –
where do we begin?

Using the example of the three horses presented at the weekend course in the Netherlands, it became clear how sensitive work and interaction with horses can be, right from the start. Many riders tread the path, and to begin with, they tend to lead and work with the horse using rather coarse signals, with the intention of generally fine-tuning them. In my view that never works. Instead, we basically should establish the level of sensitivity from the start. That is why it is so important for me to accompany each horse through a short sensitisation process, which then puts us in a position where we can complete the initial lungeing exercises, for example, with the finest signs that are almost invisible to the observer. That then transfers itself directly onto riding. At various points in this book, you can find advice and practical instructions relating to this sensitisation phase at the beginning of the work and wherever it seems appropriate in the course of the exercises. It has a lot to do

with the 'first parallelism' and the 'tuning in' during the first meeting. The principle is this – always choose steps that are small enough to always be 100 per cent effective.

100 per cent –
does it even exist?

One of the themes of the weekend course was advice on the fundamental difference between the human path of growth and the path of being tested by a horse. If you learn to play the piano, to paint or to sing, then, hour by hour, you will become richer inside and you will have more and more ways of expressing yourself. You become more authentic, sensitive, stronger inside, more self-confident and so on.

The opposite often happens with horses, because they don't differentiate between 30, 50 and 90 per cent. They only know black or white, and only recognise 100 per cent. You are either together or apart, you are either pregnant or not. Anything in between does not exist for a horse. That is why I have been able to tread my path with horses comparatively quickly. I have tried to place demands on body and spirit in many different ways before. A horse can then only evaluate the status quo and say yes or no. If he says no in his own way, then things not only sometimes becomes very dangerous, but often also very frustrating. There is practically no general growth. That is why I advise all riders to be active in as many different areas as possible, in order to experience an inner process of 'becoming and finding'. A person can then keep transferring this to the horse world, so that it can be reflected there. As I say – you don't learn to ride by riding.

Naturally no person is 100 per cent in the absolute sense. To expect that would be presumptuous and arrogant. However, anyone can be 100 per cent in a limited, 'human' sense. You can give all that you are capable of at the time. You can contribute your truthfulness, authenticity, credibility and inner strength as far as possible. Horses don't want anything more, but they also don't want anything less. But this also means sometimes sacrificing a wish, i.e. paying attention to the consequences of your actions, always being ready to meet the needs and always being ready to relativise. Dull routine and stagnation are guarantees of grey mediocrity, and horses don't wish to know mediocrity, because it's the death of the soul and an abomination for any horse.

The magic

In this sense, I am also talking about a kind of 'magic' as the quality that I always try to achieve when I am with a horse. It has to shine and move people; it has to move and be timelessly valid. Like a forest's morning scent, like the sparkle of a fish beneath the mirror-smooth surface of a calm sea, like an eagle's gliding flight, the even flight of geese, like a smile.

The circle completes itself again here, because in the moment when this stallion attacked his owner in the Netherlands, the magic ended. And my actions end there. At this point, I have to differentiate, just like any other person. I can only point out that fundamental questions now need to be asked. Namely, the question of whether this woman should really be with this stallion at all. My question implies the answer. If I continued to act, kept wanting to 'help', then I would just be pushing and bending into shape, forcing and 'making things fit' for 'everyday use'. The magic would then inevitably be lost. That is then no longer my world.

I left the arena with quiet, but emphatic words of warning. When it reaches this point, my path simply comes to an end. I know that I must draw the line here.

Rough behaviour?

Another coincidence? I've just received the following e-mail. I think it fits in with our subject really well:

'Dear Mr Hempfling,
I have been trying to work with horses like you do for several years now. I'm 25 years old and I have been involved with horses for around 15 years, But I still get the feeling that we have little idea of what is "real" and "natural" in horses, because unfortunately, despite our best efforts, we

still tend to fall back into old patterns, to become hurried or haul on the rope. Then afterwards we keep getting annoyed about this rough behaviour.

I keep realising that the background to these setbacks is that, in many respects, we are lost and despairing how we should behave.

However, the obtuse person eventually reappears and we turn to what seems "easier" – nagging and complaining, hauling the head around and giving a smack with the whip. … Which destroys everything again. […]'

For me, the boundary between the desired interaction with horses and the reality, all too often when people are trying very hard, as described in the e-mail, is the same as the boundary between magic and authenticity and routine, which often does not 'work'. It is the difference between the first and second levels, just as I described right at the beginning of this book.

The narcissistic rider, or the inability to allow closeness

I touched on this subject that weekend, and I was concerned that this book would be incomplete if I did not cover this topic at least briefly here. According to experts, narcissism has now become a kind of widespread disease and it exists or is dormant in many people. Why am I writing about this now? Because the horse world, in particular, offers so many opportunities for all kinds of projections and therefore represents a happy hunting ground for many people who have symptoms of narcissism, so this subject is very important for us, and also quite relevant in practical terms.

In broad terms, how does a narcissistic personality develop? Here I describe a clear and extreme mix of symptoms that clarify this condition:

- A child looks for and desperately needs the closeness, the very personal understanding and the direct devotion of its parents.

- However, parents are often not really able to build up this inner, individual relationship and keep it constant.

- The child now experiences a divided world. On the one hand, they escape the pain of not really being accepted and understood, by withdrawing into their own world. The loneliness in the core of their heart now becomes a kind of structure for existence and survival. On the other hand, the child hides behind a mask because they quickly learn that outer (behavioural) patterns lead to outer recognition more than anything else. Admittedly this is no replacement for real proximity, but is the only thing that the child can grasp.

- This two-part structure is eventually carried over into adulthood. This kind of person seeks closeness deep down, but at the same time has a terrible fear of it, because they have never really been able to express it and have never experienced close communication. They are alone in the world. The parents were loved as well as hated. The natural love of a child for its parents is compensated by (often unconscious) hatred of the reality and of the reality of the parents.

- These mechanisms basically form the 'home' of the narcissistic person. They continue to strive for closeness, but pull back at the crucial moment, by setting up a conflict, for example. What is really tragic here is that this conflict, this withdrawal, almost always comes from what is hidden. It almost never results in an open conflict.

- And its further consequences are also tragic: the very person who is close to the narcissist and their (apparent) love will be pulled right into this vicious cycle of life and breakdowns. The 'victim' of the narcissist is always their closest companion. They often no longer understand the world because, no matter how they seek to order and harmonise it, they cannot avoid conflict.

- Because narcissists still cannot achieve this genuine, authentic appreciation in adulthood, all that remains for them is the inner conflict with themselves; but what is this inner self? As a child, this authentic core became concealed by a mask of external behaviour. Narcissists expend a great deal of their energy on maintaining the mask, and doing everything to make it appear authentic. This mask now becomes the direct and closest companion, an anchor and replacement identity. In short, all of their love is concentrated on it. In reality, narcissists don't love themselves, but the opposite. Inside, they usually dislike themselves, but they love the mask that has become their cloak of iron. They both love and hate themselves and their imaginary identities. They idolise and judge themselves; they elevate and debase themselves, almost simultaneously.

- This division leads narcissists into very deep conflicts. They strive ceaselessly for (external) recognition but, at the same time, eventually turn away anybody that gives it to them. The inner authentic core just continues to wither, precisely because of this external recognition and, usually, an unconscious part of the narcissist's being is distantly aware of this.

- Narcissists, as self-assured as they may appear, hardly have any self-confidence inside, so the subject of power is crucial for them. As they perceive it, power gives them their only form of security, because they don't have any (inner) security at all.

- Apparent power, apparent closeness, apparent recognition, apparent success, apparent outer glamour, physical contact, warmth and, above all, an ever-silent victim, can be found by the narcissist in the horse and in the horse world. Thus, we can now understand how it is possible for a being to simultaneously appear to be deeply loved and then tormented and tested or even mistreated. The divided feelings of the narcissist cling to the horse's silence and find a happy hunting ground for possibilities and 'compensation', because the narcissist's inner and outer contradictions are not silently tolerated or honoured anywhere else. There is scarcely another place where they can hide so well, where they feel among their own kind.

Narcissism is a global aspect of our modern world. The (powerful) world of stars and starlets, politics, economy and, last but not least, religion would be impossible without the different faces of narcissism. I think it is advisable to delve into this hugely controversial topic, and I did it as well because the horse world would be completely different without these symptoms. These investigations also helped me to finally grasp the enormous difficulties that some people have in building closeness to horses, because narcissists want closeness more than anything, so that they can wilfully destroy it again, just before it is achieved. Then, even our best teacher cannot help. They can only protect themselves by creating distance. At present, specialists consider healing this clinical condition to be very difficult.

About Bert, the absolute quiet and the archer

To conclude this summary and move on to the next topic, I would like to go into another important point. On Sunday evening, I met a few managers to discuss a planned event with them. Just a few weeks ago, I had given Bert, the head of a management consultancy, some initial help and instructions by telephone, based on a video clip that he had supplied. This was the essence of my advice: he must do everything much more quietly and, on the whole, do a lot less. Bert stuck to these instructions and had already achieved the first successes as a result. His comment about this was:

'I would never have believed it possible that somebody could do so little and proceed so deliberately, yet make so many changes. Although I have already slowed down so much, I must go much, much further, following your advice. It was almost a shock for me to see and to admit how much I actually still rush about.'

I know that is how it is for many people. The consequence of the quiet and the intensive uniformity of my work unfortunately do not come across in photographs alone. It can almost only be experienced and understood in a live demonstration. To give some support, I would like to offer the image of an archer, deep in concentration, who composes himself very quietly before shooting, finds his exact position and then raises his bow, in complete concentration and with no time pressure; he takes aim and then finally fires, knowing that he only has a single shot. The moment of the actual event, the flight of the arrow, appears to be unrelated to the preparation. And the contrast between the power of the shot and the gentleness of the events surrounding it is also significant and striking. I experience something like that in my work with horses. It is like a very quiet, gentle flow, without any awareness of time that communicates purposefully, heals, animates, stimulates and reacts. If you extend the idea of quiet and economy of action to the imaginable maximum, and then multiply it with itself at least once, then you will roughly be where I would really like most of my students and course participants to be, combined with ever-increasing inner energy.

That's enough about my experiences in the Netherlands this weekend. Now let's get back to practice in detail and devote ourselves to the mother of all exercises, the shoulder-in and the beginnings of the dance together.

As the owner of a stallion led her horse into the arena on this Saturday morning, he seemed more rushed, wild, excited and even a little playful, than anything else. However, one thing stood out at me through all the chaos – the immense danger in which the woman constantly found herself.

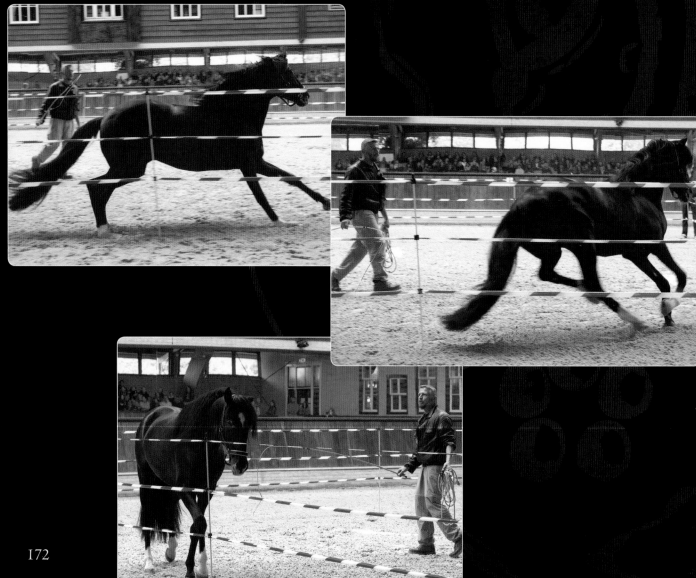

The stallion turned out to be a strong 'King', and working with him was pure pleasure.
I was quickly able to win the horse's trust with the smallest of steps in order to do precisely what he had waited so long for – to be supported with precise guidelines. He could be lunged as smoothly as if he had hardly ever done anything else.

Without changing my posture, and only using conscious breathing and the play of inner energies, I could change him from one gait to the next, where he remained quietly or sought to join me.

This little gelding was presented to me because he practically wouldn't let anyone touch him, having been terribly mistreated in the past. Any touch to his ears caused him to throw himself to the ground. After the animal had come to trust me, I was able to touch his ears with my nose and face.

Through unfettered
expression to perfection

Part 2

The golden platform
Shoulder-in, in practice

I have emphasised the importance of free shoulder-in for a horse's growth process again and again, in my books and videos. In Dancing with Horses I go into great detail about how important this fundamentally simple and natural exercise is, and how you can build it up step by step. At this point, I would again like to illustrate the important points of shoulder-in in practice.

177

Important: in the overwhelming majority of cases, free shoulder-in in walk and trot, with and without a rider, is the ultimate and, at the same time, most important exercise that the horse offers us humans as an entirely natural way of moving. The exercise maintains and supports the horse's weight-carrying ability and health to the greatest and most satisfactory extent. Horses will only spontaneously offer additional sequences of exercises from their natural environment and framework of movement in a few cases. Our role is to further encourage the horse in a way that is beneficial to him. You should never train or force a sequence of exercises or gaits. Although this may be common practice, it actually just destroys what has been achieved, on a physical and spiritual level.

A shoulder-in that is not done freely by the horse has no positive effects, physically or mentally. Quite the opposite. Only a horse that moves and carries himself freely, that can balance his head, neck, back and hindquarters without limitation, will grow, quickly and powerfully, through this exercise. (Also view the video clip *The Art of Lungeing.*) We do not always start with the shoulder-in exercises in walk, as we see in our example here. I will come to the other variations shortly. During our lungeing sequences, the horse has already shown that he is ready to be supported in shoulder-in. We can see that because he is already stepping under more in the corners, and spontaneously offering smaller circles, sometimes with a diameter of less than 3 metres, with a nice lateral bend and

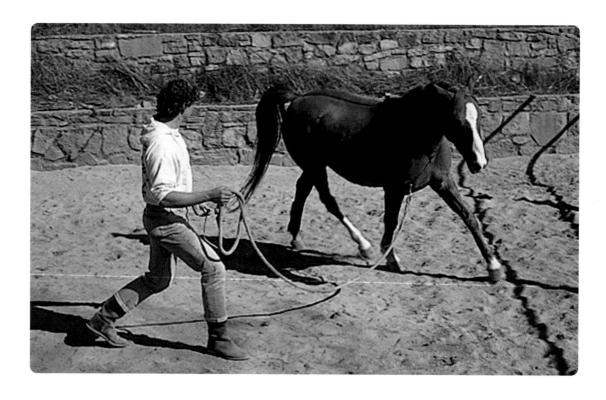

a nice inward flexion. On the whole, the horse is relaxed, springy and loose in all parts of his body.

The picture left illustrates this state very nicely. With a raised and relaxed, yet powerful back, stepping well under his weight, with a well carried neck and nice, relative submission, little Janosch walks in a small circle with correct lateral bend and with his head to the inside.

A horse that goes like that will automatically show the first steps of shoulder-in in the corners. He will simply enjoy it so much and recognise the enormous potential that it holds for his own advancement. Please observe the compactness of this little horse, an animal that first came to me with a ewe neck, narrow chest and sunken back. Simple lungeing exercises on a natural and loose basis, combined with shoulder-in exercises, create this enormous bio-positive effect.

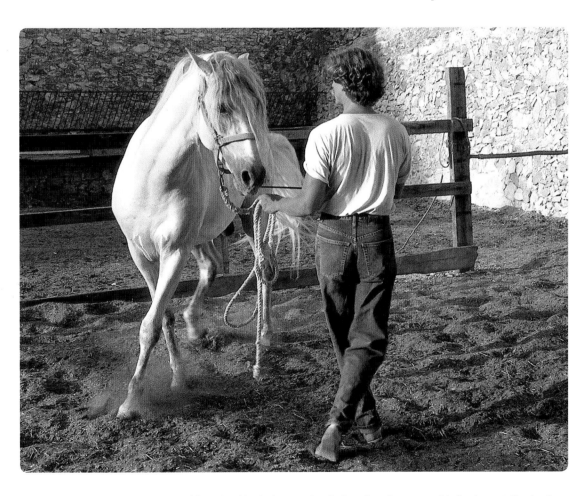

I have emphasised the importance of free shoulder-in for a horse's growth process again and again, in my books and videos. In Dancing with Horses *I go into great detail about how important this fundamentally simple and natural exercise is, and how you can build it up step by step.*

As light as a fly

*We make an offer and watch how
the horse responds*

If we have achieved a good starting point using leading and lungeing exercises, we can start with this kind of shoulder-in in walk.

For the shoulder-in exercise, we need the horse to react to minimal stimulation to his flank. I position myself in front of the horse as shown in the diagram. The tip of the whip points to around 20 to 30 centimetres behind the area where our lower leg would rest. We keep touching the horse's flank impulse-like with the weight of a landing Fly (!), to stimulate the horse to take his first step. Stop giving the signal at the very first sign of movement. It does not matter whether the horse actually moves away to the side correctly. Each step is welcome at the beginning, and should be praised immediately. Important: never touch the flank with the whip any harder than this, even if you have to stand there for several minutes until something happens. Sooner or later, the horse will take a step sideways, and then we can lavish him with praise and finish this section.

It can be helpful to position yourself a little to the side of the horse so that he is already holding his head slightly to the inside. As a result, he will be encouraged to step under even stronger with his hindlegs. End the session or start with another exercise immediately after the first reaction. Gradually, the horse will react to the slightest touch with the whip, and finally to a slight indication with the hand.

Because the horse now fully accepts your vital circle (see Chapter 9 – *Practice from the beginning*), he will understand and recognise you as a barrier and see how he can move gymnastically in front of and with you in shoulder-in. The horse will gladly accept and offer these steps himself, with increasing joy. But please note, the shoulder-in requires physical effort from the horse, something that is frequently underestimated. For that reason, please only ask for a few steps, so that your horse never loses joy in this exercise. A dialogue will quickly result because the horse will continue to offer this exercise spontaneously. We need sensitivity here to achieve an ever more harmonious dance.

A question of body language – pressure or freedom?

The art of lightness

Now it's just a question of using body language to support the loose horse in shoulder-in at walk and trot. Walking in lockstep, crossing our own legs in front of each other, and taking the appropriate position to the horse, we invite and encourage the horse to take a few steps in shoulder-in, in complete freedom. That's enough about the beginnings and form of the first approach to this key exercise. Everything else will be covered in detail in the next chapter.

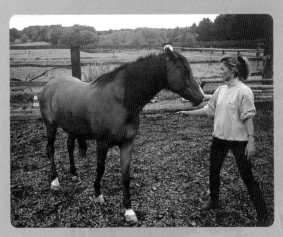

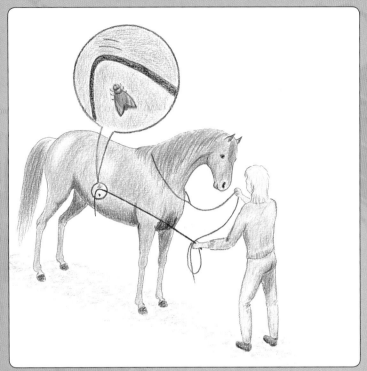

*The tip of the whip points to around 20 to 30 centimetres
behind the area where our lower leg would rest.
With impulses that weigh as much as a landing fly (!)
we keep touching the flank.*

There is just one more, really important thing for me to mention. We want free, loose play from the horse, a kind of 'calm wildness', a kind of display and movement that has not lost any of a horse's original wildness. That is the art, the magic. But why is this boundary so difficult to cross? Is it really that difficult? In principle, no, but to achieve it your own body and your own being must express this freedom and this natural power strongly and clearly enough. If you move together with your horse, then nothing about your expression should inhibit him. Even slightly raised shoulders or tension in the back or pelvic area will be absorbed and reflected by the horse. I mainly achieve the lightness that you can see in the horses that are with me through the relaxation in my own body. Do you remember the picture at the start of the book, where I look like I'm floating? Only the relaxation in your own

body will let the horse be free in the exercises. A tense body will put constant pressure on the animal. It has an enormously braking and debilitating effect!

This point is immensely important. The picture above shows PRE stallion Almendro. He moves in a friendly, light and playful way, yet he is also so proud and so noble, as we have seen in the many other horses that I have worked with. Again and again, it is a similar expression of liveliness, power, free play and natural pride. That is the fruit, the mirror and the affirmation of the unique, free, inner being or of the fact that you are on the way there. No amount of earthly violence and no trick will ever be able to produce or force this expressiveness. This gift will be bestowed on those who make an effort with themselves and with their own relaxation, their own inner freedom and independence.

If I come across as a flexible, sensitive, well-balanced and physically aware person in my pictures and videos, it is because I am always striving to preserve the qualities that nature gave me, and to become increasingly aware of them.

Fitness, stamina and artistry?

Two extremes with no happy medium?

At this point, we should briefly turn our attention to the physical requirements for completing our exercises with horses. If I look around, then it seems to me that the issue of physical awareness is primarily characterised by two extremes. On the one hand, I see a lot of genuine couch potatoes – people who have very little or no access to their body and their sensitivities, while on the other, there is a rather extreme form of fitness, artistry and physical performance.

We are all familiar with the images of Eastern forms of mediation that speak of a special kind of middle ground, which placed less emphasis on 'fitness, stamina, and artistry' – at least

initially, and more on authentic body awareness, natural suppleness and the free flow of all our inner energies.

During the past 30 years, I have developed my own body exercise system that, based on experiences and reflections with horses, combines this approach with our Western understanding of movement, body and harmony to create something very compact. The core of this system implies that the goodness is actually very close. It is not only literally, but physically right in front us, because it involves consistent further development of the most natural forms of movement and structures of the person themselves. No 'fitness', no skill, no extreme achievements, no competition – quite simply, no extremes. I have recently started to offer 'body-awareness teacher education' to pass on this simple but

effective natural system. To take part, you need a lively spirit, receptiveness, enjoyment in and the love of learning new things, and the desire to pass them on. However, there are no physical limitations. Before we move on to the next sections, I would like to say the following – if I come across as a flexible, sensitive, well-balanced and physically aware person in my pictures and videos, it is because I am always striving to preserve the qualities that nature gave me, and to become increasingly aware of them.

Personally, I spend about one or two hours a day on physical awareness exercises. It's like taking a shower under a natural waterfall. I never break a sweat during these exercises and they are never too much for me. However, I think that around 20 to 45 minutes a day is long enough. So, neither your horse nor your body need artistry, achievement or to push boundaries. Both of you desire a simple awareness of your posture, power, energy and balance that is right for you.

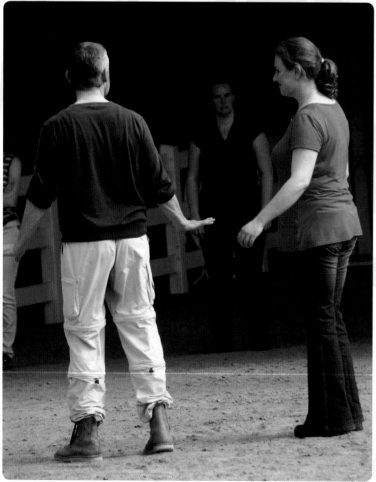

It's also about being like children – nothing more, nothing less.

A continuous changing of direction and form, circumference, gait and tempo

An introduction to the work with Queijo

Let's address the second specific and detailed case and the practical development of this horse. The Lusitano stallion, Queijo, was with me for a few weeks. The pictures were taken during this time. To recap, the bottom right picture shows the horse alone in the field. The middle and top pictures show the horse when he is being influenced by my signals. We can clearly see that the horse has gathered himself up and is submitting nicely. His back is much shorter, but above all we can see how the inside hindleg steps far under the horse's weight onto the outside track, collecting and balancing the horse further in a lovely shoulder-in.

The top picture shows how the horse turns to me and carries his head far to the inside as

he does so. Admittedly, it isn't quite the correct bend that we want to see at the end, but it is still a very positive sign that the horse is focused on and trusts the person. If the horse moves like this for too long or too often, I give a small, friendly sign, for example with a hand facing the head, to tell the horse that he can balance himself better if he maintains an even bend, i.e. doesn't turn his head quite so far to me. You can see that very clearly in the middle picture. Here the horse is positioned absolutely correctly in a wonderful, powerful shoulder-in, full of impulsion.

What is the work like at this level of training? As you can see very clearly in the video clip *Collecting a Stallion at Liberty*, no form of movement is ever the same. That is a very important characteristic of this work.

The handler keeps giving the horse new balance exercises that need to be executed with increasing precision and confidence, by moving on different tracks and circles and by changing the rein.

It is a continuous flow of changing and altering direction and form, circle circumference, the manner of the exercise, and in gait and tempo . It enables us to achieve the following:

- The horse stays attentive and highly interested, because it is only in rare cases that he knows the next step and the next direction. At this stage of training we very rarely exercise the horse on a round circle, for instance. That is mainly done in the first sections.

- The horse continually has to balance and bend in a different shape. He is very open to learning, and the lateral and vertical suppling is incredibly effective in a comparatively short time.

- The horse really enjoys his physical presence and his growth process. He is like a child at play, enjoying all of the happy experiences and the variety that such free expression brings.

- The horse is increasingly affectionate to us in our role as communicator, source of inspiration and director. He becomes more interested in what we have to offer, so that the quality of our communications becomes more and more refined. The horse begins to seek us more intensely.

In both previous pictures, you can see that I am roughly level with the horse's flank. This is very often the case at this level of education. However, the change from the back to the central position is a big step.

Let's go a little further back to the beginning to help us understand it.

Surprising and new:

the two forms of biopositive posture

The first picture shows the horse with a low head and a very long neck and back. He really seems to be creeping along. For many, but not all horses, this is a very important initial phase of lungeing work, and I would now like to talk about it in detail.

There is no tension without relaxation, no day without night. In this series of three pictures we can see how the horse builds himself up gradually in the first section, while still in a loose posture and wholly undisturbed. Let's look at it quietly, because it holds a very important key. The following is a centrepiece of my work. At most demonstrations and events, if I go into this point at all, I can only cover it briefly, because so many other things need to be taken care of first. Remember all of the first steps with Marouk, and remember also that I first had to give Marouk an idea of how wonderfully and proudly he could move. That is an important inner boost at the beginning. Queijo also went through these phases with me. However, he has now found himself. Now comes the time to expand the spectrum of expression, because he can now choose and change between relaxation and high performance. The more relaxation before, the greater and more proud the performance afterwards.

The first picture shows the stallion in an apparently 'unattractive' posture: 'long', not stepping under, and evidently lacking in impulsion. Yet it actually shows something quite different: namely the preparation for the opposite! What does that mean? I can tense a muscle

particularly well, if I have relaxed it thoroughly first. In genuine relaxation lies not only the opposite of tension, but the entire potential for perfect 'tension' and perfect performance. Understanding that and recognising it in the horse himself is immensely important!

Up until now we have seen two forms of movement in this stallion:

1. The movements of the loose horse without any communication from a person that uses their body and their example to direct the horse into a biopositive posture.

2. The very form of movement in which the stallion could show himself in all of his inner and outer power, elegance and beauty, through the active support of the person.

And now we finally come to a third posture, which like the second is very biopositive, that of potential performance.

This last posture, which we see in the first picture, is accompanied by many positive effects, if we understand that it has a transitional form and then really bring out and support this transitional form in order to develop it to the free play of power and expression.

I always stand behind the horse during this phase of work, under all circumstances. Here, I accompany the horse as quietly as possible. I allow the horse free choice of tempo in walk and in trot. If he wants, he can even creep along really slowly, as long as there is still a hint of recognisable movement. Only when the horse stands still, or shortly before he stops, do I give a signal with a whip or rope to get him moving again. During this phase, I offer nothing

other than complete quiet, constant and very clear support, always from the same position in relation to the horse, in order to be able to feel, should the horse want to gather himself up and present himself at any time.

In the second picture, you can see that both the horse and I are continuing to gather ourselves up. I am still standing at a right angle to the stallion's quarters, but no longer quite so far behind. This position can, of course, be varied, depending on the horse and the situation. However, we can clearly see how the horse gathers himself up again in the neck area. In fact, he almost rears up at this point, as he raises his back further and as he clearly puts more power and impulsion into his hindquarters. Can you imagine or even physically empathise how positive, restorative and invigorating this is for the horse? We can also see that I am holding the whip closer to the horse's hindleg, to carefully support this effect.

Important: look at the first picture, where the entire top line of the horse works and swings together in a very relaxed and loose way. Admittedly the neck is low, but look at its top line and the active muscles, especially in the second picture. This is exactly the development that the horse needs. We can easily see that the horse can gather himself up from back to front wonderfully from this posture.

In the third picture, you can see how I clearly animate the horse in the next phase to keep gathering himself up, in order to use his hindquarters with even more momentum. This sequence of exercises will also cause the horse to move his head and his neck, in a lovely lateral bend.

The top picture shows me with Queijo at one of the first meetings. The two bottom ones are taken from the beginning phase with another Lusitano stallion at the same event.

I would like to turn your attention to the communication between human and horse, to the stallion's posture and my own. Slightly bent, almost slightly drawn together, I concentrate my own energy as if in a magnifying glass, to then let it flow to the horse. The horse is not unaffected by it. He looks at me, he recognises me, responds and then builds himself up correspondingly. The horse is collected, proud and beautifully curved. Lots of different exercises and tasks can now follow for him.

As a rule, the phase in which the horse learns to develop and feel the energy reflected from me in himself, only comes then, along with the change between relaxation and high performance. The dance begins – the horse plays too and celebrates his own, rediscovered energy.

The aim: self-carriage

The pictures show other phases that lead to collection from complete relaxation. I am now standing closer to the middle of the horse already, and you can clearly see from my body language how my impulses are being directed more strongly to the horse, in order to help him to keep collecting, balancing and carrying himself.

The picture in the middle on this page shows a typical first shoulder-in. The horse is now full of impulsion and energy. He has completely grasped and understood the sense behind all of the exercises and procedures. He is entirely devoted to the person. This is clearly shown by his head, which is turned far to the inside. Person and horse are together, inside and out. Just look at the harmony of the movements. The horse is still very fast and I have to follow him with long strides. I am now positioned at the level of the withers. I hold the whip parallel to the horse and I use it to show clearly how the horse can move. I give him clear suggestions and information. The head is up and the hindlegs are clearly stepping far underneath the horse's weight. The entire expression is full of power and joy.

The last picture shows the horse in beautiful self-carriage. I am still directing and giving instructions and help through my body language, yet I am reducing the amount of instruction, because the horse carries and holds himself

more and more. That is our aim. I want a horse that increasingly internalises these biopositive suggestions, to go through the programme again every day all by himself, following his own rhythm. Horses actually do that. I have seen how they repeat the exercises in the field, alone or with other horses, just like a child that gets helpful inspiration for a meaningful game and then takes delight in continuing and repeating it all by themselves. That is the support I want for the horse.

Relaxation is still present in the collection. It facilitates the weight-bearing strength, expression and self-carriage

Because this topic has a key function in my work, I would like to spend some more time on it and make it clearer. The opposite pictures middle and lower show phases of further collection from complete relaxation. It is always the same principle, adjusted to the individual expression of each horse. In the middle picture, we can see clearly how the horse seems to release energy in the hindquarters, so that he can step underneath himself more. The bottom picture shows how the horse is still concerned with his neck and head position, so that he can bring this part of his body more and more into natural balance. Everything is perfect in the top picture. A mythical and mystical picture. Perfect form, original wildness, joy and devotion in free gestures from a horse that is still loose and not constrained by anything. The meaning of my kind of meditation with horses, based on their expression, is to achieve and maintain this.

The following points are important for these exercise phases:

- I never let the horse just bumble around, with no relaxation and no prospects. I very much hope that this has become clear. When I talk about relaxation, I do not mean a horse that is just shuffling along with a sunken back and stiff lower neck. That is precisely not what it is. Please look at the pictures and the video clips again closely. I am talking about a posture that, through the absolute inner calm of the person and through his composure and equability, signals to the horse that it can and should follow this example. This requires that all anxiety and insecurity have been removed from the horse during the previous exercises. Now it finally becomes clear why I previously put so much emphasis on the exercises and procedures that I described in the beginning using the example of the stallion Marouk. Relaxation is something active, for people and horses, rather than a passive 'letting yourself go'.

- I aim for self-carriage that actually keeps carrying the horse and changes the horse mentally and physically into a generally collected, energetic and more powerful picture. Then I do not need to 'pull' the horse together between seat and hands, using mechanical aids, each time I ride. Instead, the horse has fundamentally developed biopositively, and therefore has a considerably more collected basis.

• That also means that, in my way of being with horses, there is no warm-up phase. The developed horse is ready to move, if necessary in high collection, because collection and the ability to move in balance beneath a rider have been implanted in the horse.

The top picture shows a horse on the way there. The loose animal comes running to the person so beautifully and with so much delightful agreeableness and wonderful inner and outer posture.

Without any force, or mechanical aids because that would just spoil everything.

This basic work phase of potential performance can last a few days or even weeks. It will also not end abruptly. Instead, the sequences of potential performance become shorter and shorter, until constant self-carriage is achieved. If necessary, I will keep returning to potential performance with very advanced horses, depending on the horse's mood.

The whole spectrum

Expanse and compactness in one breath

The three pictures show the free play between expanse and wonderful compactness. Now the person, as the horse's director and mentor, has all of the options in hand, or rather 'in their body language vocabulary' to keep leading their charge in further exercises that may even place opposite demands on the horse. For me, this is the highest form of suppling from the ground, from which further collection, passage, half steps and piaffe can grow organically.

Developments into which we do not force the horse out of impatience and the need to 'want to make' something out of it. The horse will push himself in all of this, namely when he is organically ready and feels compelled to do so.

The horse will keep taking wild leaps and showing us how lively, happy and full of energy he is. We cheerfully accept these signs and use it to make our game and our further offers.

The second picture illustrates wonderfully how the horse wants to get closer to the person, how he flexibly seeks narrower turns and more new

challenges, to try out new positions of balance. I receive this gladly to animate the horse, to push his hindquarters under his weight, lower his quarters and free up the forehand so that he can offer the first half steps spontaneously. In this picture, you can already see the first approaches to passage and piaffe, and why I am now standing further forward, because it enables me to animate the horse to move powerfully on the spot, or at least without moving a lot forward. I don't want to slow the horse down, but to bring all of the power into once place for performance. In this situation, I also have my right arm slightly raised and I use this gesture to urge the horse to move without moving too much forward.

The type, shape and duration of the exercise, however, is determined by the horse and his willingness to grow further. Together, we only take in the impulses of the moment and the current state to let the further consequences result from them, as a team. This work is always so surprising and new, because each horse must follow his own path to development. A person who works and takes part in this way is basically just an amazed onlooker and silent admirer of an erupting nature that appears and celebrates a very special spectacle before their very eyes.

*The moment is determined
not by routine
and following a strict plan,
but as a result of dedication,
surprise, wonder and
inner quiet and joyful flowing.*

195

The dance begins –

the positions in shoulder-in

It looks complicated, but it is actually nothing more than harvesting the fruits. Believe me – what I am about to describe all comes essentially from itself. It is the consequence of the consistency and attentiveness so far.

On these pages, I have again summarised and presented three basic and possible positions to the horse in the shoulder-in exercise, in images, words and diagrams. The photographs and diagrams can essentially speak for themselves – please let the individual situations sink in, so that you can find an intuitive connection to them.

Position I – You should, or rather you could start with this position, and you can return to it frequently again later.

Further development in free collection and work on the spot are not yet possible from this position alone – to achieve those you then have to have changed to the position right next to the horse, at the level of his withers.

Remember: it's about keeping the horse in place more strongly by changing your position to the horse, in the direction of their withers. It's very important in the beginning that you never depart from a 90 degree angle to the quarters if possible, so you are actually always behind the horse. Only when you have established that the horse maintains his energy even if you shift the position forwards in a completely relaxed posture, and when he spontaneously offers shoulder-in at the same time, can you change the positions without the horse instantly shifting down a gear or stopping altogether. All I can do is try to describe it as best I can. In reality you will learn everything with your horse in the end

Position I

The essential basic position behind the horse is shown first. The position to the horse and the tendency of the rider's inside shoulder to really come in are crucial to being able to cross over the legs. From the position behind the horse, you have the optimum effect on the horse's shape and collection. Again, the photograph shows this clearly.

and you will recall my descriptions clearly. As we have said, it comes by itself and it's a wonderful experience. I just want to prepare you so that you already know what will happen anyway, if you devote yourself to staying on the path or keep coming back to it.

Position 2 – This diagram shows the dynamics of effect and movement from the person to the horse in the central position. In this position, the horse is practically between your arms. This enables you to help the horse to keep concentrating on moving on the spot, in increasingly high collection. The video clip *Collecting a Stallion at Liberty* illustrates this wonderfully.

In practice, the person takes the individual positions naturally, using flowing transitions.

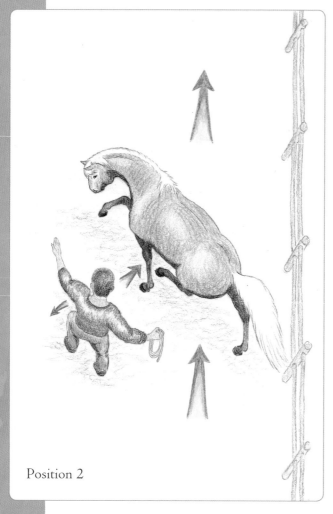

Position 2

Position 3 – Here a special dynamic develops in the position directly in front of the horse. The dance and the freedom of the horse are spectacular. The change from one side to the other in shoulder-in, in a flowing transfer, is very interesting from this position. This makes the horse more supple in the most long-lasting way and also makes it very sensitive to our signals. This is shown accordingly in the diagram.

If you approach these exercises with your horse quietly and in a natural and organic way, then it shows that you have now taken on a very positive role for your horse. You have come very far on my scale of what is possible. The inner connection and trust on both sides are the prerequisite for achieving this advanced and free sequence of exercises. The shoulder-in develops differently in every horse, so you should not attempt to follow a plan or a programme. As we have said, it will happen spontaneously, if you have just done enough preparation on the principles. The horse wants it to be that way

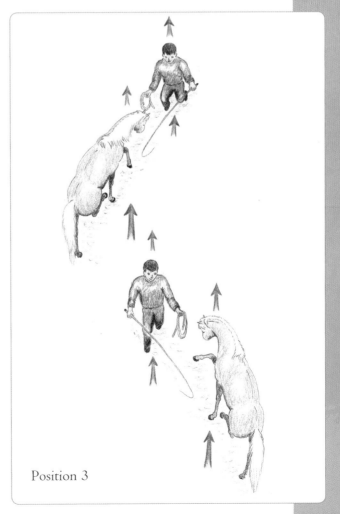

Position 3

and will do everything to bring us exactly to that point. Do we have the courage to let it happen? To trust in the absolute order of wildness? The most wonderful thing is that once we have gone into it, no longer is everything strange to us. We do it with the unique certainty that everything was already quite clear in us — long, long before.

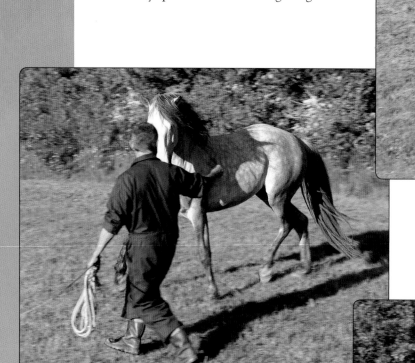

Please, always remember:
closeness comes from distance
and from inner independence.
Then every encounter
will stay free and playful inside.

Another important focus using the example of work with Xingu

Please note

Now that everything has worked out thus far, I would like to go into something important in more detail, just to be sure, because the horse will keep testing us on each new curve on our spiral of growth, and while the core of a problem may basically have been solved, the symptoms, especially to begin with, can keep appearing, like aftershocks or waves, often suddenly and unexpectedly. However, they become weaker and weaker, even when we consequently find ourselves in the 'eye of the storm' – even if the storm is sometimes just a slight draught.

The following pictures show this kind of 'ripple' effect with Xingu and, more than anything, we can see how we should always act unconcerned, waiting for the result that is important for us at the end. The video clip *Amazing Bridleless Riding* very clearly illustrates how you can manage this kind of wave as a rider. Janosch protests violently in the middle of the Spanish plains, and I have nothing other than my body language on an unsaddled and unbridled horse. More about this later. Now back to our example with Xingu.

So, the stallion stands provokingly in front of me and asks me once again whether I am really able to lead him in the long term. At first glance it doesn't look like much, but something like

that can escalate very quickly. An inappropriate reaction at this point would possibly throw him straight back into his old behaviour patterns. The messages in these pictures are as follows:

- You are in charge – always. That means that you can and must be completely quiet and composed. Time does not matter. It is always on your side. With quiet but very precise gestures, I indicate to the stallion that he should stay on the circular track around me. The horse keeps pushing in front of me, which you can see very clearly in the second picture. I remain consistently in my place. When moments like this happen at my events, I often say: 'Not a heartbeat more'. I occasionally act demonstratively, as if in slow motion.

- It is important that we don't show any emotional reactions. You should always stay quiet in these kinds of situation. If you feel anger, disappointment or helplessness, which would be completely understandable and only human, then take your thoughts straight to the perception of your body, the scents, the sounds around you and the image of your counterpart. Root yourself in the ground again – in brief, remain in the present, in the here and now, and breathe in deeply. Naturally, we assume that there is no more danger at this point and that this kind of aftershock can be quickly surmounted through quietness and steadfastness.

- In pictures 4 and 5, you can see how the stallion, initially still a little 'thoughtful', finally side-steps quietly onto the circle. We remain as solid as a rock. We win, but we don't fight, and respect and closeness to us will grow.

- If we are in the here and now, the next step is always important for us. Observe, have the entire picture in front of you and feel the next step and then the next, until you have the distinct feeling that you could and want to end this section. It is important when doing so that you feel that the 'ball is really in the pocket'.

  So try to feel when you can really end an exercise. It is important to learn to recognise, more and more easily, with time, how to not want too much or too little. After each exercise unit, ask whether you have managed it. Feel inside yourself and listen to your inner voice and, if necessary, do it better and more clearly next time.

- In each situation, especially those that we see in the first four pictures, we obviously have to ask ourselves why the horse does what he does. Why is the stallion protesting here? The horse always has the right and the obligation to draw our attention to his state by protesting. That is very important. If you cannot find an answer to this 'statement' immediately, then end the exercise elegantly, interrupt the sequence and take a break. In this case, in the situation with Xingu that meant it was essential to direct the stallion onto the circle with clarity and composure, but to stop after one circuit, in order to find out why the horse acted in this way.

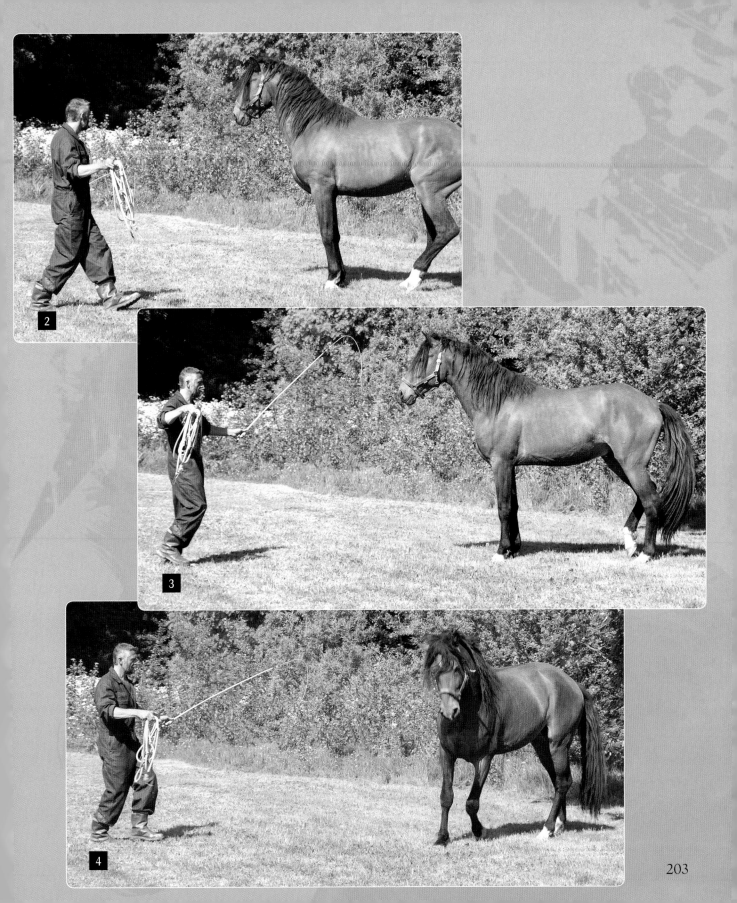

5

• Let's move on to the result and the last four pictures. In the last picture (8), we can see clearly how quietly, inwardly curved and attentively the stallion walks on the circle. It seems to be so little and, yet it is everything! Again I want to point out, using these pictures, how important the phase of lungeing the loose horse is. In these simple, but correct forms of movement, the horse expands and develops immensely, both physically and mentally, and in these balanced, constant forms of movement, the horse connects itself to us more closely. This is the key to all the forms of the dance. From it arises all of the motivation in the horse itself to develop, whenever he wants. Xingu developed a very nice, compact form of shoulder-in from this composure. However, that comes from the horse himself. Please commit to memory the posture of the horse that we see in picture 8, because that is what we want to achieve. At this point, ambition often sets in, and the person often misjudges the positive things that they have actually achieved. They are then easily lost. Had we just waited a little, the horse might have started to dance spontaneously.

• So, trust the nature of the horse. If you have reached this point, then trust in the result, enjoy the quiet and delight in the gentleness of being with your horse, and trust the development of the natural with him. You should not want to force anything, to push and press and 'winkle out' a dance, otherwise it will not really be able to develop freely and expressively. The dance comes – always in a manner favourable to the horse. Let yourself be surprised. Every tree and every horse grows differently and develops in its own, unique way. Just give them enough room. Then nature will act through you.

Here the stallion Xingu is checking again whether I am still able to lead him. Such aftershocks are common. Remain completely calm in situations like this. Stay in the here and now. Feel the present, your partner – the horse. Become aware of your body – but leave the level of emotions such as anger, helplessness, or disappointment. With calmness and perseverance you will survive these aftershocks safely and quickly, which will in turn consolidate your relationship with the horse even more.

Practice from the beginning

Always 'embrace' the whole horse

9

Practical experience based on
the first level

Genetic engineering or pesticides?

*Now that I have conveyed a rough picture of my
way of working with horses, we can again turn our
attention to the key practical details. Many questions have certainly come up, and I hope that most
of these will be answered in the paragraphs below.
But before we zoom in, let's look at the wide angle
shot — a general parable before the practical details
about horses.*

207

At the moment, there is a lot of discussion about genetic engineering and genetically modified foods. When it comes to maize, for example, we know that the genetically modified version contains a 'built-in' poison against this crop's most aggressive pest. Supporters say that it is much better than using lots of chemical pesticides. But what is the truth? This – if you were to practise natural crop rotation, i.e. plant maize once a year, then wheat or oats for example, and then plant maize again the year afterwards, then those pests would not pose a problem at all, because they need uninterrupted maize consumption from year to year. Many modern farmers no longer want to or are able to cultivate crops using natural crop rotation, because all forms of production have become specialised and because the market does not allow it. Conclusion: we are looking for what appear to be solutions, each one worse than the last, because we departed from the basis of reality and nature a long time ago, but, as we have said, there are no solutions on this lower level. I wanted to say that in advance of the following chapter. I don't offer any alternatives here either – pesticides or genetic modification – i.e. either very bad or very, very bad. I would also recommend 'natural crop rotation' here, a way of living where, in the best case, problems don't occur at all and which, at least, certainly doesn't cause them. Before we return to practical considerations about horses, here's another very personal comment on the subject. As I see it, the worst enemy of humanity isn't climate catastrophe,

but experimenting with the innermost strongholds of nature, the genes. My fear is that, even before climate change can destroy us, humanity will have beaten a retreat as a whole from the consequences of genetically modified foods, unless we put a stop to it immediately and resolutely. Until we do that, we can scarcely imagine the potential damage. What represents a few concerns, or even essentially only one major concern about the world, is a final irreversible sell-out of the inner sanctum of life. And isn't that what we are concerned with here?

How did it really happen with Naranjero?

These pictures show me with the PRE stallion Naranjero, from the former Spanish military stud in Barcelona. Despite the apparent danger that he posed to the soldiers, I led him apparently effortlessly on a loose rope to a mare in season. You can see this in the video clip *His Powerful, Gentle Leading*.

In reality, it was obviously a highly concentrated action. Much of what I have described until now can be found in the encounter with this stallion. Using this example, let's look at the precise details from the practical experience. How is it possible for something so actually or apparently spectacular to happen?

• I looked over the stallion very closely first. This horse was an impressive being in every way, with immense expressiveness and power.

However, deep down, the stallion's being was reasonable and very soft. Because of that, and only because of that, I was quickly able to gain his cooperation. He was highly intelligent, very sensitive and delicate, in his own way not aggressive at all and generally very attentive to people. In brief, he was a splendid chap inside, full of hidden softness and sensitivity. That's why I was completely certain that I could act as I did, with no danger to myself, the stallion, the mare or the people in the area. It was still a clear demonstration of the efficacy of body language and inner presence. However, it doesn't happen at this speed with all horses, not by a long way. So, everything I do always depends on the horse's being to begin with. The being is mirrored in his outer appearance. For that reason, it is possible to completely fathom it out. Using this example, I would again like to show you the precision, with which this can happen, because, imagine that I had been wrong about the stallion's being – with uncertain, possibly even deadly consequences. Please practise it yourself. It is a basis. Everyone can rediscover it in themselves.

• You have all the time in the world to doubt yourself and everything else. That leads to important questions and, finally, also to answers. But once you have stood up in order to act, any doubt will be a guarantee of failure and defeat. Please look at me standing there, between the aroused stallion and the mare, and observe the decisiveness in my physical expression. It no longer contains the slightest doubt, because otherwise the stallion would then barge through everyone, just as he had always done before. Only my decisiveness and the precision of my body language keep him in place.

This is our key point, because now we are coming to another important element of leading a horse. The entire direction is important, not just the distance, because, in reality, I am directing the horse in his whole posture, at least when it is necessary and this example shows that so clearly. Here it was a spectacular action before the eyes of the initially sceptical soldiers and the video camera. Yet the principle remains the same, even with any other normally well-behaved and less spectacular horse.

Always 'embrace' the whole horse –
with arms like a giant

Let's look at the pictures on these pages. It immediately becomes clear that I am having to work quite hard in this action. It was not easy, although it almost looks like a dance in the flowing movement of the film. The pictures that I have chosen for you show me as I simultaneously guide and lead the horse. In the second picture, you can see that I am always ready to maintain and create distance by keeping the horse at bay, using all

of my groundedness and decisiveness. Mentally, I give him no hint of a way out. It simply has to be that way now. My actions, my appearance, my body language and my decisiveness are seamless. Everything must merge together into one entity – even the slightest deviation from this would lead immediately to disaster.

The basic principle of my body posture is always one of downward-flowing, downward-directed energy. If my shoulders are low and my breathing deep, I can use my arms powerfully; I can signal with the rope and play or give an actual warning. Against the background of inner peace and 'physical gravity', this all makes an enormous impression on the horse, on which I am wholly and completely reliant.

In the first picture, you can see clearly the other dimension, because the hands, which are always raised, also guide the horse sideways with great precision. As a principle, that is immensely

1

important in daily interaction with every horse, because I would like the horse to acknowledge me and not run out to the side. The mare is now standing to the left of us. This powerful lad wants to get to her with all his might, and until now, under the leadership of the soldiers, he has actually always managed it, even if sharp leading bits have caused him pain. If the horse simply broke away at this point with his head to the left, which would be easy for him with just his halter, then he would be on top of the mare the very next second.

What should I do? My arm and the rope tell the stallion that that is precisely why I am there, and that I know it. With this horse, my body language is enough. Naranjero understood it immediately. Xingu, on the other hand, who I have already spoken about several times, would hardly react to it immediately. That is

why I would not get involved in this kind of undertaking so early on with a horse like Xingu. However, the principle would be and was the same with him, as with all other horses: I always control the whole horse. I make my gaze wide, like that of a painter who sees the whole picture and lets the overall impression soak in. Naturally, I always look at the animal's head, but I pay equal attention to his hindquarters and his whole body. It is important that I hold the horse as if he were between my arms, speaking metaphorically but in a certain respect also literally. You can see this clearly in the first picture. I will explain this entire process again clearly on page 214, using a diagram. Imagine that my left hand was 5 metres longer. It would then form a kind of wall for the horse that would prevent it escaping out to the left. In the event, the stallion actually follows me away from his lady friend, as if there really was a wall (pictures 3 and 4).

I always control the whole horse. I make my gaze wide, like that of a painter who sees the whole picture and lets the overall impression soak in. Naturally, I always look at the animal's head, but I pay equal attention to his hindquarters and his whole body. It is important that I hold the horse as if he were between my arms, speaking metaphorically but in a certain respect also literally.

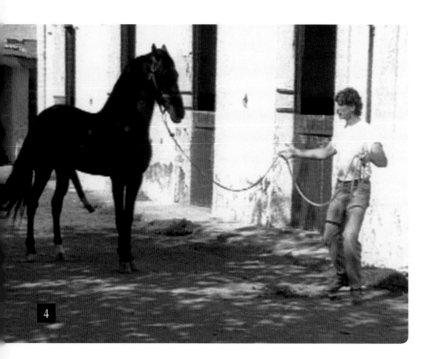

In a very few cases, I actually erect this 'wall' – with the help of a guiding signal whip. Naturally, I won't touch the horse with it at all, but I initially show the animal my wide space, the space that I absolutely must claim. Here, the 'spiritual dimension', the precise image down to the finest detail and decisiveness were enough.

I basically do the following with Naranjero:

- I keep the distance decisively and then I keep giving direct, often very tiny, signs forwards to the horse, when he comes too close to me.

I build up mental 'walls', to the right and left of the horse.
My hands and arms show this very clearly and without interruption.

- I always show the horse the path that we should travel together, in the interests of everyone, as clearly as possible.

- I trust the fate that encouraged and challenged me to go against my initial fear and concern about going into this situation and surviving it.

212

About our 'vital circle', the natural reference and the natural competition

In essence we want to hold the horse in a comparatively narrow frame, as if we had giant's arms, for the benefit of everyone, especially the horse. In diagrams 1 and 2, we can see a person with a horse in front of them. In the diagrams, the person is surrounded by a circle, a kind of 'clear drum', which I call the 'vital circle'. That is very important for my work.

There are people who, when talking for example, sometimes get unpleasantly and uncomfortably close to the other person. This kind of violation of our private space is very much the order of the day for the Western world. There are countless examples of it. Many people have forgotten to recognise and respect this vital, invisible circle in themselves and consequently in others. The diameter of this vital circle naturally does not stay the same. I would allow somebody close, a family member, a partner or a friend much closer to me than a stranger or a person that seems suspicious. In any case, injury often results if this invisible boundary is crossed! Sooner or later it will hurt, to a lesser or greater extent.

You can only be really harmonious with horses if you are aware of these circumstances. They live completely in these worlds. Depending on the herd member and their status, they differentiate very precisely in the wild about who can come how close to whom and

when. We should adopt this practice so that we can communicate with horses in a way that is beneficial to them. Depending on the horse, I therefore allow different distances and ways of behaving. This follows the immediate feeling, not a fixed rule.

About the individual drawings:

Diagram 1. Here we can see how the horse stops at the boundary of the vital circle. In the event that he doesn't do so, there are lots of often tiny signs and gestures that can be used to gently make the boundaries clear to the horse at the right time. Their clear demarcation makes the person more positive (+++) than the horse's environment. Therefore the clear reference.

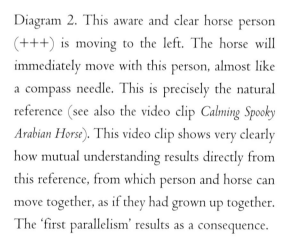

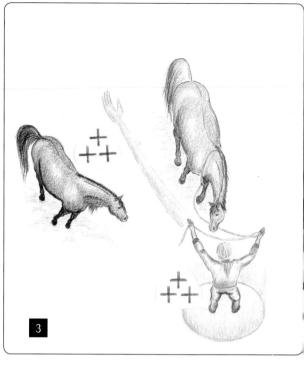

Diagram 2. This aware and clear horse person (+++) is moving to the left. The horse will immediately move with this person, almost like a compass needle. This is precisely the natural reference (see also the video clip *Calming Spooky Arabian Horse*). This video clip shows very clearly how mutual understanding results directly from this reference, from which person and horse can move together, as if they had grown up together. The 'first parallelism' results as a consequence.

Diagram 3. This shows an aware horse person in a genuinely competitive situation (also +++). Naranjero, for example, had completely acknowledged and accepted me, but the awaiting mare in season was certainly of no less importance to him. That is why the person has three plus signs, but the mare does too. In this kind of situation, I have to use my arms to amplify the effect of natural reference. The horse will then no longer take the initiative to do something, even if the attraction from the outside is really considerable. Naturally, in a situation like this, the person has a good chance of being at least as important to the horse as the mare in season, because of their inner presence and their body language.

214

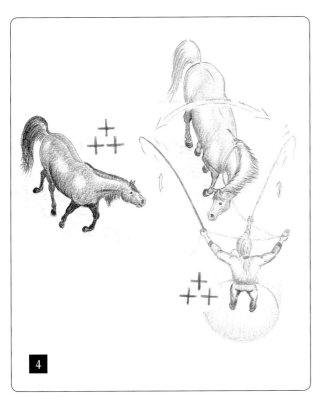

'Embracing' the horse when leading

If possible, always lead your horse with a whip (diagram 1).

I have described the individual leading positions and the exact use of the whip in *Dancing with Horses*. I want to go into more basic forms again here. The drawing makes the possible actions clear.

With the guiding radius of the whip (diagram 2) you can both influence the area in front of the horse, and also the area of the hindquarters. Even if the horse clearly moves his head or hindquarters away from you (diagrams 3 and 4),

Diagram 4. Here I show the maximum possibility of communication. As I have already said, I was able to work freely with Naranjero right from the beginning and lead him past the mare straight away. With a horse like Xingu, I would actually have to extend my 'giant arms' with a whip. I clearly show the horse the boundary by raising the whip over the horse's head from left to right. This is a very effective means that must only be used with great care and awareness, and it is only likely to succeed if the person really sets an example using their character.

the leader can shake the end of the whip near the quarters to 'align' the horse again. It is important that we stick to this description and the procedure when leading the horse, but it is also relatively simple. I cannot emphasise that clearly enough. It is important that you always act and react gently, but immediately. The secret behind it is to anticipate the possibility of acting. The horse person is now in the same state as the trained master of Eastern martial arts who no longer has to assert themselves physically or defend themselves, because they already know that they can do it. The possibilities and the richness within them, the security and the radiance put them in a position where they practically no longer need to use everything that they have practised. This is possible because of the vigilance of growth and because of awareness of the means that are available to them in case of

doubt. All of these positive imprints and experiences in us form an enormous platform where we can move and live freely and authentically.

Come or don't come –
just do whatever you want

Now we come to another essential behaviour that makes nearly all horses hesitate or stay when they want to run away. Even if it doesn't happen right away, they at least keep playing with the thought, like the grey stallion on the photo top right that is following the soldier. Why does he look a little strained? Because the person wants the horse to follow him and because he expresses that very clearly in his gestures.

I, on the other hand, do not care in the slightest whether the horse follows me or not! Let's

therefore I cannot rely on you and you might even be dangerous.' And the band would get tighter and, in cases of doubt, may even tear, with obvious consequences.

In this respect, the long rope is also an important tool, because I can easily extend the distance to the horse to more than 5 metres. Important – the person must know and tread their path unconditionally, decisively and consistently. I think that both of these pictures make the difference clear (see also the video clip *Breeding Stallion Harmón Reborn*).

look at the bottom picture. I am watching this little guy out of the corner of my eye, but here you can clearly see that I am not the slightest bit concerned about whether the horse is coming or not; yet that is precisely why he comes! Without ever questioning it. Naturally there are some situations where I 'invite' the horse very clearly with my body language, but that is only at the beginning, and on occasions that are always very well justified. However, once this initial phase has finished, I simply 'am': I stand, I walk, I run and that is enough. The horse will too, and wants to adapt to me, my directions, my rhythms and my speed. The horse seeks me!

If I cannot do all of that consistently, even the easiest horses will keep breaking away from me and they will go their own way, because I am not going my way. For the horse, that says: 'You're not leading, you don't know what you want, you are uncertain, undecided and

- You will find that you are experiencing a feeling of pleasant heaviness and warmth in your body.

- You will feel that you are physically and mentally more 'there', more awake and more 'present' in your body than before.

- However, the most important thing is this. While you focus on experiencing the here and now, you no longer have any time to devote to yesterday or tomorrow. You have achieved something quite essential with this little exercise, namely made a start at 'overcoming time'.

About the power of pausing –
overcoming time

Now let's consider the immense power of taking a break, interruption, saying stop and waiting.

A simple exercise – at the same time as you are reading this, be aware of your feet. How do they feel, how do they touch the ground, how warm or cold are they? Now, as you continue to read, please be aware of the sounds in your environment and, at the same time, how your feet feel. Keep alternating until you are as clearly aware as possible both of your feet and of the sounds in your environment. And now, please be aware of any scents as well, at the same time as the other sensations – your feet and the sounds. Just pause for a moment and try to realise this experience. Now you can gradually perceive your whole body more and more without neglecting the sounds and scents in your environment.

What do we gain from this exercise?

- You will very probably find that you are more relaxed on the whole, even after these brief moments.

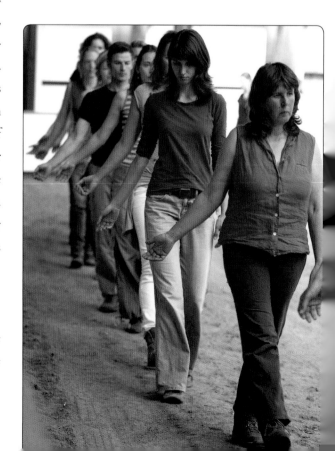

Children and animals experience time differently, especially the abstract concept of the future. For them, everything is now and immediate.

Today, many people have either too much or too little time. First they rush, and then they get bored and need distraction. In one way or another, time governs their being — time eats up experience in the present and therefore their enjoyment of life. And, because of that, they manage to take a break less and less often, because even if the body finds a certain peace, the world of thought keeps returning, along with all of the pressures that can go with it.

The type of break that I am trying to describe is one where nothing happens inside or out, while the momentary, expanded sensory/

authentic perception is sensitised to the maximum. Such high levels of concentration on the apparent nothing during the break have an enormous effect on the being in general and certainly with reference to horses. That is fundamentally important for me. In my courses, I practise this very intensively with the participants. First I try to focus their perception on the moment, in order to find the exact transition between action and pause, the apparent nothing. This kind of pausing has its own special quality and beauty — you almost always want to make it last longer. Actually, only a real impulse or an inspired stimulation should end the pause. The exact action comes from quiet, not from a hectic inner pace.

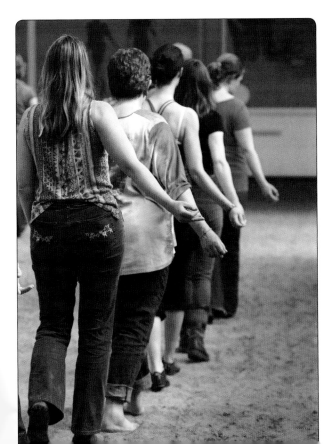

I convey the simple yet essential principles of leading a horse, halting, opposing oneself to the horse and their energy, to my course participants. Experiencing that the quality of inner peace, the pause, can be rediscovered directly from the action is crucial. Actions like those seen here would quickly trigger resistance or even aggression in the horse, without the experience of inner peace. That is why I practise the transition and the change from outer passiveness to very decisive action, without losing the inner experience of quiet and 'pause'. An important key to my work lies here.

Pressure or stimulus

Important: the right way to use the whip

What was said in the previous paragraph paves the way for the immensely important part that now follows.

We want to allow the horse free rein through his own relaxation, and to open up and offer him a free path forward. However, when we want to 'liven up' the horse using whip signals, the opposite often happens. The person makes themselves 'firm' and the horse reacts stubbornly and sluggishly. So we now move on to the next important constructive step, namely the correct use of the whip.

Firstly, when you are giving signals with the whip, it is important that you stay calm and relaxed, breathe deeply and keep your shoulders low, because now we are also using muscular strength. On the one hand, you must try to keep the whip quiet and consistent while, on the other, giving exact signals where appropriate. The whip is a very important and effective aid to give stimuli, and this is how it works:

- Whenever we want to give a horse a stimulus to move forwards, sideways or backwards, we start with a tiny signal with the end of the whip, given loosely from the wrist (diagram 2). We do not leave the relaxed posture as we do so (diagram 1). The acoustic signal was given about a second before, e.g. 'ter-rot'. Even if I know that, during the first encounter, this horse won't trot on, I still give this minimal signal. That is crucial for everything to come. Then I give the horse one to two seconds to react to my request. Afterwards, I reinforce the signal with the whip constantly, until the moment when the horse shows at least a small reaction (diagrams 3 and 4). It is crucial that the frequency of the signal is quietly increased, i.e. that the dynamic is continually increased. I then repeat the exercise after a break, or the next day, so that the horse reacts to smaller and smaller impulses until, after a very short time, it just reacts to the tiniest gesture. That is naturally our goal.

- This work is only effective if the horse is actually able – both physically and mentally – to complete this exercise, if he completely meets its requirements. We cannot use this handling to get a horse to go organically into canter, for example, if he is not ready for this gait. Please be very aware of this.

- The ever-increasing signal using the whip is given continually and then ends abruptly the

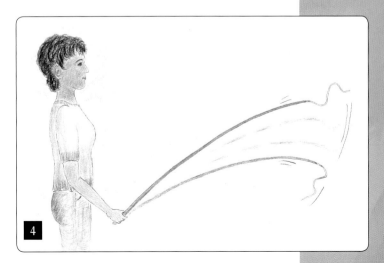

very moment that the horse reacts. This also is very important.

- Thus, the horse experiences from the beginning that we always want to communicate with one another in the most delicate and quiet way. This then transfers itself directly onto riding.

Please practise what is described here well, and get used to handling the whip the right way by repeating the exercises. I know that we quickly overlook and forget such small details. However, once you really see the enormous effect, then you will be further convinced of how immensely important all of the 'small things' are in the end. You hardly see all of these things in my presentations, because I use them so minimally and so quickly. But something wonderful results from the whole.

Our body language gives us a very conscious and important option: distance

The topic of distance is the consequence of what has developed so far. It is also very important for interacting with horses. I have lost count of how often I have had to discuss this subject in telephone coaching sessions all over the world, because in many cases not enough attention had been paid to the factor of distance. In many cases, it is one of the first tools for help and change for the better, along with quietness and general groundedness. From feedback and reports, I can conclude that success often follows closely once distance is understood.

What does it mean? A shy horse will automatically keep its distance from an unknown person – even someone familiar. A pushy horse, however, will try to get close, very close or even dangerously close to any person, familiar or otherwise. With any horse, the subject of distance is of considerable importance, and we can only move freely and creatively in this important area, using body language. In each case, it is important that we decide about the question of 'distance' and that we consciously organise events to match the requirements of space and time.

To begin with, many people enjoy having a horse following them, but in reality it is more like a 'coincidental intrusiveness' on the part of the horse. The horse 'creeps' into the person's pockets, squashes past them, shoves them whenever they like, but sometimes also trots behind their human colleague. The very minute the horse is tempted by the smallest blade of grass, the neigh of a friend (not to mention the lure of a mare, in the case of Naranjero), the fun is over. Then our friend does what he wants again and unfortunately we no longer have any control over him, in many cases.

Choosing the right distance is of fundamental importance. The distance and timing of an action are as important as the action itself. I would even go so far as to say that the distance or proximity to the horse can make the difference between, success and failure. If you consider the meaning of this point in depth, then you can gradually develop a feel for it – but this is something that you must work on.

222

This is a typical, dangerous scenario, because not even the slightest positive thing can be built on this at any other stage of interaction.

The shy horse must be made familiar and the pushy one has to be persuaded. An important key to this and much more is the right distance and the time that is filled out by distance or proximity.

In these four pictures, all taken in Namibia, you can see me making normal gestures, namely dealing quite consciously with distance and proximity. In the top picture, I am creating a distance that I have precisely determined. This is a very shy horse, whose owner could not even touch him. I am working with distance and proximity with the dark horse, because it was very pushy. To summarize: Whether the horse is shy or pushy, aggressive or timid – the right distance is extremely important, in order to be able to grasp, understand and finally transform every possible manifestation. Only in comparatively few cases will I go straight to a horse and touch him, in the first encounter. However, there is always a very good reason for that and it always happens very consciously.

In all four pictures you can clearly see how versatile and expressive body language can be.

If you try covering up the horse in the pictures with your hand, then you can see from my body language how the horse moves and behaves at that point. You can always sense a connection between the person and the horse, even if the horse is further away from the person in purely physical terms.

However, keeping a distance – how does it work?

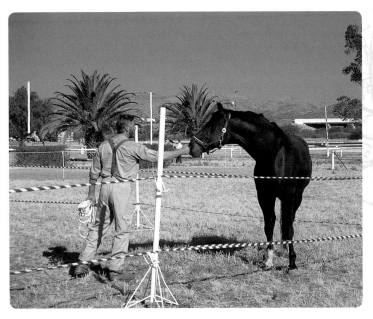

A double dose of success –

closeness and respect through distance

As with any subject that, in the end, is determined by feeling and looking at the details, I cannot go into everything that could be said in this respect – there is simply too much. However, I will try to clarify the basic structures that convey the principle, so that you can experience everything else yourself and through practice learn to handle your horse ever more subtly and sensitively through constant development of awareness.

In the top right picture, you can see two things happening simultaneously with the stallion. On the one hand, the woman can lead him close to the mare safely, although he is not even wearing a halter. That was the main aim of this exercise. We also see that the horse not only allows this, but the stallion does it with a very calm and trusting expression in his eyes. This is all the result of very conscious work on distance. What happens, in detail?

- When working on distance, we almost always automatically move in a very safe area. Distance is also always a question of angle to the horse. Namely, the angle gets smaller and smaller, the further away the horse is. For example, keeping a stallion in a corner requires lots of steps if I am close to him, but just a flick of the finger if I am at a distance – an important fact that you should consider.

- Distance always encourages the horse to be independent. A fairly important point for everything that will follow your interaction together. Distance creates self-awareness in the horse.

- Pay very close attention to the rhythm, because the horse will soon express a wish to be close to you. Merging distance and time together successfully requires a fine feel. Pay attention to the horse's reactions, to his expression and signs of wellbeing, calmness or irritation. Think back to the pictures at the beginning of the book – the relaxed horses that are so close to me, with such contented expressions and such soft eyes. The game of distance and time always came before the result here too.

- The moment when I allow the horse to come to me is particularly important. That is why this point is often an important topic in my demonstrations. For the participants, I try to show how I can cause very different horses to eventually show me closeness and familiarity, using the sensitive interplay of time and distance. If the horses then come to me, the originally nervous ones behave almost exactly the same as the originally aggressive or dominant horses.

To put it in a nutshell, if the horse is close, the change must already have taken place. Hardly any more changes can be made to a spatially close horse. Then, in cases of doubt,

I am in a passive, led and crowded situation. This is a very important point.

- The woman in the pictures is still acting with very raised shoulders, the energy is still too much in the upper part of the body and she is not yet sufficiently grounded. However, she is full of concentration, she is in the here and now and she has a very strong will. All of that can be read from her body language. Decisiveness in particular is expressed clearly. Devotion and sensitivity will keep growing, along with softness and gentleness.

- Here are some more crucial key words on the subject: move as little as possible, and only do what your intuition tells you is really required. Keep making long breaks. If you are in the centre yourself, sometimes seconds seem like minutes. However, they are still only seconds, and the picture seems chaotic from the outside. So, lots of calm and long

because everything is really decided here. The miracle happens here – often in seconds.

- It goes without saying that we never rush the horse – quite the opposite. My distance work is always very quiet or even static.

- You should check the horse's being very closely, first to establish whether proximity or distance are appropriate at this point. If you are unsure, then you should wait. Search for a clear entry in yourself and then act gently but decisively.

breaks! After doing something quickly or actively, always reorganise and re-establish your body and your posture. I often take this opportunity to sort out my rope. I return to the status quo with quiet, deep breathing and relaxed shoulders. If you want to use a rope or whip, you should always make sure that you are calm and relaxed first. Then the end of the rope that you throw near the horse will never seem aggressive. A smile on your face makes everything softer for the horse. If you create distance, make sure that you don't startle him. I am often bold or even loud from a really great distance, especially with nervous horses. Contrary to all expectations, this calms the horse down. Why? Because he absorbs all of my composure.

- For me personally, work at a distance is one of the best parts of working with horses,

- Please observe yourself, using video and photo analyses. Take advice from friends and colleagues. Become more aware of yourself –

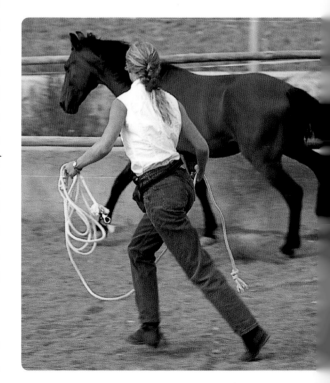

a never-ending journey. In the end, the rider in our pictures is very close both to the horse and herself. The direction was good and the result is too. That is what the horse wants, nothing more. He does not want us to grow out of ourselves. He just wants us to trust ourselves, to discover our boundaries so that we can then expand them, very carefully and with great joy, so the journey becomes the goal. Here we have a wonderful example of it.

- Distance is created and maintained through clear pictures, clear images, clear and upright posture, minimal gestures, use of the whip and rope against the background of an inner being that is always friendly and, naturally, a background of ever-increasing amplification of the signals, as discussed.

The most important lessons concerning closeness and distance so far

I took the little three-year-old colt in this picture from a wild herd just a few days before. I clearly show the horse that I do not want him to come to me or move in any other way. I want distance. The end of the rope is on the ground. Within a very short time and almost without him even noticing, the horse learns not to move from the spot when the rope is on the ground. Almost as an aside, it happens in a short time, as a consequence of the rest of our exercises. Just look at how the horse reacts with all of his gestures and body language.

We have got to know all of the important issues concerning closeness and distance. I always explain the main form of interaction that we are currently dealing with to the horse very clearly: whether I want the horse to keep

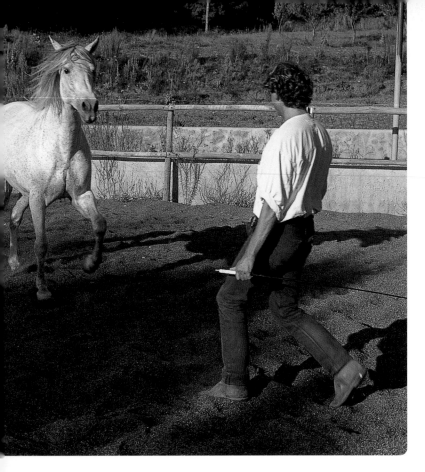

A very natural process –
lungeing comes from distance

Lungeing follows spontaneously from the forms of distance. Closeness results from lungeing and leading comes from this closeness. In turn, the body's signals send the horse away and the entire process renews itself on a different level of the spiral.

In the picture top right, we can see very clearly how the person automatically achieves a lovely, correct and quiet position behind the horse, as a result of distance. One follows gently from the other, a wholly natural process. Now the person 'pushes' the horse, like a lead stallion, carefully, but determinedly in front of them. The gelding is very quiet and respects the distance and the person. The situation shown clearly in the second picture then spontaneously results in turn – the horse will turn to the person, in a gentle and trusting way. Just look at the horse's eyes and his careful inward bend – towards the person. We already know this horse from other pictures in this book. Again, these are the beginnings. Can you see how gently and consistently this all works in the end – how the individual building blocks form a whole? Above all, it is consistent for the horse. Is what we have discovered here not, in principle, a very simple and easily comprehensible form of interaction with horses?

Now this horse also shows a strong desire to come to the person. It is time to help him to do so. We give a small sign to tell the horse that he

standing still, come close or remain at a distance; whether I want the horse to go away from me; or whether I want to give the horse the chance to joyfully come closer to me. This can clearly be seen in this picture. It is only from this kind of distance and use of clear body signals that the horse can develop both independence and the desire for closeness to you that this happy cooperation shows. Now the horse can also clearly be led. The vital circle is taken into consideration, and success or failure are no longer a matter of circumstance and environment, but solid, determinable, and reliable factors in being with the horse. The result is clarity and safety – and a good basis for the work to come; riding and lungeing.

can come to us. Now a pushy horse will keep exactly the same distance as a shy one, namely an arm's length or more. From the outside, you will no longer be able to tell which horse was which. Both are equally familiar, horses that respect the vital circle of the person and themselves, with all of their individual forms of expression.

Lightly and with the smallest signals, we can now direct the horse outwards into the distance in order to lunge him. One comes from the other – the transitions are soft and flowing. Everything is ready for the dance.

As we come to the end of this chapter, there are still a couple of matters to clear up – how do the invisible changes of gait work? And what about the breathing trick?

The invisible transitions between the gaits –

and what about the breathing trick?

First, we need to create some structure, because again we are introducing some important themes.

Let's start with an overview of the human being's four most important zones of strength, as I experience them. We have to use them quite consciously when interacting with horses, and naturally we can also do so in life in general. One of these zones of strength is intrinsically linked with breathing.

THE FOUR ZONES OF STRENGTH:

1. The area from the shoulder to the solar plexus. Here it is important to achieve a 'relaxed width' that allows us to almost let the energy 'flow through'. There is a very important energy centre here, and this is where people today often have blockages. As a result, energies that are essential for life are trapped there, instead of flowing, and our breath gathers there too. However, it does not belong there at all, because our pear-shaped lungs extend right down to our stomachs. That is where our main lung capacity actually is. People with asthma do not primarily have a problem with getting enough air, but with releasing the air that they have used. A very common picture in our Western world – more about breathing a bit later.

2. Another important energy centre is right next to the solar plexus – the diaphragm area. The diaphragm can be thought of as a kind of dividing membrane, but it is actually much more. The upper part of the stomach, the spleen, liver and gall bladder are all in the 'sphere of influence' of the diaphragm. Together, all of these organs form our physical centre, i.e. the centre of our body – not our energy centre. Many physical issues originate here – as well as the feeling of wellbeing and happiness. The harmonious interplay of the organs here and relaxation of this part of the body are crucial. Many apparent heart and lung problems actually originate here. The 'physical centre of love' is located in this part of the body.

In colloquial language, we talk about having 'butterflies in our tummy' when we fall in love. While the first and third energy centre areas can be stimulated and harmonised by spiritual influences, we can affect this centre best by changing our lives. What and how we eat – what and how we drink. How we sleep, what the rhythm of our lives is like etc.

3. The third energy centre is around 5 centimetres below our navel. This is both the location of our energy centre and, at the same time, the collection point for our breath. This area is very important when it comes to balancing, forcing or guiding energy, but also accumulating life energy on the whole and making it available.

4. The fourth area is right next to the third — it is the area of innermost life energy and sexuality. In physical terms it is located in the pelvis, kidneys, bladder and reproductive organs. This area is particularly influenced by the energy potential of our food and the proportion of fire and water and hot and cold. Colours, shapes, scents and, in particular, moods have a crucial positive or negative effect on this area. In German, if somebody is deeply affected by something, they say that 'it affects their kidneys'.

Zones one and two should, above all, let energy through and let it flow. However, in reality they often store it. That leads to widespread diseases that hide behind names like whiplash injury and irritable bowel syndrome. Trapped energy is usually experienced as tension, cramps and often as 'indefinable pulling and dragging'.

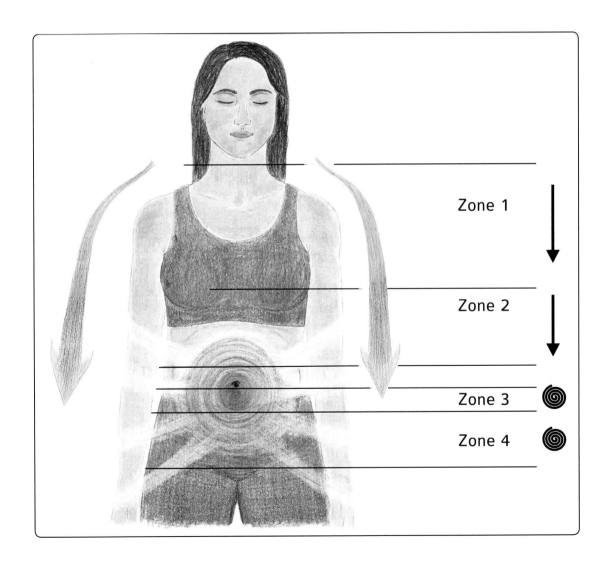

Zone 1

Zone 2

Zone 3

Zone 4

Zones three and four, on the other hand, are where energy should gather, for all of our lives. If you aim at this and achieve it, then ageing need not be a process of slow decline, but, in the best case, one of ever-increasing energy and power. A person who lives consciously will die at the high point of their power – they depart at the best time.

Studying these four zones is especially fascinating, also in being together with horses, because the horse 'scans' us immediately and checks whether energy is flowing where it should be flowing, and whether energy has been collected where it is required for survival. I have already gone into these things in this book before, and I will do so again where it is unavoidable in relation to the horse.

The upper zone, in particular, determines our posture, our openness and willingness to communicate. Our voice forms here, carried from the depths of the fourth zone, and our moods are first articulated here. The fourth, lowest area is our 'turbocharger' – the energy is either there or not. Occasionally we can cover up a lack of energy or squeeze out the last remaining drops with stimulants, but that does not change the reality and the consequences. Latest when the 'tank is completely empty' the real problems will start. What does that mean? For your activities, never go beyond 30 per cent of your abilities, if possible. You should always try to stay between zero and three out of 10 conceivable portions

of your energy, muscular strength and endurance, because anything beyond that is a kind of 'emergency' for the body. The body can cope with a lot of emergencies without suffering, but it cannot withstand a 'constant state of alarm' in the long term. Therefore: no cross country run over 30 per cent, no work situation, etc. So, if you feel that you are almost always making use of all your available energy, you can be certain that you will pay for it one day. Instead of voluntarily and consciously changing something, you may one day be forced to. Just ask people who have recovered from burnout syndrome and listen to them, when they describe how many small things they can now enjoy in life that they just used to rush past. 'Small things' that are now everything to them – life!

The third zone of our quartet of power is the one that I often tackle first in my training sessions.

Naturally, all zones are connected, but the third area is really crucial for our work with horses.

About changing gait smoothly

How it shouldn't be – during almost every transition to a different gait, the horse changes its posture, jerks or tosses its head, swishes its tail, hollows its back and becomes longer, harder and more tense. Correspondingly, the rider is thrown about or loses their seat.

Why does this happen? Besides the inappropriate use of reins when riding, there are essentially three factors:

- On the one hand, the horse is often led or pushed into a faster gait, canter in particular, much too early and without preparation. That means that the horse associates this gait with unpleasantness from the start, and not only reflects this feeling in the precise moment with tension or even panic, but basically comes to associate changing between gaits with stress. He learns something negative. That is why it is hugely important that the change between the paces is done in the gentlest way possible, right from the start.

- On the other hand, the horse is usually simply overwhelmed by the commands. The horse is in walk, for example, and then the next moment is asked to trot or canter, with no preparation.

- Every harmonious change of gait, in any direction, in the wild, is preceded by a moment of collection. The horse always has to use his hindquarters more strongly and actively in order to execute the transition smoothly and comfortably for horse and rider. That is why it is essential to have a collecting 'intermezzo' before each transition.

How it should be: in principle, a horse should change gait in a sequence of movements when it is already carrying itself as well as possible, according to its present level of skill. A horse that is not completely balanced in walk cannot go into trot in a harmonious and 'rounded' way. So we have to create this balance first, right before the change. This 'self-carriage' is then taken over into the new gait, so that the horse does not lose his quiet, relaxed self-carriage. The result is a precise, but soft transition. The effect is that the horse's top line does not change at all. The overall look and impression remain the same, and there is no sign of tension or displeasure.

How do I do it? Something that greatly surprises many spectators is the moment during a demonstration when a previously tense and nervous horse that I did not know before trots on, in or immediately after a specific corner, without the spectators being able to recognise a signal. I comment on the individual steps, clearly emphasise my breathing and then, as soon as the horse starts to leave corner X, he trots on wonderfully softly and quietly.

Here's how it works. We have numbered the corners of the Picadero in the following drawings.

Diagram 1: Here I am working the horse in walk from the ground, in the first corner, for example. The horse should trot on the second he has passed this point – exactly one lap later.

I am already thinking 'trot' very clearly here. From here on, I very clearly visualise the image of the trotting horse. Nothing happens physically yet. We pass corner number three and the following happens: I move very slightly further behind the horse. However, I make sure that the horse does not come any closer to me, but stays on the track. This all fits into my forward movements so well that it can hardly be seen from the outside. I can balance the horse really well using these actions.

As a result, the hindquarters are further activated, although I make sure that the horse doesn't trot on yet (I mainly control this through my general position to the horse: closer to the withers = braking; further back = accelerating) because he is supposed to change gait at the spot and on my signal, from the beginning.

Diagram 2: We have now reached corner four. The horse now knows exactly what is happening. He is prepared and already full of excitement. Once we have passed the third corner, I again step a little further behind the horse and let my breath flow freely in my lower abdomen, i.e. in area 3 (see diagram p. 231). My posture remains upright and opened up forwards; my shoulders are very low, my pelvis slightly tilted forward with my buttocks naturally held together (zone 4).

In brief, I centre my energies so that I can use them to control the energies in the horse. That may sound strange to some people, but this is how I experience it: with a deep, quiet breath into the third power zone, I cause the horse to practically do the same. He breathes in deeply and quietly, and so builds himself up again, gathering more balance, impulsion, energy and joy, in order to pick up a trot in corner one, precisely on my tiny signal (waving the end of the whip by less than one centimetre), quietly,

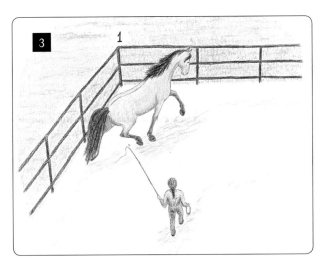

without changing his carriage and full of inner power (diagram 3).

The horse immediately transfers this experience to all of my requests and also to riding. If possible, I try to prepare all of my intentions in this way. As a result, the horse is practically never ambushed, but always supported and 'guided in' to every exercise.

More on breathing: a whole book could be written on this subject alone.

• Please never force your breathing, although this is recommended in some (mostly misunderstood) oriental practices. Instead, visualize your breath flowing very calmly down to your lower abdomen, into the third power zone. Your shoulders stay low and pleasantly relaxed with every breath. You should never breathe in and raise your shoulders at the same time.

• As far as I am concerned, it isn't about breathing in more deeply, but observing your breath. Basically, you will even notice that you breathe less, with lower frequency, but that you have 'more air' and a 'longer breath'.

• Occasionally, place a hand on your lower abdomen and imagine how your breath touches the surface of your hand. Always work quietly and carefully.

• With low shoulders that 'sink' towards the floor, surrender yourself to the image that your breath does not flow through your mouth or nose, but through your lower abdomen. You will quickly feel the calming and strengthening effect of this kind of deep breathing, and your body will guide you further.

• Before adopting breathing techniques from books or teachers, please check very carefully whether you feel your best every second, right from the start. There is certainly some very good advice in this area, but also some very bad. The principle should be naturalness, simplicity and the constant acceptance of your own feelings, wellbeing and intuition. It isn't about learning something new, but remembering something original and authentic. We want to breathe as we did from the start when we were babies.

The impulsion for the gentle change into trot or canter comes from the hindquarters.

You can see clearly in this picture how the horse brings his hindquarters underneath him, forming a lovely top line as a result and making the smooth yet powerful transitions from walk, into trot and then into canter. The picture below shows how I am clearly behind the horse in the transition, after I have prepared it well.

Now everything comes together

Body language
in detail 3

10

Memories of Gotland and the first moon landing –

of foals and other wild animals

+

We have already celebrated the fortieth anniversary of the first moon landing. I personally believe that it really took place, although many say that it didn't. For me, the fact that the twelve astronauts who eventually visited the moon found life after the moon landing difficult is much more interesting. It is generally known that they needed a very long time to adjust after their return — and none of them seem to have fully succeeded. What does that have to do with horses?

Well, evidently being one of the twelve people who have actually been on the moon isn't enough to make you happy. It would seem that the opposite is the case. Perhaps experiencing some kind of spectacular high point in your life leaves you in a trap from which it is difficult to escape. I see the same thing in exemplary fashion with the horses. Here consistency, second by second, counts from the very beginning.

It is about celebrating the evenness of time in taking and giving, as consistently as possible. That is what must be meant by the 'middle way' of the Far Eastern masters. Outbursts are to be feared, as well as steep climbs and the pitfalls that follow them. That is why I am very concerned about achieving clear, steady consistency from the beginning with horses, and why it is a recurring theme at my events.

I recently conducted a seminar on the Swedish island of Gotland. It was significant that this event was attended by so many professional riders and teachers. Yet there were enormous problems and some very striking horses. The general pattern that I would ascribe to this event is one of extremes. For almost all of them, I had to find the centre, the essence, the core, the summary and the overview. I am going to write about it briefly at this point, because it is generally so important for us.

Horses are and always will be wild animals, even if they appear to be tame. Children are and always will be clear and straightforward people, even if many adults misunderstand them. Clarity and straightforwardness are at home in children and animals. That is why we adults are so easily exposed by them. I see our present time as one that neglects one thing above all – namely clarity – because of all of the apparent opportunities. There are explanations and apologies for almost everything, and I get offered many of them.

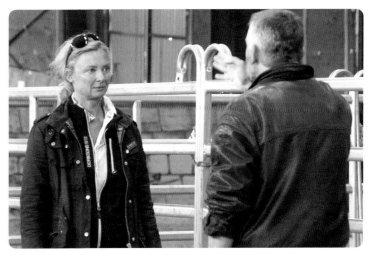

The fact is that the nervous, aggressive and/or sad horse too often remains, so one of my most important concerns is directing the gaze forwards and straight ahead. I often even do it literally. The kind participant in the following photos does something that many contemporaries do quite unconsciously – they often don't really look straight ahead. A horse will then become at least as nervous as I do. It was only when I drew the participant's attention to it, while solving the problems with her horse that she really became aware of her circumstances, so we practised keeping the eyes and hands directed forwards and keeping them there as she threw a rope as a signal, for example.

As a result, she achieved an encounter and clarity with her horse that she had never experienced before. I am writing all of this as an aside, but believe me, this topic could not be more important for me and the horses.

The organiser of the course, herself a very successful dressage rider and instructor, also showed us her horse. She was often afraid of this horse and he had almost killed her. He actually behaved terribly to begin with, but then

became the favourite of everybody at the event and a wonderful and very quiet and wise teacher for many participants. What was the key? Understanding, clear communication, clear gestures; indeed clarity on all levels. Fear and a lack of confidence can force us to walk serpentine inner and outer paths. Initially this begins in the sphere of the conscious, but it increasingly sinks to the levels of the subconscious.

This brings me to a quick sidetrack that still has a lot to do with horses and my work. People say that old people end up strange, eccentric and 'childish'. For me, this is very often an uninterrupted line that goes through your whole life until the point when it becomes blatantly obvious. To put it in a nutshell, if we look at people through a horse's eyes, there would only seem to be 'old' people. Staying young in mind throughout your whole life requires that you decisively set the course very early on – making a constant effort for clarity in communication with yourself and the world, and in this respect, there is no better being to check than the horse – and, of course, children.

The horse took on completely different behaviour after the event, and the owner found her way back to new confidence.

There are still wild horses on Gotland – the Gotland pony. I didn't know that at first, but they showed me two lovely examples of the breed. One, a little yearling colt, kept on standing on his hindlegs and greatly troubling all of the bystanders. The horse was not intended for work during the course, but I just could not let it continue. So, without hesitation, I demonstrated how, with very little effort and in a very short time, you could help this little colt come to a completely different way of behaving with rooted trust, feeling 'at home'. I want to use this event, which took place at the demonstration, to say just a few words on the subject of foals.

- Everything that a horse learns before the end of his third year becomes part of him, just like his genes, i.e. his colour, his size and his body shape. Hardly anything about it can be changed later. We should never forget that.

- A foal will get the best education in a large herd in the largest possible area. He should have as little human contact as possible.

- Foals are completely different from children. Each attempt to convert them to our human/ childish world using well-intended behaviour patterns eventually leads to complete lack of orientation and leaves the horse confused.

- Because of their lack of ability to arrange themselves in a healthy relationship of respect and hierarchy, the consequences are often dramatic for a horse that then experiences an excessive and mainly false interest from people and a maladroit approach.

What should be done? We will need less than ten minutes for the case to be completely cleared up.

Let us look at the pictures:

In pictures 1 to 5, you can clearly see that I have no interest in the little colt. I go my way. I only dealt with a large tarpaulin for a moment and that was it. I did not look at the horse once as I did so. Of course, he did not know that I was naturally observing him very closely. My movements are round and grounded, so I quickly managed to get the horse to trust me deeply, but also to respect me.

To begin with, the little horse gives me a wide berth. Everything about my body language tells him that I am trustworthy. The colt then overcomes his fear of the tarpaulin and his curiosity increases. It is important that I clearly demonstrate to a foal from the beginning that my world still revolves without him, because a foal is right at the very bottom in the hierarchy of an equine herd. Of course, this little chap had completely forgotten that, and things that are not repaired now – virtually in the last minute – will remain a problem in the long term, and indeed can often become very dangerous. In any case, the horse's being and behaviour remains disturbed – he does not find his centre or his inner balance.

In pictures 6 and 7 we can see how the stallion slowly comes to trust me. The way he does it is significant. He does not come into my vital circle, even at the start.

Pictures 8 to 12 show how the horse can now be easily led and you can see how the colt is relaxed, how he keeps yawning and is completely calm. He has found his 'master', his trusted person and partner who builds him up, supports him and who can introduce him into the world of people, but who is, at the same time, also so strong that his position is never at risk.

Picture 13 very clearly illustrates how everything else builds on it. Naturally the foal now gives me his foot without him being tied up – why would he run away? Why would he fidget?

It took less than ten minutes for the case to be completely cleared up. The owner of this lovely horse was happy to promise all of us that she would continue on this way. She had lost her heart to this beautiful breed and now she saw very clearly a way to approach even the youngest among them with respect.

Being with foals is so simple. Their souls are still very trainable and malleable, but for that same reason they can also be spoiled and injured very easily. Clarity, straightforwardness and an awareness of the horse's being that should never be confused with sentimentality, are immensely important. Please never feed foals by hand, and be mindful of your 'vital circle' right from the start, both gently and clearly. Your body language and your being should simultaneously signal inner strength and absolute trust.

Spotlight –
focus on the important points so far

Here we can see how Maria is working with a soft, leather cavesson. This is a very important tool. The horse receives very fine stimuli to the bridge of his nose, even when the lunge line is slack, i.e. a fine vibration, caused by opening and closing the fingers. This provides additional support for the horse's posture. It is important that the horse has first learnt not to leave the lungeing circle, i.e. no longer pull on the lunge rein, or at least seldom and then minimally.

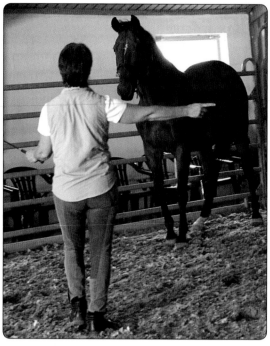

These top pictures illustrate clear body language. Both course participants had practised it first, because in the beginning, it takes quite an effort to relate clearly to your body language and to stand by it. However, both horses understand it and begin to react. Naturally, the 'body signals' become finer and finer with time, but we return to the clear gestures whenever necessary.

Here we can see I am 'pushing' the participant 'forward'. I do that to show them that the horse will follow when he is not asked to do so obtrusively, and he actually follows.

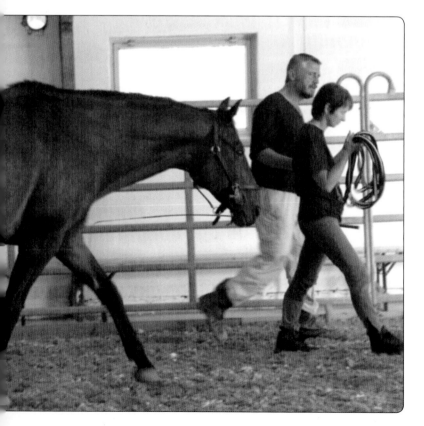

Here the participants have the task of leading a partner as gently as possible, while their partner keeps their eyes closed. Try it out with a friend. It will give you many impressions, primarily of how a horse feels when he is completely dependent on us.

When riding or working from the ground, many people hold their heads either up, down or to the side. The position of the head is the first communication signal – combined with the person's whole posture. Try always to look straight at the 'horizon'. The position of your head has a great influence on the posture of your body – and vice versa. Please become aware of this.

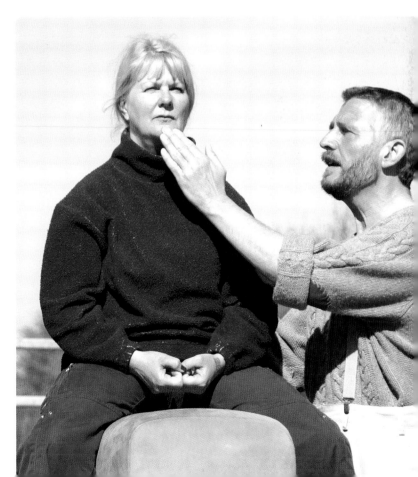

Exemplary leading, exemplary body language. Good distance from the horse. The left hand is always ready to react, the rope is held loosely yet consciously. What else could happen? This man is well prepared.

Clear body language – the horse understands and reacts immediately.

The young stallion still has to find his position and his self-image first. Here, it is important to keep the horse at a distance. The leading arm is raised high, the posture clear and strong.

The stallion learns to wait, to stay standing, to be patient. Again, the raised leading hand consciously shows the horse the importance of distance.

There are still 'murmurings' in the young stallion. Of course, this is not 'first parallelism'. We are working and leading here. Using the mares, the stallion learns to stay quite close on the left side and walk past quietly and correctly. The grounded, clear posture of the man forms a centre around which the horse can orientate himself.

Exemplary body language again. After leading, the rider makes a quarter turn to face the horse and thus clearly signals to him to halt and stay standing. The arm is quietly lowered and a pause follows.

Now everything comes together

Before we turn to other themes in detail, we will see how everything comes together on this page and the next – closeness, distance, moving in and out, leading and proximity. It all causes an unbelievable and touching change in a very short time in this horse, the third stallion from the Spanish military stud. Yet everything has now become considerably clearer and more familiar to you, because the individual steps that must flow into one another, to lead to the result, can now be clearly recognised. Nothing happens here other than that which we have already discussed and worked out by this point.

In his confusion, the horse was extremely aggressive. He attacked me immediately and constantly. Let us look at the pictures again, but this time against the background of what we have already learnt:

- The person is not afraid of the horse – the body language shows that clearly. He is at a distance. As we have already discussed, even the smallest signals have a great effect from here. At this distance, if necessary, the horse can even kick out and let off steam safely. It is just a matter of minutes and the horse will want to be close to me, and will eventually enjoy being near me. He will find trust, understanding and healing in my proximity. Naturally, something like this is still a task for a very special person, and I do not want

to encourage anybody to do something of this kind, as I said at the beginning of the book.

What is crucial is that every case can basically be cleared up and solved using what we have already discussed.

- In the third picture, you can see how the horse stops on his hindquarters, together with the man. I can keep the horse at a distance without even touching him, or even stop him abruptly with his hindquarters right underneath him. This creates great respect and trust at the same time. This form of stop was appropriate here.

- In the fourth picture, you can see how the man's body is obviously totally unconcerned by the horse's attack. This stoic calm and composure make a very strong impression on the horse, which can see that all of his actions will be without consequences. Shortly afterwards, each horse starts to think about it and change his concept.

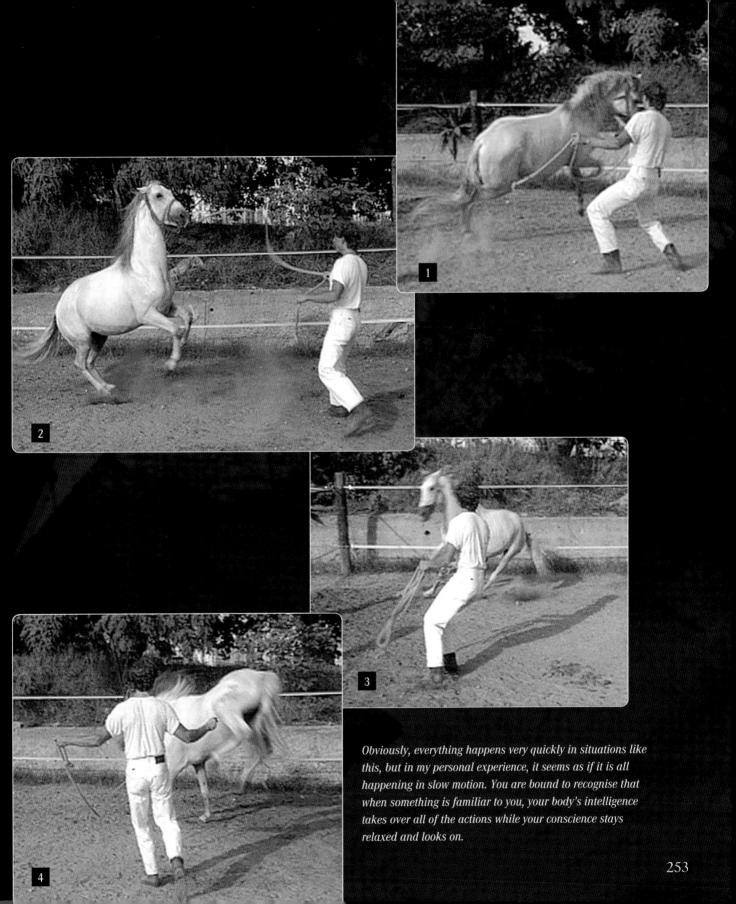

Obviously, everything happens very quickly in situations like this, but in my personal experience, it seems as if it is all happening in slow motion. You are bound to recognise that when something is familiar to you, your body's intelligence takes over all of the actions while your conscience stays relaxed and looks on.

253

Closeness, devotion and unity come from fighting, doubt and protest

In the first picture, we can see very clearly how I give up my very upright posture for a moment and lower my head invitingly, demonstrating absolute placidity. The right hand holds the rope so that it is just lying loosely over the fingers. Everything is soft and modest. This posture is consistently continued in the second picture. I am practically 'hugging' the horse. He keeps showing me the reference – remember, if you will, the drawings on the topic of leading. The 'first parallelism' follows from reference – the stallion will keep following, like a compass needle. But what do the horse's eyes reveal? What praise for our reservation, our efforts and our constant scrutiny around an ever more original standpoint.

You can see very clearly how I am concentrating. Alertness, paired with gentleness and sympathy, are expressed in my face and in my

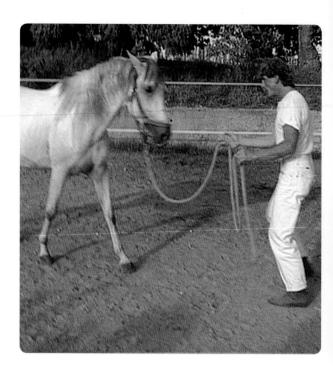

body language. The right hand is always ready to protect my vital circle, because this stallion was now so 'with me' and inwardly so close to me that he wanted to express this tendency through contact too. You can see this very clearly in the video clip *Wounded Horses Can't Cry*. Any aggression leaves the horse like a layer of dust washed away by the rain, what remains is an expression of pure sadness and endured pain, mixed with the purest devotion to a man who embodies a completely different image of human beings, for the horse.

In the last picture we can see very clearly the stallion's expression, which is directed inwards, because after an episode like this, he has to go through many stages inside. This is mixed with the most varied feelings. After such an encounter,

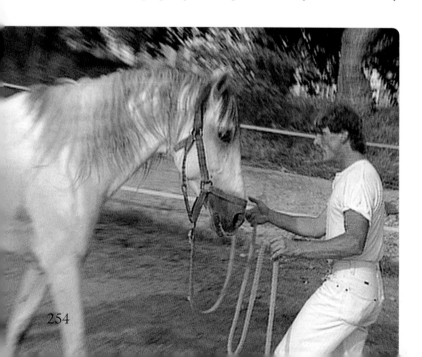

254

to be dreaming. At the same time, the shell breaks and the horse opens himself up to the person, even if he is alone in the world.

I find it hard to describe in words what happens between myself and the horse in moments like this. The pictures speak for themselves. But what is gained in terms of inner experience and authenticity in these seconds and minutes cannot be taken away by anything or anyone in the world.

horses are usually very quiet. To begin with they withdraw, even physically – standing quietly in the corner of their box and appearing

In my eyes, that is real wealth.

255

Solving the problem 'incidentally'

I have already written about the problem described here at other times, in a different context. I would like to explain it again against the background of the theme of this book. Essentially, we cannot find anything 'special' here – a comparatively 'normal' encounter with a horse that was causing his owner problems. However, the body language has been captured very precisely in the photographs – along with what is 'special' about the 'normal'.

First the horse turns his head into the corner to threaten me with his hindquarters and stands there impassively. Unlike the example with Marouk, this behaviour was already very deeply ingrained and also coupled with signs of aggression. Every case is special and individual. I proceed differently here than with Marouk, but in the end the result is the same and the way is equally effective. In the third picture, we can already see that the horse now comes straight out of the corner. The pictures on the next page show how his expression has changed considerably and how he is very close to me, after scarcely two minutes in all.

Here, the result can also be attributed to the fact that the man in the pictures is completely decisive on the one hand – everything about his body language shows this – and on the other hand, because he completes the task 'inciden-tally' and extremely 'modestly'. I would now like to refer to this important point, in particular. It would not have been possible to solve this case in this way without a 'whatever, it's not important' approach. In the first picture you can see that I do not go straight to the horse. I tend to claim the space next to the horse. I do not look at him and I do not actually have anything to do with him. I plan to use myself as a 'wedge' between the horse and the fence. You can see how low my shoulders are – it is almost as if they are pushed down. In this case, the effect is that the horse yields immediately. He gives the space to the 'leader' without complaint.

Some people want to fight at times; but no horse in the world wants to fight – horses want to live, survive and win, and that is exactly what I want too. Being with horses means keeping and bestowing peace on the highest conceivable level. I forbid myself any form of fighting and arguing, any form of conflict-ridden interaction with horses. This means that the body language must not ever express the opportunity for a fight.

It is very risky to walk up to a horse so close from behind and claim his space as shown in this example. The horse would then be challenged to fight by the tiniest signal from the person. Please do not ever approach a horse like this, unless the situation is absolutely clear. This way seemed to me to be the clearest, most definite and also the quickest, in this case. If I do something like this, then I know very precisely beforehand how the horse will react – I often describe it to the spectators before the actual action. However, the condition is then that I do

not have an attitude of expectation or making demands. Everything also happens 'incidentally'. This apparent indifference, this refusal of any passion eventually guarantees me success and affirms my inner strength, but also my absolute placidity to the horse.

Winning, not fighting

In the fourth picture in this series you can clearly see that I still do not look at the horse. The right shoulder is still demonstratively pressed down and the whip low on the floor, but the horse is still acting clearly. He is simply acting consistently – he cannot do anything else because he is following his nature. Finally, I turn openly to the horse, bring him to a halt and give him the opportunity to turn to me as his mentor. From here, the story takes the path that we now know in detail from the pages before.

In the sixth picture you can see that the horse stands in the corner with his head turned to me. The earlier problem has been wiped away with a tiny stroke, never to appear again with me.

This example clarifies that I am not willing to 'waste time', even for a moment. I take all the time in the world, appear patient to the last, but at the same time, I am always highly effective. Nature appears to be extravagant, but she does not waste anything. I do not want to lose a second without making direct progress. There is no standstill. I may stand motionless for minutes and then perform any, possibly unexpected, action the next minute. You will then see that the problem is solved and it becomes clear that not one second of the waiting and persistence was useless.

As in the previous examples, the horse comes to me and I can further quieten him with new offers and activities.

The moment that was captured in the last picture occurs immediately before the first steps of 'first parallelism'. Yet, when you look at the horse, it is clear that this horse would not hesitate for a second to follow me in immediate proximity.

The circle completes itself again...

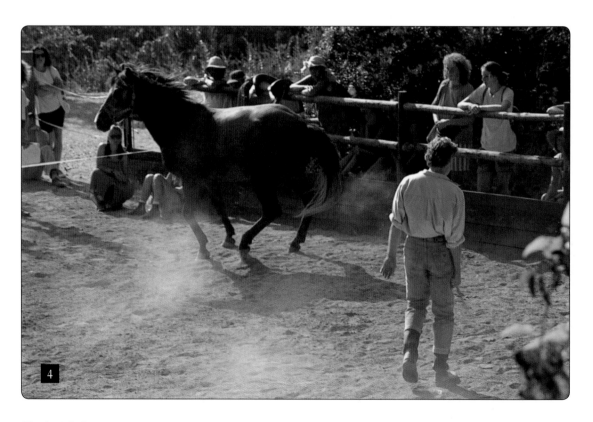

4

The denial of any passion guarantees me success. It assures the horse of my inner strengths, but also my absolute inner placidity, because passion is also always a kind of fight – it means idea, will, usually also a plan, and being too close.

5

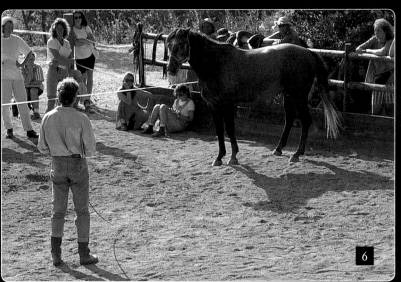

6

Do you have the courage to reach the highest level of trust?
It is less a question of skill and more a question of being decisive. On the door to paradise there is a sign that says: Decisiveness.

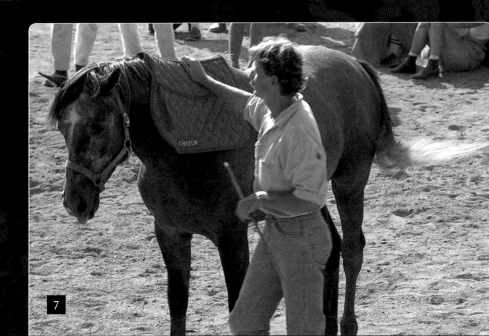

7

Do what has to be done, even if you have never done it before

In this picture, I am 'pushing' a horse over the area, but look at the horse's expression – he is not at all 'amazed', unlike the people around him. On the contrary, he is quite calm. In the end, it no longer seems important what you do, but simply how you do it.

I have done the 'craziest' things in events, if necessary, and only the success that came immediately made people stay. There is no single way; there is no logical sequence if you follow the nature in yourself in order to experience it thoroughly, because there are no logical consequences in nature. There is only renewal, natural limitation, surprise and absolute precision. Nothing ever happens twice in the same way.

Before the next chapter, I would again like to encourage you to feel your uniqueness that awaits discovery (or rediscovery) beneath wants, fears, imagination, worries and future plans. The devil loves copies, poor imitations, the masses, their frenzy and their susceptibility. However, horses love the original and the individual, the unique, in brief, the authentic. And they love the brave.

People come to me because I am successful, but they are only surprised by the path to success until they succeed themselves.

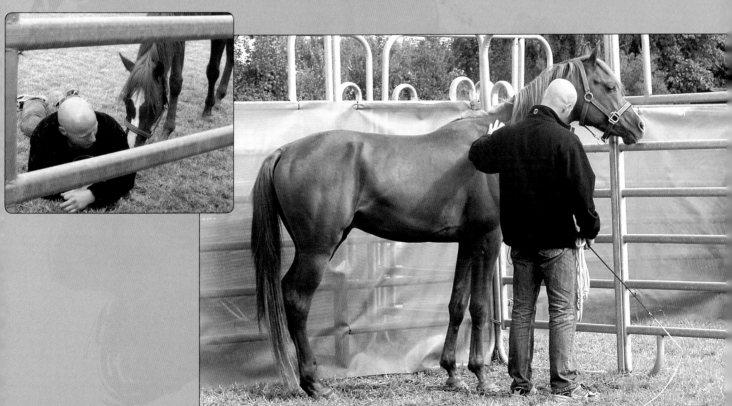

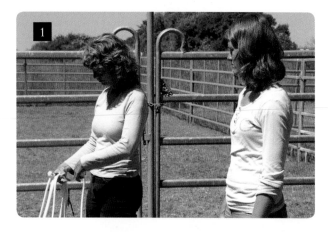

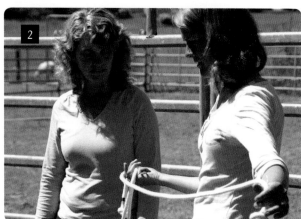

A few more observations from practical experience

Pictures 1 to 3: Please try to become as familiar as possible with the tools of your trade. When you are using the rope or whip, it is very important that your posture is absolutely still and upright, that your shoulders are low and relaxed, and that you can direct all of your attention to the horse and not at the instrument in your hand. These are all important details, that together, make the result possible.

Picture 4: Here we see the practical 'walking on the circle' exercises again. All of the participants in this picture are advanced. Nevertheless, I keep coming back to these basic exercises before we go to the horses. I cannot over-emphasise the importance of these apparently very simple exercises.

3

Pictures 5 and 6: I am always correcting my course participants' postures when lungeing. Please look at picture 5. It does look quite nice, but if you compare this picture with the next one, you will easily notice how much more directly connected to her horse the young woman in the white T-shirt is now. This exercise, in particular, is anything but easy. It is correct when we are on a small circle behind the horse and at the same time with our chest facing the horse. Then it is as if we are aiming our inner energy straight into the horse's energy centre. The effect, on our 'human coach' too, is immense. Please study these two pictures very closely and compare them with others in this book where you see me working.

The Magic Circle

11

The Magic Circle –
on the path to the secrets of horses

Before we turn to riding in a new way, we first come to another very special topic, which I call the Magic Circle.

One of my greatest wishes is to show people what it is really like to interact directly with horses, when you share in their innermost secrets and communicate with them directly. To be completely accepted by them, and live connected with them in their world for minutes or even hours, is completely different from a conventional riding experience and the usual interaction with a horse. It is as if you had flicked a switch and lit up a dark room. The two forms of experience are almost opposite. This is my wish.

The reality looks quite different. To me, it seems as if I might have to describe the entire process, step-by-step first.

Only this, together with time that gradually changes everything, increases the chance that more and more people will also get this direct access to the world of the horse. This book is a considerable part of this whole picture and a further part is the work in the Magic Circle, which I describe here for the first time.

The Magic Circle is an instrument for practice. It has been born out of the necessity of giving as many people as possible a basic idea of what I am trying to put across. It is – briefly and honestly – a compromise. The Magic Circle is to a rider what a centrifuge is to an astronaut. A centrifuge prepares an astronaut for departure from the earth, for starting with the rocket, basically for the big adventure, for the magic. But the centrifuge is not space travel. You do not leave this world with it, and that is how it is with the Magic Circle. It does not open the doors to the mysteries of horses, but you can get closer to them. But you must not confuse one with the other, because then you would lose the hunger for the real thing.

Before we deal with the subject properly, here are some key points:

- The Magic Circle is a concession to reality. It makes dealing with horses easier and takes us to their mysteries. However, it can be misused. In spite of this danger, I will describe the principles here because I have the bigger picture in mind.

- Personally, I never work in the Magic Circle, because it restricts you to a few important initial areas in dealing with horses, but that also means that it excludes other areas. Therefore it represents a restriction for me. However, it is really useful for the beginner.

- An important rule in the Magic Circle is that you only work in it for a short time and only work through short sequences in it.

- The following can be achieved in the Magic Circle:

1. The dominance relationship to the horse can be considerably improved. The dominance relationship, and at the same time, the horse's trust in people, can be increased by working in the Picadero or when leading. It is different in the Magic Circle, which is initially and primarily about dominance. However, the present relationship of trust is not disturbed.

2. You can experience and test out the effect of your own body signals. This is a particularly important experience and requirement for the work in the Picadero that follows. However, it is important that you observe and monitor yourself

closely. Preferably, you should have a really good and sensitive coach at your side, whom you can trust.

3. The horse's sensitivity can be increased considerably. That can happen, but it does not happen automatically. It is important that you completely understand the basic principle, and take one step at a time, with great confidence and composure.

The Hilary revelation

The bottom picture shows me with the Warmblood stallion Jack. He will accompany us through this chapter in his own, inimitable way. Before we return to practical concerns with this horse, I have another important duty to perform – I have to explain Hilary's revelation to you. I do that with both a tear in my eye and a smile on my face.

Why? On the one hand, Hilary's revelation summed up something that had long been part of one of the biggest riddles of my entire work. On the other hand, it would seem purely and simply fanciful to anyone who had not been through the many processes themselves. Indeed, it appeared so odd at first that I did not get it myself for many years. Hilary, a very nice course participant from Australia, blurted out this revelation once – at the very moment when she was going to be overwhelmed by its consequences. She allowed me to name this phenomenon after her – the Hilary revelation.

One is that the time in which we live makes it so difficult for people to exist on a single level of experience, trust and communication, as horses or children do. Instead, so many people switch subconsciously between the various levels and keep creating new areas of tension, consciously, or usually subconsciously, that can largely no longer be penetrated. I experience this as a major problem and it almost always fills me with sadness when I am near it.

The other problem is directly related to the first and leads us straight to the Hilary phenomenon. In my twenty years as a teacher working with horses, I have not been able to explain why people are so different from horses. Here a person still seems strong and self-confident. Here they still have all of the important things in mind. They know how to hold the whip, how they can use the rope, how they should stand, walk and signal. That was how it was with Hilary too. That is how we all experienced her. Until the moment when I offered her a horse. Then there suddenly 'wasn't anything there'. Even Hilary, a strong, experienced woman from Australia, stood before us as if she could have been knocked down by a breath of wind. In front of her was the horse, who was not paying her the slightest bit of attention. We were there again and I asked my question again: 'Hilary, why aren't you doing everything that we discussed before?'

And – for the first time – I actually got an answer. And what an answer. Hilary said: 'Klaus, I have been watching you with horses for weeks. I have travelled halfway around the world to experience a man live, who gets such different results from horses because he leaves everything behind when he is with them, essentially the great uncertainty, seen from the point of view of a person, and just follows his feeling, and that is exactly where I am standing. Nothing of what I know and have ever experienced can help me. Nothing else but my feeling. It is as if I was standing in front of a chasm, with a cliff wall behind me. Every step could lead to disaster or I have to fly. I know that I should fly, and I also know that I can fly. I know that one day I will fly, but in front of me there is only the abyss. And it cries for trust. And this abyss makes me catch my breath. It lets me forget everything and first of all it takes my strength. And around me I see only sheer, naked fate. And right in the middle, on a tiny island, in the middle of this sea that is both everything and nothing, the horse waits for me.'

We all sat there with our mouths open. There was, and still is, nothing I could add. Hilary's revelation opens the way to the practical Magic Circle experience for us all.

Hilary, a very nice course participant from Australia, blurted out this realisation once – at the very moment when she was going to be overwhelmed by its consequences.

After Hilary's convincing statement, I suggested to her that she should simply follow me into this 'ocean that is nothing and everything'. I was working with a young Arab gelding and asked Hilary simply to be my 'shadow'. This gave Hilary the opportunity to experience everything from my point of view. She found the composure and the uninterrupted flow particularly remarkable. Everything builds up organically and merges together. For her, it was like going through a strange landscape, but it was as if we already knew the next step, because everything was so familiar, despite it being unknown.

A wonderful practical lesson –
KFH's Magic Circle

This is an unbelievably effective type of exercise to do with a horse. These exercises are an excellent preparation for leading, and above all, lungeing. What does it mean? When we build a Picadero in the middle of an arena, a free track is automatically created, the 'magic circle'. Using body language, you can very precisely steer, stop and control the speed of a horse that is moving on this track, as well as guide him into various exercises. The benefit here is that the horse reacts and responds with accuracy to the approach, appearance and fundamental being of the person.

Another important benefit is that the teacher and the student can usually keep some distance apart from the horse, and yet experience directly how it reacts to their signals with great sensitivity and 'plays along', despite the distance. The extent to which the horse person has already learned to approach the horse with essentially 'relaxed' body language becomes particularly clear during the exercises in the Magic Circle.

The exercises are very versatile and can be varied and adjusted individually to suit each person-horse pair. The most competent and helpful accompaniment possible is important in the whole procedure, because precise 'assistance' from a friend, helper, coach, mentor and teacher will quite quickly lead to new insights and successes in the end. If you practise alone and without suitable observation and checking, there is

the risk that you will become 'fixed' too quickly and get lost in a blind alley, and everything will simply become tight and then difficult.

In the following pages, I will show you a few basic exercises that you can change, vary, extend and expand according to requirements and corresponding to your intuition, naturally relating to the horse. Everything we have discussed so far applies to all of these exercises.

What should you pay attention to, in particular?

It is crucial that you go about this work as quietly as possible. The Magic Circle is the ideal place to practise how you can let the horse find his way forward without inhibition, in a completely calm way, using minimal signals and movements. The tasks chosen should always be simple enough that they will lead to foreseeable success with lightness and joy. That creates steadily increasing self-confidence for the person in a very simple and powerful way, especially in their ability to positively and gently dominate the horse with minimal signals. The principle of the Magic Circle consists of moving the horse in front of you, and therefore automatically taking on the position of a high-ranking stallion. If they are done correctly and in a grounded way, these exercises make an enormous impression on the horse, so that you will be able to find your deserved position in the hierarchy without any further problems, or at least a lot more easily.

On the one hand, we achieve relaxation in the person, minimisation of their body signals, the experience of correct dominance over a horse at a great distance, action, reaction and communication with the smallest gestures with a great and optimum effect. On the other hand, the horse's options for acting are comparatively limited by the outer and inner circle, so that it is relatively easy for an intuitive and correctly coached person to build up a completely new dominance structure in relation to the horse in a relatively short time.

In my teaching sequences I pay particular attention to the following details:

- The correct, relaxed but upright posture of the body with low shoulders, comparatively small but precise steps, the correct gait, stepping and stopping.

- Very clear signals from the body that make unmistakably clear to the horse what is supposed to be communicated at that moment.

- Becoming aware of emotions and thoughts that can be communicated and discussed, with the aim of the greatest possible presence in the here and now, alertness, sensitivity and receptiveness.

- It is also important that the immediate reactions of the horse are translated and made clear to the student at the right time and in a way that is easy to understand. Because the tasks set are essentially very easy to complete, the student can direct all of their concentration and attentiveness to the smallest reactions of the horse and changes. The learning effect is immense!

- You should also be aware of ensuring a slow but steady increase in the exercises in the Magic Circle too. The exercises should be interesting and full of variety for the horse as well. By slowly but steadily increasing the level of difficulty, the student can learn and recognise the dynamic that can be discovered in the organic processes and sequences with horses.

- Even if the exercises themselves are not difficult, they require very great precision from the student, enormous concentration and presence. That is why it is important that these exercises are only performed for brief moments.

- It is very important that the horse is not impeded in its forward movement by the 'restrictive' emotions of the student, or through any possibly constricting body signals. It may seem easy but it is actually one of the most difficult and important areas of experience. If a student manages to make great progress here and to convey direction, position, turning points and so on, to a horse with relative ease, then they have created an excellent basis for further natural positive interaction with horses. As we have suggested, the function and role of the tutor are of great significance in the Magic Circle.

An overview of the first possible exercises in the Magic Circle

PREPARATION FOR THE EXERCISE

Basically, everything that we have said at other points applies here too. The student should approach the exercises with great calm and as open a timeframe as possible. It is important that they can already use the whip and rope correctly. It is also very helpful to complete some physical and contemplative exercises, beforehand.

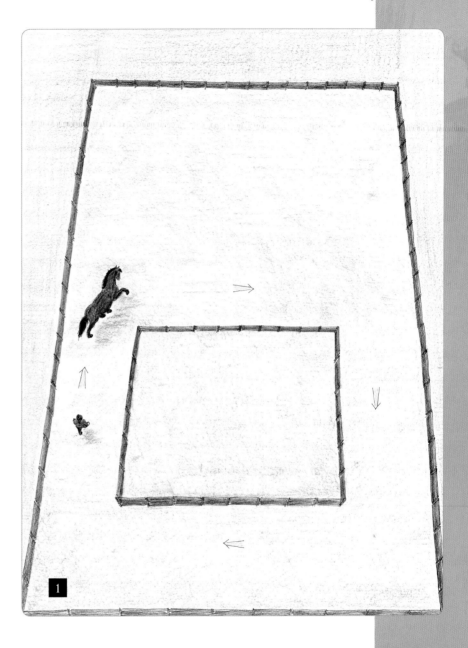

Example exercise 1: The student has the task of moving the horse in front of them, quickly but quietly, for around three to five circuits on the track of the Magic Circle, maintaining a distance to the horse of at least 4 to 5 metres. The horse is then praised and the exercise completed.

Example exercise 2: The student's task is to gently direct the horse into a predetermined corner of the riding arena and keep him there for a few moments. The distance to the horse should not fall below around 4 to 5 metres. Once the student has called the horse to himself out of the corner, the horse is praised and the exercise ends. It is important that the task is performed with as little complexity as possible, and if possible, with minimal body signals.

Example exercise 3: The student has to direct the horse into a predetermined corner using body language, keep him there from a distance for a moment, and then guide him from there into the opposite corner of the arena and keep him there for a moment too.

Example exercise 4: One side of the Magic Circle is narrowed by an 'obstacle'. Now the student has to move the horse in front of them past this obstacle, quietly and with minimal gestures. Again, the distance to the horse should not fall below around 4 to 5 metres. The trainer should make sure that the remaining

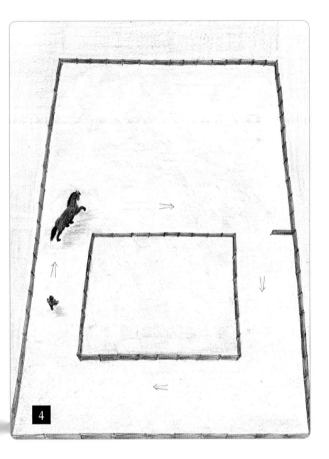

path for the horse is such that a certain degree of hesitancy and spooking should be expected. The obstacle should not exceed a certain size under any circumstances, so that the task is not too difficult or impossible for the student. The trainer needs to have a high degree of sensitivity here. If carried out neatly, with a good posture and minimal gestures, this very exercise can have an enormous learning effect for the student. To begin with, the horse will try to avoid the gap so that he can run past the student in the opposite direction. The student will only manage to get the horse through and over the obstacle at a distance with perseverance and clear body language.

Example exercise 5: In this version, the student has the task of leading the horse through the open door of the inner Picadero in the inner area and back out again. Here, it is important that the path next to the entrance to the inner Picadero is not closed, so that the horse always has the option of choosing this easier route. The student's task is to guide the horse in the right direction using only body language, position and inner and outer clarity.

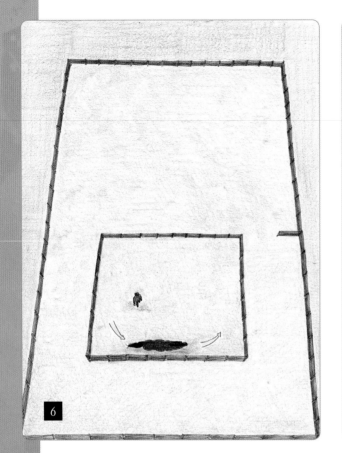

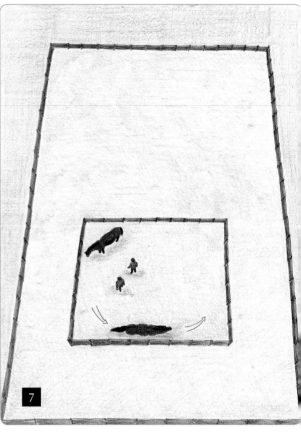

Example exercise 6: The experience gained in this way puts the student in a position where they can lunge the horse in the Picadero itself …

Example exercise 7: … stopping and holding in the corner.

Another reason for the particular success of the students from my last Compact Schooling in June 2010 was that we expanded and extended the work in the Magic Circle. The work that I describe in detail in the following pages cannot be valued highly enough.

(See video clip *Magic Circle*)

1

Working with Jack in the Magic Circle

— making the leap into practice with an example from experience

The owner got a lot of enjoyment out of her eleven-year-old coloured stallion, Jack. However, he occasionally played up badly and then became quite insufferable, and for example, would not tolerate any veterinary treatment at all, either by a vet or by the owner. After I had worked with the horse for a short while, the case became clear to me. It was not too difficult, but it had to be treated thoroughly. Jack was a mix of the characters 'Guardian of Fire', 'Friend' and 'King'. A very good-natured, basically soft guy, but the

king within him was strong and always wanted to rule as well. Once he got something into his head, it was virtually impossible for the owner to dissuade him, so first and foremost there was a clear problem with dominance.

Pictures 1 to 3 show me with the stallion in my 'normal' work. Jack built himself up well very quickly, but also showed me his current 'problem areas'. I then had to communicate with him at a distance and quickly build up and clarify the relationship of trust and dominance. Again, more clearly, I would now continue to work with the stallion in precisely this way, just as I made clear using the examples of Marouk, Queijo and other horses. As you can see very

2

3

on the following pages show both: for one, the reduction which you can primarily recognise from the horse's posture and his expression. You will search the following pictures in vain for a posture like the one in the first picture, but they also show the success of the student, namely the first really feasible steps to an improvement, to a closer and clearer relationship between person and horse. An intermediate stage, but a workable one – a compromise, if you proceed with caution.

Picture 4 shows us in the 'first parallelism'. This naturally cannot be accomplished by working in the Magic Circle. However, because I wanted to work with the rider in the Magic Circle, I brought the stallion here and showed him the new work area.

clearly in these pictures, I am working with the posture of the horse, his sensitivity, impulsion, distance and proximity, dominance and trust, all at the same time. In the Magic Circle this is now reduced very consciously to a very small area, together with the owner. The photographs

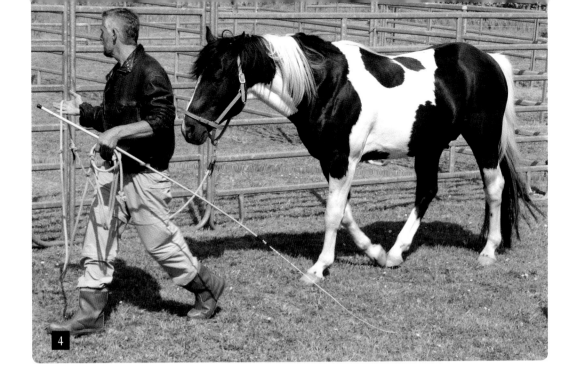

Pictures 5 to 8: In order to prepare the training for the owner, I brought the stallion into a very crucial situation for him, right at the very beginning. He was supposed to stand very precisely in a corner within our Magic Circle and stay there, at a distance.

6

7

As you can see from his expression (pictures 6 and 7), the horse protests briefly but then stays quietly and attentively.

In picture 8 you can see me explaining to the rider how she can now best manage these tasks herself. Naturally, this part came right at the end of the exercise sequence. We will see that the horse owner's problems lay at exactly this point. However, everything worked out well in the end, after successfully building up the lessons. Thus the horse was able to transfer much of what he had experienced through me onto the owner. Please look at the man's flexibility again and his short and pared down but 'dance-like' movements. What I want from the horse is really a lot for the stallion at the moment. Yet I almost remain on the spot. My body language is absolutely unmistakable for the horse.

8

9

Pictures 9 to 12: Before I hand over the horse and the sequence of exercises to the owner, I direct the stallion around the square for another lap. When doing so I guide the horse simply by raising my right hand and occasionally clicking my fingers. The horse is very friendly and does not show even the slightest sign of displeasure or aggression. The ears are pricked very forward and the horse is moving quickly and at a great distance. The horse is now sufficiently prepared that he can continue to be worked successfully by the rider herself. Naturally she has to do all of this alone at home or with close friends. However, I will concentrate on describing the following photographs in great detail so that you have some good starting points and hopefully can avoid the pitfalls. You can clearly see how the person automatically always assumes the position of the dominant stallion in this exercise. If the appropriate behaviour still has a corresponding supportive effect, then the positive effects will not fail to materialise, and that is why we now want to turn our attention to the appropriate behaviour.

10

11

12

13

Pictures 13 and 14: Everything begins with leading the horse here too, and we also keep coming back to leading in the Magic Circle. This is very important, especially in this exercise, because the horse is very consciously kept at a distance throughout. It is particularly important to get closer to the horse again after just a few laps and then to lead him neatly for two or three laps. Please pay very close attention to that point!

The student has the whip and the rope in her hand in order to give a signal with one or the other alternately.

14

In picture 14 we can see that the horse keeps a very nice distance, but at the same time, starts to 'grind his teeth' a little. This is because of the rider's posture, which is slightly fixed in her shoulders, and the way that she is still holding her arms slightly away from her body. In this kind of situation, I say to the student that she should relax more, simply think about something else, smile and walk as if she hadn't a care in the world. Then the horse can go more freely and contentedly.

15

Pictures 15 to 17: On the whole, everything looks great here. The distance between the person and the horse is particularly nice. Let us look at the pictures one by one.

In picture 15, the woman's expression is still too strong. The signal with her right hand is too unsubtle, because the horse just walks indisputably. It is very important to always differentiate between a neutral and a very relaxed posture and a 'signal posture'. If signals are required, please always give them minimally to begin with and then slowly build them up. We discussed this in relation to using the whip (see page 221).

The rider's posture is very relaxed in picture 16. The horse is content. The signalling with the rope is almost at a maximum in this picture. If the horse does not react to this information, the rope is thrown clearly past the horse.

This can be seen in picture 17. Here the rider shows nicely how you have to keep the shoulders quiet and low during this kind of action and convey a very placid impression on the whole.

The aim of signalling with the rope is to eventually be able to control the horse with just a hand signal. You must always keep that in mind. You have to keep moving on quietly, but constantly.

Pictures 18 to 20: In picture 18, the horse challenges the person. Composure and clarity are required here. The person quickly gets too close and everything becomes too narrow, inelegant and an argument can eventually follow. However, the Magic Circle always prevents this because of its inner structure, if you stay collected and convincing. Then progress is always possible. Here the choice is to relax completely and to quietly direct the horse forwards with correct, i.e. increasing, signals with the whip. It is always about your own posture, your own development of awareness.

The pressure in picture 19 is also too strong. What is the most remarkable thing? At the very moment when the distance is right and everything appears to be working, pressure can very quickly lead to a counter-reaction in the horse. You can experience the connections between stimulus and reaction very directly in the Magic Circle.

Please do not deceive yourself: it might look as if everything is quite simple, but it is not. It requires concentration and body awareness to execute these exercises elegantly and eventually without any pressure – for that, the effect is unbelievably great when it works. It is an interim exercise, but I recommend that you

take it very seriously. In our case, with Jack for example, the owner was actually able to 'treat' her horse in a simulated consultation afterwards – for the first time!

In picture 20 you can see how the horse now takes the exercise as a game, joins in and is very relaxed and happy. Our rider has already gained trust and now behaves more quietly and in a more grounded way. All of these experiences are worth gold for the leading and lungeing work that follows. Please always take a break between the individual laps – after around two to four minutes. Less is more here as well. It is better to stop at the right time and start again later or the next day.

21

Picture 21: Here Jack is trying to hide himself in one of the corners that we have made with the fencing panels. The rider quietly approaches the horse to get him moving again, using tiny signals. However, it could be gentler and more confident with regard to expression. Here, the coach's task is to find the right instructions and comments. Can you see that too much energy is still gathered in the chest and shoulder area? A horse's willingness to be led by a person, to be accompanied, depends directly on the overall appearance of this person. Success in the Magic Circle is determined by the student's willingness to turn all of their attention to it. It is recommended that these exercises are prepared and accompanied by body, awareness and expression exercises. The importance of this should not be underestimated.

In picture 22 the 'relationships' are turned around – now the horse is 'leading' the person; simply turn round, wait for a moment and then continue the exercise in the opposite direction.

22

Jack and his owner go through their first task

After all of the preparations, we had now reached a point when the first tailored tasks could be set up and managed for both. As we have said, it was about dominance. It turned out very quickly that we had hit the nail on the head with the following exercise. The rider was supposed to direct the stallion as gently but as clearly as possible into the top right corner of the Magic Circle and keep him there, and she was very surprised at how difficult she found it to complete this apparently 'simple' exercise. Before we look at the steps in detail, here is this essential point again.

The moment that a horse like Jack notices that something very specific is wanted from him, he stands on his hindlegs and protests. Not because he does not want to stand in that corner. That does not really bother him. No, he is protesting on principle! In doing so, he demonstrates that he does not really trust his owner to lead yet. The pictures talk a clear language. Please look again at the four pictures that show me with the stallion in the same exercise right at the beginning (see pictures 5 to 8 on page 279–280). You can clearly see that the stallion hardly protests with me at all. Again, it is not the horse, but the person.

On the one hand, my role as a coach particularly consists of ensuring absolute safety, i.e. always giving a warning at the right time, before it gets too 'tight'. On the other, I always give a pointer in these situations if the trainer seems to be tense. Otherwise, I give the events as free a rein as possible so that the owner solves the problem themselves. In a preliminary talk, it is again made clear that all of the signals start off minimally and are only increased by the required amount until the horse reacts.

Pictures 1 to 8: In all of these pictures, it becomes clear how much the stallion expresses his displeasure by tossing his head. The Magic Circle actually 'compels' the person to always stay in the right position – an invaluable aid at the beginning, because the student at least does not have to worry about that. If the fence block were not in the middle, the horse would quickly look for his strongest position in the arena and the undertaking would take on a whole new dimension.

First the rider tries to direct the horse in approximately the required direction. She has to proceed very carefully, because if the signals that she gives are too strong, the horse will run to the other side, out of the corner. That happened several times, but here we are just showing the important pictures that eventually led to success. In almost all of the pictures we can see that the woman is still 'creating too much pressure' with her body. That is why the stallion reacts with such indignation, among other emotions. He reflects the 'rigidity' in the woman's expression with his gestures. With time, with the help of

the right body exercises and by observing the immediate reactions of the horse, the rider will develop a different inner and outer balance of her own volition. Here it is crucial that less pressure, more relaxation and greater quiet do not let the horses reactions occur at all, because that would just lead to more pressure in turn. A paradox that can and must only be experienced if you want to solve it. The Magic Circle is a wonderful first place for this.

5

6

7

Pictures 9 to 16 show the exercise being completed. Pictures 11 to 13 again show very clearly how fiercely the stallion was fighting. Unless such behaviour is dealt with immediately in this kind of exercise, disaster could happen at any time. But there is more, the horse himself does not feel good, because all he wants is peace and quiet. After all, he stands relaxed in the corner and appreciates the praise and happiness of the rider. We ended this exercise at this point and did not repeat it again. It is very important that you leave enough time, and if possible, only continue the next day. The point when you can finish an exercise is much easier to estimate in the Magic Circle because the horse can clearly see the solution to the task. That way, he also knows that a temporary, very positive end point has been reached.

Naturally everything about the stallion Jack, and his owner must, and will, get better in the coming days. However, it has now reached a successful end.

8 288

9

13

10

14

11

15

12

16

17

Pictures 17 to 18: After a break, we built another little obstacle that was accepted by the horse playfully with no problems and without any protest. Naturally you can get any horse over an obstacle with lots of fuss. However, it will certainly have become clear by now that this is not the point of the Magic Circle. Rather, the results of the gentleness, the active participation, understanding and minimisation of signals are sought. As you can see, the owner is still far behind the horse, who has since overcome the obstacle with his ears happily pricked.

At the end of the sequence of exercises, we have a relaxed horse that has really understood, by himself, what was asked of him, which was what it was about. He has not only fully grasped his task but also that of his owner. The stallion knows that he is helping the person to become closer to themselves and to their authenticity. He now knows the individual steps very well, because they have been clearly defined in the Magic Circle. Both horse and owner were successful; both had meaningful experiences, insights and not least joy. Was I able to explain the principle to you?

In responsible hands, may it blossom into what corresponds to its meaning and purpose.

18

The all-important – plan and programme or feeling and being?

It is important that we become more and more confident from one small victory to the next, gain trust, and that the horse realises that the person reaches higher, step by step, to reach his level.

Careful observation and critical self-analysis are of the utmost importance here. The problem is never with the horse – it is always with us.

To conclude, I would like to mention a 'pitfall'. Work in the Magic Circle in particular is based on the fact that small exercises can be carried out. We saw this in the last photograph. But here, in particular, it is important to almost immediately 'forget' the task and the aim of the journey again. I naturally have to keep them at the back of my mind, but on the first level, the seconds in the 'here and now' and the feeling remain crucial. Afterwards comes the task, the next step of the way. Human life will always have a plan and a programme, but it all only becomes really human because feeling is above everything. The willingness, the counterpart and his feeling of always being in first place.

Naturally a Magic Circle can also be misused. But that is not what we want. So, proceed quietly, with consciousness and with the constant effort to make yourself and your own inner and outer posture into the object of the exploration.

1

2

Magic Circle highlights

Pictures 1 to 3: Here we have a few participants joined together by a rope. This allowed them to play 'horse' and try to react like one. We did this exercise before the activity in the Magic Circle – it was very instructive for all participants, because the people who represented the horse could see very clearly how a horse must feel if a person lacks clarity and confidence when they act.

3

Pictures 4 to 6: Pictures 4 and 5 clearly illustrate how Jo's body language shows that she was not quite sure of herself at this point. The 'horses' react correspondingly, indeed some-times with very oppressive actions. The best way to solve this is always with a short break. First take a breath, collect yourself, ground and centre yourself and naturally smile as well.

Picture 7: Now the moment has come. Jo approaches the horse in the Magic Circle. She quietly sorts out the rope and waits. That is exactly the right thing to do. Leave yourself time and maintain calmness. Collect yourself, and above all, feel the energy of the horse.

Picture 8: Quietly and with an upright posture, Jo now signals to the horse that it should

give way. It is important that it all happens with plenty of inner relaxation and with an inner and outer smile. With time, Jo will learn to keep her shoulders lower and more relaxed. Then the horse will not swish his tail as he is doing here. Horses react to everything – simply everything!

Picture 9: A confrontation is starting here. The horse is not standing straight in front of

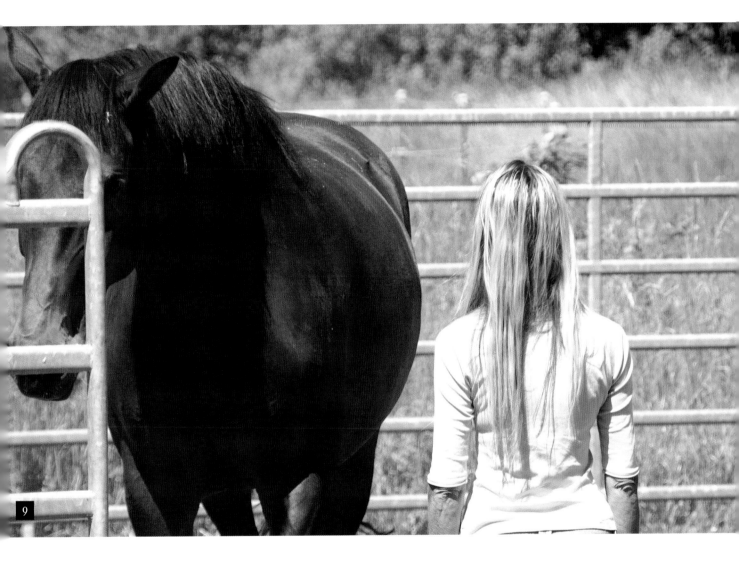

9

Jo and his expression seems rather questioning. Here, it is a matter of complete inner confidence, quietly demarcating your own vital circle, matter-of-factly and gently, waiting for the right moment, and then, with inner joy, giving your horse a clear signal to yield. How much can you learn in situations like this – if you are open to it?

How fragile and vulnerable Jo seems on this picture, in front of the being that she wants to impress, persuade and, in the end, lead gently. We can all only grow beyond ourselves inside – with a horse this is not an option, but the only possible way.

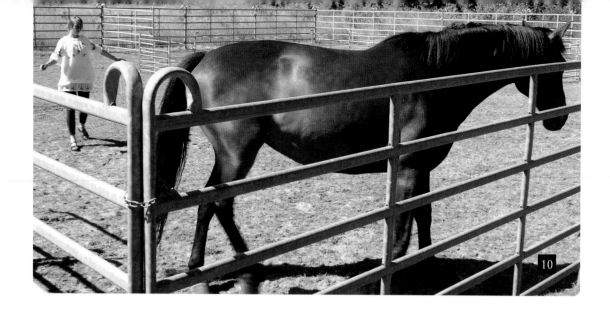

Pictures 10 and 11: Two similar situations are depicted here, and in both the horse reacts gently, and in principle, willingly. In the bottom picture, Hilary is very grounded and her overall position is stable. Only the left hand signals a little uncertainty to the horse. That is why he 'asks again'. Over time, these gestures can be refined more and more and improved utilising the horse's reactions.

In picture 10 the posture is basically grounded, clear and gentle but she could be more upright. The position of the head, above all, is slightly questioning and unsure. Also in situations like this it is important that the person steps far behind horse. Here it could be appropriate for the person to take another step to the left, from where we are standing, i.e. in the direction of the fence, to open up the path more clearly for the horse.

Pictures 12 to 14: Here, Alexandra, the owner, is working with her horse. We can see, especially in the second picture that the horse is still a little 'grumpy' in her reaction. That is related to past experience. Here it is important that you clearly understand why a horse shows this kind of reaction. On the whole, Alexandra is clear and gentle in her work in these pictures, but in the first two pictures, we can recognise a tendency to be pushy and demanding. The horse associates just that with memories from the past and reacts accordingly. You can see this more clearly in the third picture, there the distance is right, the shoulders are low – only the arms are a little too high and that is why they appear pushy. However, the horse is now very relaxed and quiet on the whole.

Body language
and biopositive riding

72

Riding – the basics

My approach is to build up the riding lesson in the following stages:

1. The rider's seat at rest.
2. The rider's seat during slow movement, paying particular attention to the movement dynamics, 'sitting in the movement' (in-balance).
3. Feeling the horse's movements, his legs and his rhythm in walk.
4. Halting and getting the horse to walk on using only body language signals and without using the reins at all.
5. Changing direction as a result of balance and body signals (cross-balance).
6. The rider's seat at trot and canter on a circle.
7. The path to riding that benefits the horse is now open and you can keep following it using the basic principles and skills that we have just given.

Now let us take a bird's-eye view of these things as a whole.

My world of riding

Principle 1:
Riding, dream and inner images

Everything that we have said, done and discussed thus far can be transferred to riding, one-to-one. As an introduction to our final topic, *Body language and biopositive riding*, I want to try to go into the fundamental experience of riding as a whole. I invite you to follow me into my world of riding. I would like to present it to you as a whole to begin with, before we turn to the individual areas and details again.

The pictorial world of the imagination is very important for me personally. According to modern research, the majority of our life is actually controlled by images, primarily subconscious images. All forms of contemplation, meditation and relaxation are actually based on the power of inner pictures and the world of imagination. It was not for nothing that the world of dreams, as a purely pictorial world of imagination, was so important for our ancestors. Inner pictures have an effect – there is no question about that. However, the question is whether or not we want to influence these pictures and their effect.

REMEMBER THE RAILWAY WORKER?

In my book *Dancing with Horses*, I recounted the story of a railway worker who was locked in a refrigerated carriage overnight and froze to death. In the morning, the man was found with all of the symptoms of having frozen to death. However, the real drama was that the refrigerated carriage was not working at all because of a defect. It was summer and the temperature in the refrigerated carriage had not dropped below twenty degrees overnight. Yet the man died as a result of physical hypothermia. This example is far from a one-off. The idea of cold convinced the man that the cold and his subsequent death were real. He knew that you could not survive the night in a refrigerated carriage. That was what killed him.

Our modern world, in particular, is a world of images. In contrast to moments of contemplation and meditation, these images rush by us outside, leaving their impression in the subconscious. I wrote about this subject for my masters degree at the University of Cologne, almost ten years before I got involved with horses. I was interested in the power of pictures, primarily as a tool for manipulation and influence, for example in the spheres of advertising, politics and mass media. The fact is that any product usually does not depend purely on its inherent qualities, but on the image that people have of the product – the myth decides. Just think about cigarettes, cleaning products, cars and so on. Open an average bottle of wine at home and pour it into two different glasses. One should be elegant and high quality, one ordinary. Put two price tags in front of them – one low and one high. Then ask a few friends to taste the 'wines'.

You are likely to have similar results as I had as a student: Nine out of ten subjects will evaluate and prefer the apparently more expensive wine. I was even able to mislead recognised wine experts. What is so crazy is that the wine really does taste better; and the railway worker does die inside the warm refrigeration wagon. Our perception of reality is always a complex overall impression composed of many individual elements in our final perception, where the facts often play a subordinate role, and it is no different with riding. Yet, on the contrary, when we ride we are in a very specific area of life, because beneath us is no more and no less than the embodiment of all symbols and all myths.

The more conscious and authentic a person becomes throughout their life as a result of experience and inner growth processes, the more their experience is orientated to the real facts. In the same way that I encounter the 'real' horses, with their 'real' ways of behaving. Real meditation and real contemplation are actually the opposite of escaping from the world. They are an attempt to see the world as it really is, to take off the tinted glasses. I think that great confusion reigns on the meditation 'market' itself, i.e. where meditation is offered as a commodity, because it is another world of 'glossy images' that affects us and often pretends to be something. Recall the first chapter of this book.

With horses, I am different from most people, closer and more direct, because I want more than anything to understand how they really are. The astonishing thing about it is that the world an authentic and conscious person sees is more real, but at the same time much more fantastic. Not one image of the world can approximate the magnificence of the real world. No romanticised image of a horse can match up to its reality, because only the real world merges in the conscious human being with the world of dreams. There is hardly anything more complex than the experience of sitting on an ever-wild animal. Only, how close do we allow this extremely complex, deeply natural and therefore real experience come to us? Or how many mechanical things do we squeeze in between?

SHAPING SOMETHING POSITIVE WITH POWERFUL ENERGIES

The railway worker could have turned the events around. There are many fantastic stories of children, animals and even drunk people who have survived life-threatening situations. I mention these together, because a drunken person no longer holds on to pictures, even in a very dangerous situation. In this case, as with animals and children, the body's survival instincts can run undisturbed by negative influences, in hopefully the best case scenario. Start by imagining that the railway worker had instead been locked in a working refrigerated carriage. Conscious work with positive images could conceivably have had the exact opposite effect. He could possibly have survived those powerful energies by using the mental images that actually killed him, that 'suggested' to him that he would freeze to death. Does that seem like an exaggeration? Allow me, modestly, to report on an incident of my own, a documented case.

Around four winters ago, I capsized in a small boat on the bitterly cold Baltic Sea — a situation where somebody might actually only remain conscious for a maximum of three to four minutes.

I stayed in the water for around 15 minutes without losing consciousness, and for a further 40 minutes at extremely low temperatures, completely soaked through, on a tiny island in a stormy wind. I managed to get a woman ashore — she had only been in the water for three minutes and eventually almost lost consciousness. To get both of us out of this deadly situation, I had to go back into the water to get the boat, which was now drifting far out, and again for the paddles, before I could bring us to safe shores.

The woman showed all of the signs of deadly hypothermia — her whole body was dark blue and she was shivering. Personally I was just a little red — that was all. In this situation, I did exactly what I always do when faced with horses like Phaeton and Naranjero, because these situations are also life-threatening. To a certain degree, I was, and am 'used' to it. While in the water I did not, even for a second, give a thought to the picture of apparent death or to the danger, but to the unshakable awareness of smoothly and easily completing a task to its end. Despite wearing fur boots and a fur jacket, I managed to swim without difficulty, because I had the image of a swimming man in my head, as clear as crystal, just as I had trained the principles in my exercises for decades. I had the image in my head of reaching the tiny island, getting the boat and bringing the woman and myself safely to land. I had a crystal clear, unshakable image of survival in my mind. I actually did not freeze, nor did I even feel cold, or catch a cold.

What is your reality of your life? What is your reality of your riding? My reality in the ice cold Baltic Sea was the fact that my life could not, and should not, yet come to an end. My reality was the fact that, as a wonderful part of creation, we humans have no limits to what we can do. My reality was the fact that everything is possible for fate — even allowing me to survive for 15 minutes in freezing water, completely unharmed and fully conscious. My reality was the belief, and the belief is like a dream, and the dream shapes the world.

YOU CANNOT 'LEARN' RIDING. YOU CAN ONLY KEEP DREAMING ABOUT AND EXPERIENCING RIDING

I want to tell you about images of riding like this, about such dreams that are taken straight from reality. That dream that I dreamed around twenty years ago, namely the one where I am dancing with a black horse, came true in many different respects. It became the title of my first book and has since then become part of my reality. I hope that, by now, many new pictures have also become reality in you. However, riding is nothing more than activating pictures. Riding is the image of a world in which images can be realised unhindered, because they are as real as our dreams themselves. Do you follow the pictures of people that guided your childhood? Then you will actually still be affected by these people in reality. Do you follow the pictures that caused you anxiety? Do you follow the pictures that showed the stereotypes of an outward and alienated world? Or do you allow yourself to dream and to believe in the inner freedom of

your dreams, so that they can eventually come true? Then you can set off on your way to authentically riding a horse. You only need to dream it – in the middle of the day.

You are beginning a long path that will lead you endlessly forward. A kind of dream path that you cannot see, but that you have to find your way back to.

What is special about this path? Wherever you are on the path – everything is whole, everything is there, everything is complete and valid. Even at the very beginning. There is steady growth and steady change there. However, the amount of quality and sensation is the same –

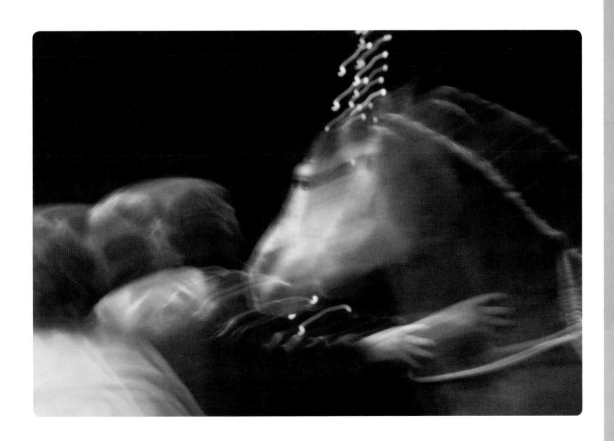

After the battle
Original graphic
K.F. Hempfling

always the same level. It is the path of life – of constant birth and death.

Principle 2:
The birth of movement

'Roll on the ground, roll on the horse, roll with the horse.'

This strange sentence describes an important experience for me. The picture shows a drawing that was created quite incidentally years ago. In it, I wanted to express this very energy. Walking begins as the crawling, rolling movements of an infant. However, it becomes clumsy and stiff if the basic thought of rolling and flowing gets lost as the years go by. A person's walk can make them appear old or young. Stiff, ponderous and bent – this kind of walk is attributed to an old person. A young person whose movement is temporarily impaired because of injury or illness will quickly say that they feel like an old person, and they will really give off this impression. My body exercise principles are therefore especially

based on the importance of this never-ending, rolling, soft and flowing form of movement.

The phenomenon of posture comes from softness and the image of rolling. I will talk about this in the next section. I have something else to add here. For me, the path from rolling and crawling to walking is a preliminary to riding that, when everything is taken together, represents a kind of circle. If you run now, you should always feel the youthfulness and roundness of rolling within you. When you get on the horse, this experience should still be in you, even when the horse finally walks on. The effect on the horse and the togetherness with him, as I look for it, is essentially an uninterrupted rolling movement. It never stops and never starts. That is why the horse does not feel overwhelmed by a signal. He is together with you in an uninterrupted 'rolling' flow.

Think about the paragraph above. First it is a question of the images that you have inside you.

The creation of
movement
*Original drawing
K.F. Hempfling*

What kind of image do you have of yourself, of your appearance and age, and how they correlate? The image that you have within you will always have a deciding influence on the reality. Rolling, flowing, crawling, walking, stepping, dancing, riding – a cohesive original experience whose principles we do not even have to learn. They are already in us.

Principle 3:
Solidity and posture

Some of you will still remember Twiggy – the first ultra-thin model. I met Monique, a friend and colleague of Twiggy, once in Spain. At our first meeting, the now older lady said to me:

'My dear Mr Hempfling, you only walk with your hips. Your upper body is always completely composed. What do you do for a living? I had to practise for a long time, to even get a hint of this posture.'

I actually think that it is of fundamental importance to maintain the small child's way of moving, where all of the leg movements are absorbed by the buffer of the hips. What is the most remarkable thing? Stiffness is usually expressed by the whole body 'rocking' so to speak and being affected by every movement.

Rolling softness and the idea of physical 'flow' will put us into a position where we can allow movements that are exactly appropriate and which can be directly 'requested'. As a result, my upper body can be kept completely relaxed and poised when walking, running, dancing and riding – so that it looks balanced and upright as an overall picture. This image of 'attractive' walking is often almost caricatured today in models. Yet how gracefully do members of communities and peoples that still live naturally move? Grace, softness, elegance and dignity always go hand in hand with inner and physical posture, 'uprightness'. If that is not observed in day-to-day life,

how is it supposed to appear in the horse? Here we have to remember what was once definitely in each of us – posture and uprightness – without a horse to begin with. No path leads past the origins within us – I cannot convey ridden posture to anyone who does not have it 'on the ground'.

Pictures 1 to 3: Upright posture, the ability to 'control' individual elements of the body separately from one another, is an important requirement for clear communication with horses. It is an essential basic condition for riding. I actually think that it is of fundamental importance to

1

2

maintain a way of moving, like a small child, where all of the leg movements are absorbed by the buffer of the hips. Rolling softness and the idea of physical 'flow' will put us in a position where we can allow movements that are exactly appropriate and can be directly requested. As a result, my upper body can be kept completely relaxed and poised when walking, running, dancing and riding – so that it looks balanced and upright as an overall picture.

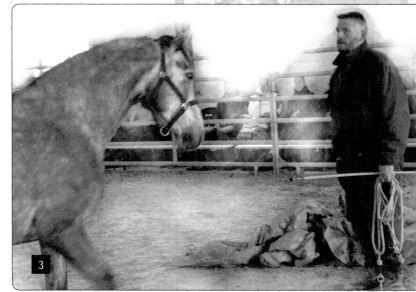

3

Pictures 4 and 5: When a picture from the series with Rico was chosen for the title, it was precisely because a posture becomes clear that is both soft and flexible, upright and complete. Riding essentially means taking a person who has been prepared in this way and putting them on a horse. If this preparation is missing, then it cannot be made up for, especially on the horse. It is an essential preparation for riding!

Pictures 6 and 7: It is essential that you recall positions and posture by yourself, and with the help of teachers and advisors whom you trust, and that you change and improve them to benefit your whole life.

Picture 8: Finding a natural position and a natural posture and uprightness on the back of a horse is the first and most important riding exercise at my events. Once this foundation has been laid, together with exercises from the sphere of body awareness, everything else can flow and develop almost spontaneously. This 'recalling' and remembering is so important. I am spending a lot of time on this topic in this chapter, because it will later determine riding almost 100%. The earlier pictures of riding were taken of me when I had been riding for just a few weeks! I did not learn to ride, but I spent years pondering and practicing the upright posture.

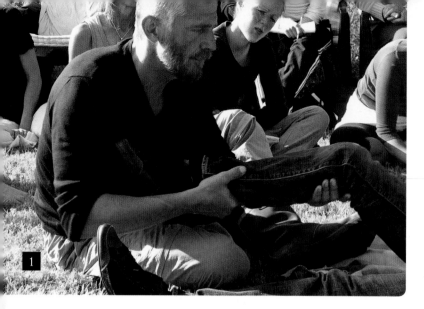

1

BODY AWARENESS PREVIEW

Riding is a highly spiritual as well as highly physically activity. This appears to have been forgotten. Here I would like to mention a few more keywords on the subject of body awareness.

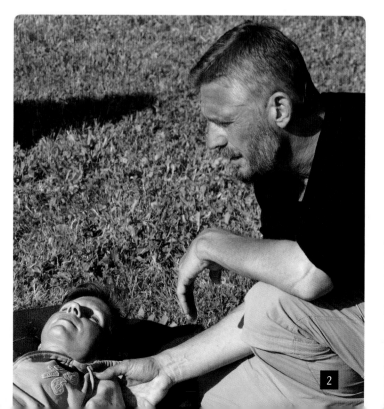

2

Let us look at the following pictures from practical teaching experience:

Pictures 1 to 3: Becoming aware and relaxation are at the beginning. During the initial exercises and support, I try to familiarise the participants with profound awareness of the phenomenon of relaxation and conscious body action. Without this basis, which each person can naturally adopt in their own unique way, nothing can work when riding. Find your way to relaxation and find your way back into your body.

Pictures 4 to 7: My exercises are actually very simple. The aim is an open and upright person. I always use the natural range of motion as a point of departure for humans as well. My examples are people that move naturally and the way children move. In my opinion, everything else is rather damaging in the end. It may look spectacular but when it comes down to it, it is not helpful, but weakening. I cannot allow that in my interaction with horses. It simply has to 'work'.

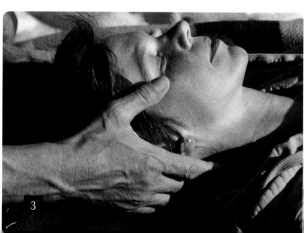

3

5

6

4

7

Here I am working at an event with a long stick. You can develop excellent sequences of activities from it that always help the person to be upright, and at the same time convey a clear sense of the individual movements. It is fun, so you will definitely want to repeat it and that should always be the case.

Pictures 11 and 12: Alternating with other exercises and games, I keep coming back to the basic posture of the person in my seminars. When doing so, nothing may be forced. Everything happens softly, with lots of information and help from the teacher. However,

Pictures 8 to 10: Ideally, the body should always know, by itself, why it does something. That is why I try, under all circumstances, to remove everything abstract from body work.

you can read the participants' experience on their faces: deep relaxation, the feeling of being centred and grounded. The eyes are looking towards an imaginary horizon and the head is held straight over the spinal column. With the sense of your bodyweight as seven parts down and three parts high. The feet are as far apart as the shoulders are wide. The pelvis is light and tipped under naturally so that the spinal column is as upright and straight as possible. Everything feels light and correct.

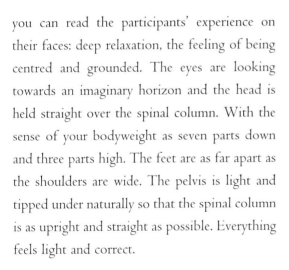

Picture 13: Here is an exercise for you: Klaudia has the task of moving her leg slightly, but keeping her arm very relaxed. I gently move her arm and ask her to keep it quite relaxed. As soon as she stiffens or moves her arm, I help her with a brief comment and appropriately soft movements. Try it yourself with a friend or partner.

Principle 4:
Sitting in the movement

I will also go into this point in more detail later on. This is where we are in the list of principles – when riding, a kind of natural dynamic results from posture and uprightness that helps to avoid a basic error, namely falling behind the horse's movement. That happens in most cases. The rider is then not with the horse, not in the movement nor in the communication, but always at least a little behind. They are then always 'a little too late'. We will deal with this crucial topic very intensively at the end of the chapter.

In our ancestors' world, the horse was only ever intended for people who had proven themselves in other areas and could strengthen their personality. Being allowed to ride a horse was a sign of a high level of inner development. Don't we find a great deal of truth in what our ancestors said?

Principle 5:
Riding is like walking

It sounds trivial, but in the end with the last of my five formulas, I have solved every riding problem that I have encountered, because in cases of doubt, I have dismounted from the horse and made the movement sequences quite clear to myself by walking on foot. Riding is like walking, jogging and running. All natural mechanisms can be transferred one-to-one. The art of riding, in my opinion, consists of never turning it into an art. Riding is nature – and affected by its laws and requirements. We will also deal with this important topic in great detail at the end of this chapter. But first I want to continue with our 'fly-past' and get a bird's eye view of the subject. Then the details will eventually make more sense and be easier to categorise and understand.

Riding – a gigantic iceberg

Look at the 'iceberg of riding'. Only a little tip pokes out of the water – a tiny amount compared to the part we cannot see. As I see it, riding is the smallest part.

The 'iceberg of riding' –
the visible fruit

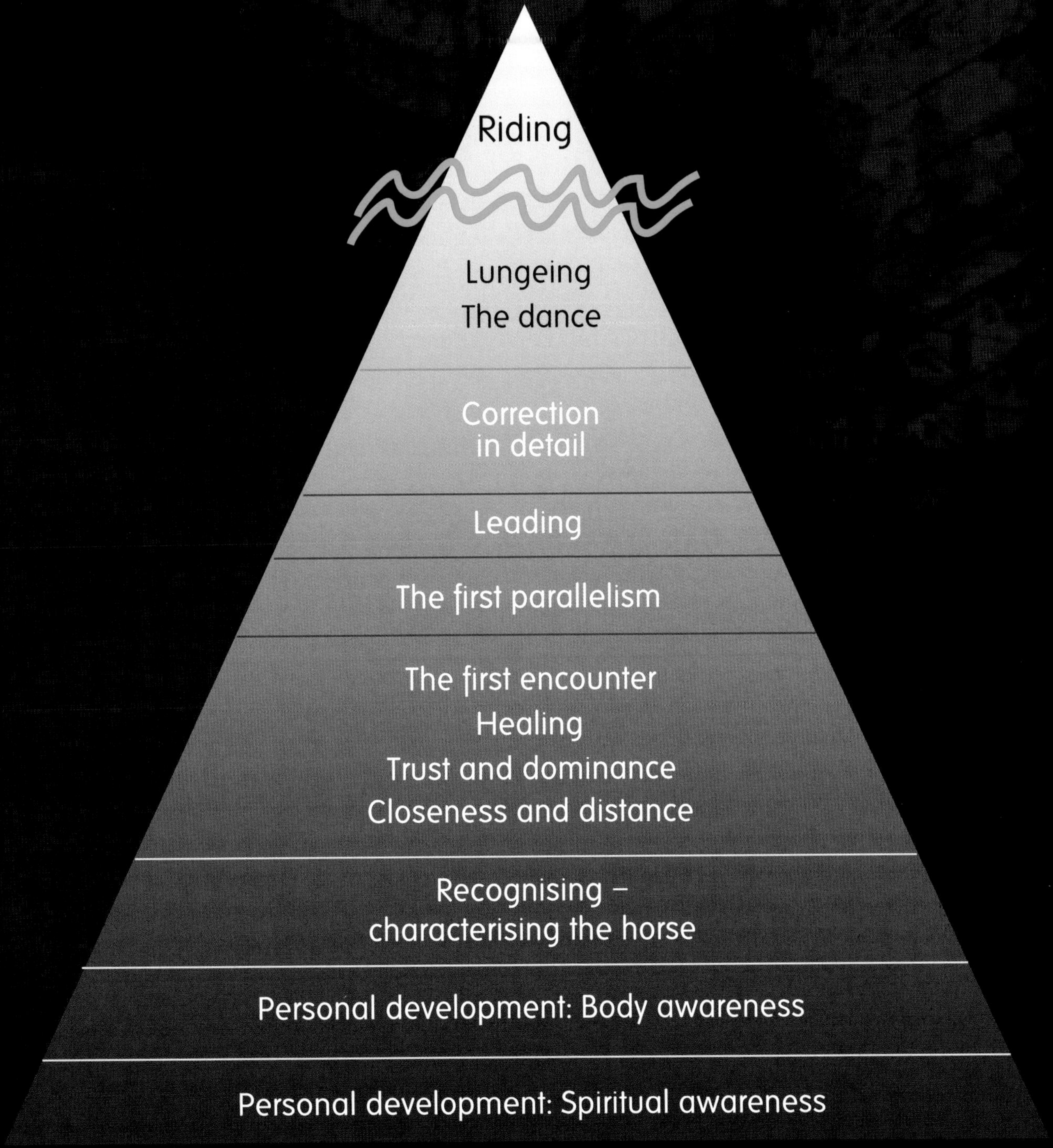

Riding

Lungeing
The dance

Correction
in detail

Leading

The first parallelism

The first encounter
Healing
Trust and dominance
Closeness and distance

Recognising –
characterising the horse

Personal development: Body awareness

Personal development: Spiritual awareness

How the pictures compare

In reality, everything is almost the same, whether on or next to the horse. We often see riders who appear to be moving securely on the horse, but hardly seem to have any control over events from the ground or when loading their horse. However, the signs are actually similar. In reality, these are both a coherent whole, inseparable from each other. You can see this very clearly in the pictures below. The physical expression of the woman and the expression of the horse are as if copied, both scenes are different parts of a single, complex event.

Problems on the ground and misunderstandings are either transferred quite clearly and visibly to riding or are hidden in one way or another. But they are always there! I have never met a horse – human pair that was an exception to this. It is true that many riders come to me and say, that every once in a while, they find it hard to control their horse from the ground, but when they are riding everything is quite different and comparatively easy.

On investigation, I have never been able to confirm this – quite the opposite. In an exact

These scenes can also be seen in the video clip Wounded Horses Can't Cry.

analysis of the situation, I have usually established that the riding situation was actually rather more problematic. How do these kinds of misjudgements occur?

Let us have a look:

- The instruments of external power that the rider has at their disposal are considerably greater than those of the person on the ground. The violence when the reins are pulled, and naturally, the intolerable pain that results, are accurately estimated by very few riders. Horses cannot audibly express their pain; they can only suffer and cry inside. A smack with the whip is painful but nothing compared to the permanent impact when a curb is pulled, or from tight reins.

- The method of choice of the rider is unfortunately too often a 'lazy compromise' that is usually not recognised. Namely, the rider secretly senses where the boundaries of their apparent control actually are. They know that they had better not approach the object of fear. They know that they should not ride along a certain road, or better, should not even leave the safety of the arena. They know that they had better not let the horse gallop a certain way, and avoid a certain field with other horses. However, if an unexpected moment arises, then hardly any riders are really aware of the risk on the horse. The accident reports that I often come across in my career tell a clearly horrible story.

In reality, to correct behaviour on the ground is essential. Then you can get on an unridden horse and have the feeling that it has already been ridden very well for years. That is my concept.

Translation, formula and code – or nature?

Let us look at a person on foot, a person driving a car and a person riding. When we are walking, moving as naturally as possible, like a child for example, then every sensory impression, every perception and also every thought will be more or less clearly shown and expressed in our body at the same time. We will possibly then become a little more upright or a little more crouched, a little quicker or move differently in some other way. If I am out on a walk and I see something interesting to my left, I will adjust my walk and my outer physical posture automatically to these inner processes.

That is not the case with the motorist. Quite the opposite – this kind of reaction could be very dangerous for them. There is always a kind of translation between the motorist's perceptions and a possible simultaneous or delayed change in driving behaviour of the vehicle. There is always a code that underlies the technical device. A translation into a different, technical language is always required. After years of practice this happens very quickly, indeed almost automatically, but it is and will always be a translation, a conversion from perception into a different technical dimension. Correspondingly, the degree of implementation will always be limited. Outside observers will be able to interpret almost every movement of a pedestrian, but the even movement of a car does not usually betray the perceptions and the emotional condition of the driver – or if it does, it is only in an extreme situation that is almost always dangerous, when they are drunk, for example.

Looking at the many different riders from around the world, I have usually found exactly the same thing – a kind of translation into another, reduced dimension. In principle, this does not change from rider to rider, but only in the form of the style of riding. That is, as if one were travelling in a train, the other in a car and the third in an aeroplane. Many do the same using different 'technical transport vehicles'.

The woman on the Lipizzaner does just that. She reacts to the problems with her horse practically by translating in this way. As if in a car, she tries to take control using the gear stick and using technical instruments. Yet the horse does not have these methods of translation programmed within as it is indeed a natural being, and a rider can only transfer these technical mechanisms onto the horse through dressage training.

As I see it, dressage training is therefore the attempt to make a functioning device out of a natural being.

It all fails in our picture – just as dressage training must always fail at a certain point. Namely at the point when you have crossed your boundaries. Then the person moves as if in an airless space. In the same way that pure technology, a brake for example, would fail. Here 'technology' fails. The woman trusts the reins and spurs and forgets all of the options for communicating with other beings in a natural way that she would have using her body and body language. The result is misunderstanding, pain and fighting.

No time for physical – mental moulding?

For a long time, the horse was military equipment in our world – a 'vehicle' for soldiers and no longer an independent being that carried fighters and hunters. Wars become more 'equipment intensive', technical devices, masses of people and horses were sacrificed on battlefields. It became important from the point of view of the military that both people and horses hurried through as quick a 'training' as possible, i.e. became of less and less value, so that they could then be easily sacrificed. There was no time for a deep, physical, sensual and spiritual moulding. Unfortunately, this historical approach still affects many areas of dealing with horses today, even if it can no longer be recognised in its external form.

In addition, the horse in its significance as a 'holy being' of our forefathers was banned by the Christian-Roman occupiers. Consequently the horse was pushed further and further into the role of a technical appliance – to this day horses are used as sports equipment, leisure equipment and as objects of prestige and gambling.

The pictures show me with Janosch – with no bridle, saddle or neck strap, in a precarious situation. Janosch was one of the most intelligent horses that I have ever met, and he was hugely sensitive. He knew exactly how explosive the situation was. Here, dressage training no longer counts; there is only pure physical communication. The horse did not want to go through a

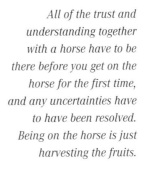

All of the trust and understanding together with a horse have to be there before you get on the horse for the first time, and any uncertainties have to have been resolved. Being on the horse is just harvesting the fruits.

319

dried-up stream bed, but it was on our way. There was a real 'discussion', because the horse always has the freedom to 'discuss' with me, to tell me his wishes and needs.

I can only keep the horse in place through my body's signals (see video clip *Amazing Bridle-less Riding*). But is this situation dangerous because of that? No – not at all, because even if I give in to the horse, I would still have it completely under 'control' again even right next to the apparent danger. What am I getting at? That all of the questions of insecurity, becoming acquainted, trust and understanding when interacting with a horse must come before you first get on the horse – before riding, because only then can they be really treated and answered. Being on the horse is just harvesting the fruits. On the horse, you can no longer thoroughly heal and no longer thoroughly correct.

An unreachable expectation?

Because there is no level of technical translation between the horse and myself, when everything is right, it means for me, that i must let go of any rules that correspond to this translation. I therefore had to find a more direct language, one that was naturally in both of us: in me as a person, and at the same time, in my horse.

The picture shows a horse with an endlessly soft, sympathetic and understanding expression in his eyes. The horse is with me. I am apparently not quite clear at this moment. I have, as

so often, reached a new boundary. I am seeking, searching and perhaps also unsure. However, I have not been left alone with it – the horse, the PRE stallion Almendro, is with me. From his expression, I can read that he is by my side, that he understands me and empathises with me – that he wants to help me.

In detail I may be unsure and have to find new ways, or take unfamiliar steps, however, on the whole I am connected. Despite the moment of inner searching or inner weakness, I am still on target. I am searching – but with my horse.

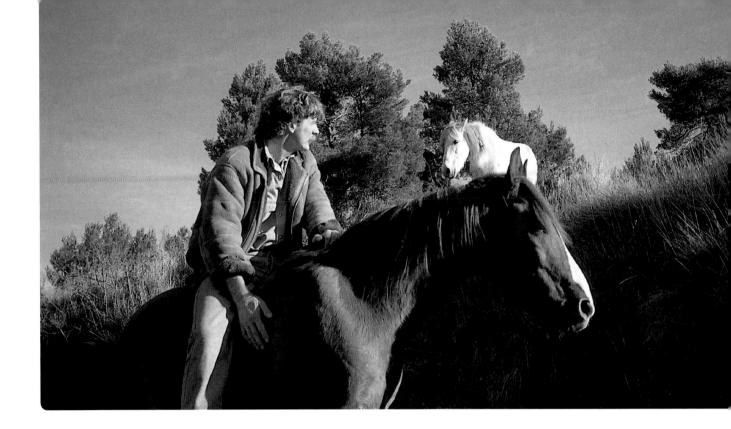

I lose my way, but am carried by my horse and his co-operation, his input and his understanding. For me, that is the most important thing — that I never lose this connection that I have gained so attentively by being on the ground.

Then, for all our mistakes and weaknesses, we can constantly move on the path of harmony.

Essential agreement –
agreement of the essence

This series of pictures show different moments of riding, as well as different connections to the horse's mouth — namely, no connection, a halter, and connection with a curb and a loosely held rein. However, I would like to draw your attention to the respective expressions of the person and the horse, because they both express the same thing with their body language. Right down to the position of the head. Please compare the pictures again.

Look at the top picture — the turn of both heads, the position of the heads, the position of the neck and body. Everything is parallel, everything is the same and everything is one. A coincidence?

321

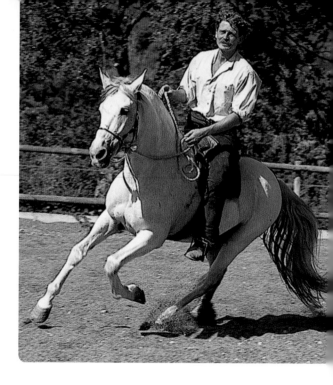

In this picture (right) the turn and position of the head are the same, and the body posture and shape are the same. Even the eyes seem to have the same expression.

The bottom picture: both are absolutely congruent here too — the observant posture of the head, neck and shoulders of the rider and horse. They are the same in all pictures. I have not selected the pictures from hundreds. I have just selected the ones that you can find in the video clips *Horse Dream* and *Art of Riding*. No dimension of 'translation', just harmony in body, feeling and soul.

Without convention?

The pictures on this page again show the similarity in expression and shape between person and horse. Just look at the third picture. The rider has a young stallion under him and is sitting cautiously. Both are going through the same experience and show the same feeling in their body language.

And look at the first picture. The gaze of the rider and the horse are both directed into the distance — both see the same, think the same, want the same and feel the same.

Let us stay with this picture and come back to the concept of decisiveness. We have discussed it in relation to leading a horse. I have shown how a horse can be held between the spiritual arms of the leader. You can see that in these pictures, but now I am sitting on the horse. This decisiveness then leads to body language and signalling that do not follow set rules, but simply the natural rhythm of the momentary movement, without any 'translation'.

Let us interpret the pictures again: the top picture shows me with Janosch. You really cannot claim that I am sitting on the horse in any kind of 'classical posture'. In this sense, nothing seems to be 'right', yet in fact everything is 'right', everything is harmonious. My posture does not correspond to a single riding style in the world, yet you can see how close together man and horse are, and how much they understand each other in all phases of their being.

For me, that is direct riding without translation. The expression on both sides is one of decisiveness. My decisiveness is transferred directly to the horse.

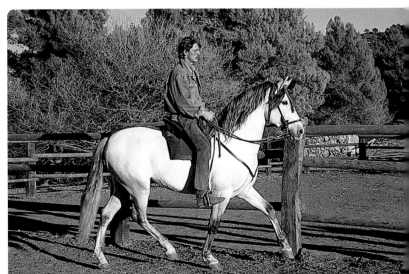

The key aspects of biopositive weight and posture aids

Now let us turn to the details: the video clip *Art of Riding* gives an overview of the individual stages. In my view, riding is reduced to a few key aspects that I will describe and summarise here again, and that I would like to explain in detail using the following pictures and drawings.

I have called the following 'in-balance': the rider's balance is in the movement of the horse. Pictures 1 to 3 show three ways of being in balance. Picture 1 shows a relaxed, natural seat. The rider's pelvis is loose and slightly tipped in a natural way, so that they can then sit upright. The aspect of the rider sitting absolutely in the movement of the horse is crucial. This is fundamental! It is one of the first steps that I want to convey to students. In my eyes, being in balance forms the basis of all riding. You can recognise the correct balance of the rider, in that practically no movements by the horse, even if they are sudden and unexpected, cause the rider's upper body to rock backwards or forwards. (See video clips: *Horse Dream* and *Riding in the Herd*.) Throughout my entire career, I have only seen a handful of riders, including professionals, who possess this most important aspect of riding. By far the largest group of all riders are behind the horse's movement, because of their seat. The majority of show jumpers do that, even though they sit on the horse with the upper body forwards.

Picture 2 shows me riding a piaffe. Here, my upper body is a little further forward, in order to stay with the movement of the horse in this exercise and to keep the horse in place without any rein aids. These fine nuances are determined by being 'in-balance'.

Picture 3 shows me in a rather unusual position, responding directly to the horse's balance with my upper body. You can see two things: on the one hand, the overall impression of the person and the horse is harmonious. On the other hand, you can see that my upper body is relatively far back. You can clearly see how much the tilted pelvis and the inside leg, which is wrapped around the horse's body, activates the horse's inside hindleg. Despite the slightly backward upper body, the rider is sitting absolutely in the horse's balance. That is a photographic snapshot. Immediately before and after this moment, I am sitting on the horse again in a normal position, as in the first picture. This vertical balance on the horse, the option of always staying in the movement of the horse by slightly changing the upper body around the optimum seat is, as I understand it, the basis for communicating with the horse through body language.

*In my eyes:
everything else
requires dressage training
or mechanical aids.*

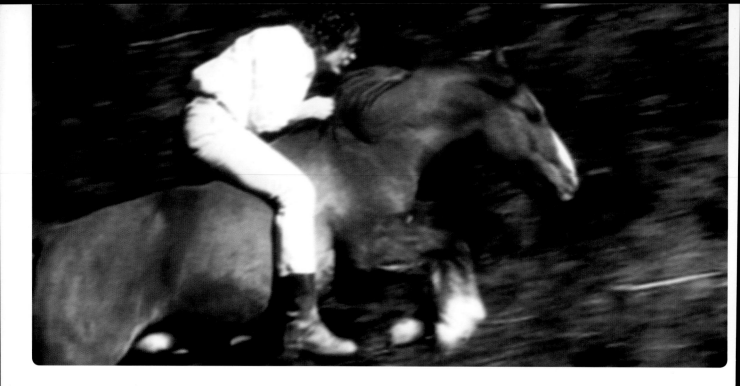

The two bottom pictures also show this 'in-balance' very well – the rider's seat in and with the horse's movement.

This can easily be seen in the jumping movement in the top picture. Even very experienced riders and professionals who have an 'in-balance' lesson are very surprised at the end at how different this experience feels while on the horse and how the horse adapts to the rider's body signals, directly and without any support. They often seem to be just tiny moments, yet there are worlds between them in the rider's perception. It is actually a different riding experience. You can only try it out. Please look at the pictures and try to feel what is behind them and these descriptions.

The drawings 1 to 4 help us to understand the principle of 'in-balance' better. Drawings 1 and 2 show riders who are in the horse's movement. Each change in tempo can now be directly balanced by firmness, dynamic and balance. Rider and horse are as one in the direction of movement.

In the second drawing, the upper body seems a little stiff and we can see a slight tendency to be behind the movement. I am describing it in such minute detail, because it really is so delicate.

Yet just think about walking. We maintain an absolutely fine balance, automatically, from childhood. Even minimal changes cause postural and balance problems.

When riding we sit even higher over the balance centre of gravity. So everything has to be even more finely balanced.

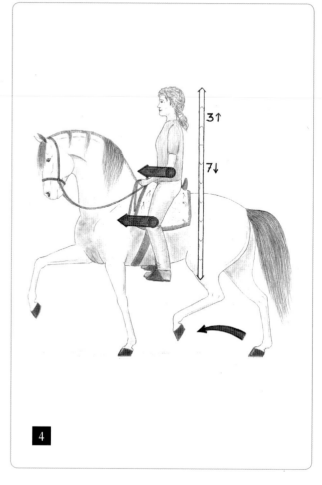

Drawing 3 shows how it should not be, but often is. Most of the energy goes up, the rider is not grounded, not in the horse and not 'in-balance'. The upper body rocks back and forth almost constantly and the horse is automatically forced onto his forehand. The hands on the reins are still much too high and the horse is steered and stopped using the reins. Regardless of how many of these riding lessons you have, nothing will improve, even after years. The basis is simply completely wrong.

Drawing 4 shows us again how it can and should be. The shoulders are relaxed and low. The rider sits deep in the saddle and in the movement. The hands on the reins are relaxed and very low. The legs hang long and gently against the horse's body. The movement dynamics of horse and rider are in harmony – person and horse are as one.

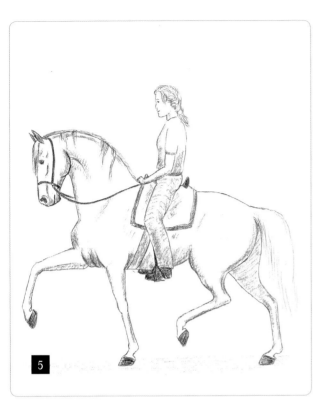

5

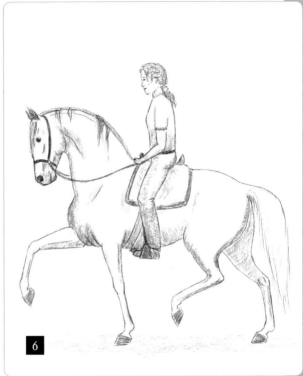

6

Drawings 5 and 6 show us positions that may be taken once for a few moments to give the horse a brief weight aid. However, these examples are not suitable postures on the horse. In drawing 5, the rider is clearly behind the movement of the horse and the entire upper body is bent.

In drawing 6, the rider is in front of the movement in a cramped posture. The horse would then immediately fall out of the balanced movement.

For me, it is fundamentally important to tackle life's challenges with as few demands as possible and that applies to riding in particular. For me, biopositive riding is like a roof resting on a few pillars, where everything is very clear and we can focus on continually strengthening these few pillars.

We now come to what I call 'cross-balance'. Regarding this point, I agree in principle with all of the riding schools in the world, namely that the rider's shoulder must, under all circumstances, be on the axis of the horse's shoulder. Unfortunately, this theory is rarely learnt, taught or conveyed in reality. Cross-balance corresponds to our normal posture when walking and running. However, if the first point of 'in-balance' has been felt and physically 'understood', then this aspect is easier to feel and put into practice. You can see a correct example in the following sketch and in the picture that is shown afterwards. You can see that the line of the rider's shoulder is parallel to the horse's shoulder – in all riding situations – really all!

The three drawings bottom right of a rider at canter also show how it should and should not be. Everything is correct in the first coloured picture. In the second, the shoulders lean inwards and the pelvis outwards. The outside leg is rather stretched away from the horse and the inside leg clamps and pushes. The third picture shows the opposite. The rider is thrown outwards and therefore loses their cross-balance.

We come to an image on page 333 that shows and unifies everything at once. I have tried to cover myself with arrows in this way so that everything eventually fits into a picture. The result was the 10 most important points of riding – from my point of view.

1. The rider's slant corresponds to the horse's slant. The rider is neither pushed inward nor outward. As a result, he can keep the horse exactly on the line even in the volte and make himself very clearly understood in the turn, without reins. The seat is firm and merges with the horse's back.

2. The axis of the rider's shoulder is at a right angle to line 1. Whatever movements the horse or rider makes, this right-angular relationship will remain unchanged.

3. Hips, upper body and head turn in the direction of movement so that the rider's body and gaze point straight in the direction of the path to be taken.

4. Through the rotation (3) of the body in the bend, the respective inside leg automatically lifts from the horse's body and frees up the path into the bend.

5. Through the rotation (3) of the body in the turn, the respective outside leg gets closer, automatically, to the horse's body and directs it into the turn.

6. The rider's weight is shifted inwards and the inside shoulder stays at the same height, but the inside hip sinks in the direction of the movement. The distance from the inside hip to the shoulder is now greater in comparison with that of the outside hip to

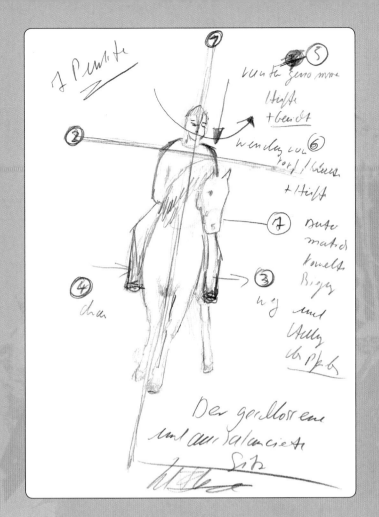

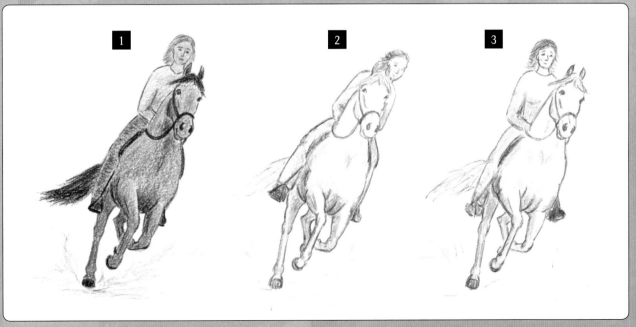

the shoulder. All this also happens when we make a turn on foot. When riding, we just have to make this unconscious process conscious again. Then we can create clear and unambiguous information for the horse so that he can follow this impulse directly.

7. The horse's head and body organically follow the rider's weight aids and bend evenly into the turn. In so doing, the horse remains completely in balance, because it is not thrown out of balance by disruptive movements of the rider or the reins. The result is complete harmony of both beings, which now perform as one. Communication through body language and balance replace any force and any inorganic 'commands'.

8. The respective outside hand moves closer to the horse's neck because of the rotation of the body. This causes the outside rein to touch the horse's neck. This also gently shapes the horse's bend and balance.

9. The rider's inside hand automatically moves away from the horse's neck because of the rotation of the body. This gesture is understood by the horse as a guiding signal. Initially the rider, as we can see on the photograph, can further amplify this effect and let his inside hand move further away from the body in the direction of movement. Normally both hands stay close together.

10. All of the signals mentioned above are made completely precise by the correct 'in-balance'. Now horse and rider have merged together into an organic unit of movement. These principles should now be transferred to all gaits and a constantly relaxed seat should be achieved.

When I ride, I personally do not feel as if I am burdening the horse with my weight, but that the horse is stuck to me, as if I were pulling it on like a magnet.

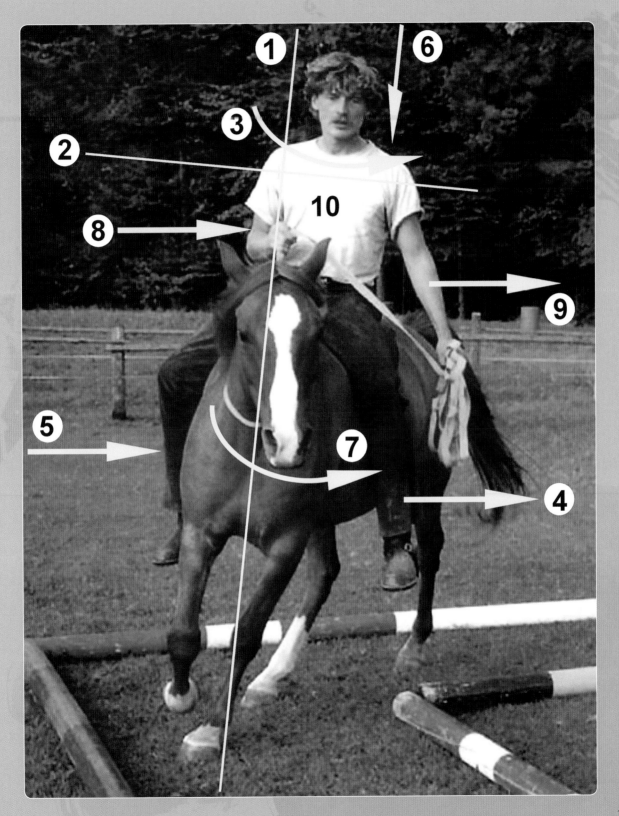

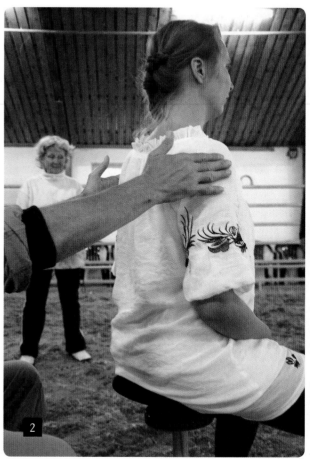

Here we can see how to practice on the ground what has just been shown in co-operation with the horse. We can clearly see how Alexandra lowers her inside hip but keeps the inside shoulder at the same height. Only awareness of these movements will put us in a position to transfer them into riding.

A chair with a seat that moves to all sides is great for practising these principles and making them tangible. Picture 2 shows how I am trying to convey the feeling of a straight shoulder for a course participant using this kind of chair. Take a look in the mirror — some people carry themselves with their shoulders at different heights, even in a normal position. This is not a problem if you approach the exercises in a laid-back way in order to solve them softly and organically and 're-mould' yourself to a certain extent.

Picture 4 shows Jo after this kind of correction. Her seat is now splendidly straight, upright and in perfect balance on the chair. Your task is now to feel your way into this posture in order to find your way back to it more quickly and organically. This posture will soon become an automatic part of our being – also when riding.

Picture 3 shows Jo in the next exercise. Here, it is about keeping the shoulders at the same height in the direction of movement and tilting the inner pelvis down, shifting all of the weight in the direction of movement, and at the same time, keeping a straight axis to the ground.

Anything that we achieve mentally and physically in the areas discussed here has a direct effect on being with horses – as well as enormously positive effects in all areas of our life.

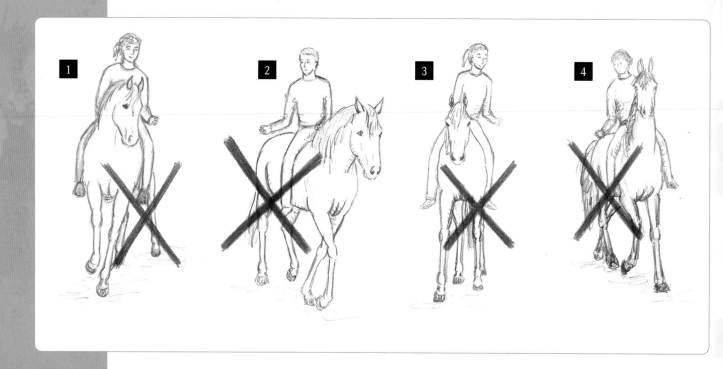

Now we have eight examples of how it should not be, but often is. These pictures show different errors in variations and combinations, because I would like you to really know what you have to pay attention to.

1. The inner shoulder is too low. The rider slips slightly to the outside. The head tilts to the side – on the whole, the posture seems hunched. So, shoulders at the same height, move the weight inward, move the inside hip down, keep the head straight, turn into the bend, and overall, be pleasant and open.

2. The rider lowers the inside shoulder too much. Althouth he lowers the inside hip, he slips to the outside instead of keeping the weight to the inside overall. The arm that is showing the way should always be relaxed and held as close to the body as possible.

3. Here the rider really tries to move her weight inwards but her upper body has now moved much too far to the inside.

4. The rider's weight is to the inside, the inside hip lowered, but the upper body turns too far to the inside and the inside shoulder is too low.

5. The weight is also to the inside here and the shoulders are at the same height, but the upper body is very tense and bent to the inside.

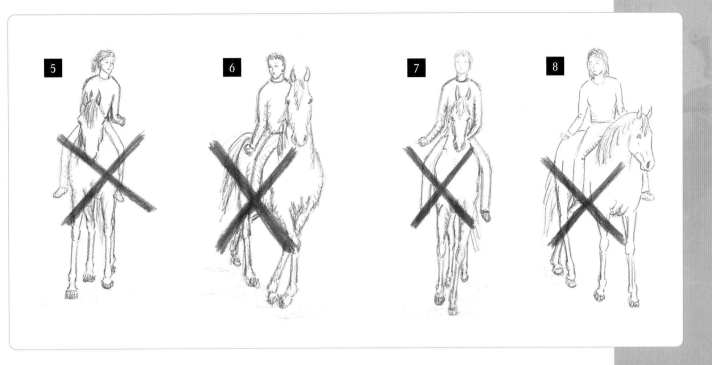

6. It is not bad at all here. The rider is sitting upright but his inside shoulder is too low and he is still slightly buckled at the hip.

7. The rider wants to turn to the right, but does not turn in this direction. As a result there are no correct aids and the horse does not understand him.

8. The rider's weight has moved inwards on the whole. However, the shoulder is too low here and the inner pelvis is not tilted downwards enough.

The principles of my kind of riding are too simple for many people. However, beauty never shows itself in complexity, and neither does depth. With this sentence, at the very end of my book, I would like to emphasise again the extraordinary power of simplicity.

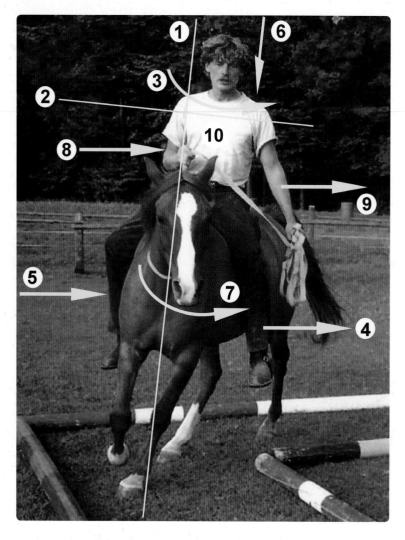

3. Hips, upper body and head turn in the direction of the movement.

4. Because of the rotation (3) of the body into the bend, the respective inside leg automatically moves away from the horse's body.

5. Because of the rotation (3) of the body into the bend, the respective outside leg automatically moves a little closer to the horse's body.

6. The rider's weight is shifted inwards, the inside shoulder stays at the same height, but the inside hip sinks in the direction of movement.

7. The horse's head and body organically follow the rider's weight aids and bend evenly into the turn.

8. The respective outside hand moves closer to the horse's neck because of the rotation of the body.

HERE IS ANOTHER OVERVIEW OF HOW
IT SHOULD BE:

1. The rider's bend corresponds to the horse's bend.

2. The centre line of the rider's shoulder is at a right angle to line 1.

9. The rider's inside hand automatically and organically moves away from the horse's neck because of the rotation of the body.

10. All of the signals mentioned above are made completely precise to a maximum through the correct balance.

Fascinating shoal of fish

The following concludes this chapter:

I love to think about a powerful shoal of fish, how they move as a whole, as if each of the thousand fish knew, at that precise moment, which direction was right. In reality, if a single fish turns, all of the other fish do the same. That is also how I experience a human being. If something changes in them, then everything else changes too. If they are happy about something, then all of their expressions will radiate happiness. If something annoys them or depresses them, then this will be reflected in everything. Only a small switch has to be flicked — for good or for bad. Isn't that fascinating?

What if...?

A colourful mix of possibilities – certainly not exhaustive, but you might find the answer to your question here:

- YESTERDAY EVERYTHING WAS GREAT – TODAY IT IS NOT. Take a break, do something else. Sometimes, don't do anything for a few days. Consider whether you have been asking for too much. Was there anything that was unfair to the horse? Have we moved too fast? Learning is not linear – just give yourself and the horse some creative 'downtime'.

- THE HORSE SEEMS TIRED. CHANGE OF FEED? WEATHER? Problems with field mates? Does the horse keep problems bottled up? Am I holding him too rigidly with my body – do I just need to be more relaxed? Is the horse getting enough hard feed? A grass-kept horse, even if it is not being worked, needs oats for its digestion. As a rough guide 150 to 300g of oats per 100kg of bodyweight of a horse in light to medium work. Even a little Shetland pony that is actually just kept at grass should get one to two handfuls of oats a day. Avoid sugar beet pulp and other by-products. It is better to feed fresh hard feed like whole sugar beet and carrots. Make sure that there is little, if any, molasses in the cube or cereal feeds – it makes horses very tired. Is your horse getting enough salt? Please only use pure salt licks for horses, because of false mineral additives in other licks. Do not give too much mineral feed – you should only feed 20 per cent of what the manufacturer recommends. Keep changing the mineral feed – i.e. do not always feed the same brand. Are there too many flies and other pests in the field? If in doubt, turn the horse out at night and leave him in the stable in the day. Is your horse bored? Is he jealous of another horse? Parasites? Insufficient water – is the water supply unsatisfactory?

- MY HORSE SUDDENLY DOES NOT LIKE ME ANY MORE. If he does not come to you as normal or greets you grumpily, then you should first establish whether he is healthy, in pain or has digestive problems etc. Asked too much? Are you grumpy? Have you been unfair to your horse? It sounds crazy, but sometimes this can happen if you are wearing a new and strange scent – a new perfume, a new soap – I have seen that before. Has somebody else been getting to your horse? This is often the case because the horse then transfers the unkind treatment to you. Pay attention to who approaches your horse. It may be better to prevent anyone from going into your stable with your horse. Happy medium: find the cause and then, if in doubt, take another break. Taking a break can often be very beneficial, alongside tackling the cause.

- THE HORSE SUDDENLY LOSES CONCENTRATION. Here, you should consider much of what has been said above – as well as this: are you just too quick, do you give too much information? Make sure that your body language is clear, and in particular, make sure that there are breaks and highlights in your work. Most people 'chatter' too much with their body, causing the horse simply to switch off. Make sure that the programme is varied, alongside phases where your horse can get into the rhythm. Always make lungeing exercises varied (see the work with Queijo). Above all, avoid asking too much. Keep to the point and stay focused. Look for beauty and joy in the present and never train the horse for an uncertain tomorrow.

- YOUR HORSE SUDDENLY SHOWS SIGNS OF AGGRESSION. Again, keep in mind what has been said above and this: you should always take signs like this very seriously, and try to eliminate them under all circumstances! What is your mood? Are there traces of aggression in you? Do you have unresolved problems of your own? Are you fair? Were you angry? Too often insecure and undecided? Do you let your horse get too close? Did you rush him? Find the causes in all of these cases and take a break for a few days or more. Has somebody else treated your horse roughly? Is your horse becoming increasingly dominant and you cannot deal with it? Then keep coming back to basic exercises. Begin again with simple exercises. Concentrate on clear leading. Occasionally stand and stay near your horse. Occasionally keep your horse at a distance. Make sure that your body language is very quiet and relaxed – pay particular attention to having low shoulders. For a while, do not look at your horse straight in the eyes too frequently. Pay attention to your arms – do you hold them too high too often? Do you wave the rope or whip about too much around your horse? Reduce the signals. Does the horse come too close to you when lungeing? Then many of you quickly show signs of aggression. Send it back to the circle in a friendly, yet clear and consistent manner.

Concluding thoughts

At an event in Denmark, a middle-aged woman, an artist, brought her horse to me. He looked alert and was standing boldly next to the woman. She wanted to jump right on and show us everything she could do.

'Stop, stop', I shouted 'not so fast – the horse is actually completely exhausted.'

The rider looked at me in surprise and complete disbelief, and there were murmurs in the audience. An older lady finally stood up and said:

'Klaus, I follow you in just about everything, but now I am lost. This horse is the liveliest of all the horses that we have seen so far.'

I listened inside myself and could not feel anything else – the horse was totally exhausted. What should be done? I asked everyone to be patient and told the rider that she should just stand there and not do anything under any circumstances.

'Okay', she said.

The horse, who was in this arena for the first time, went to her after a little hesitation, but then quickly turned away, immediately walked to a different corner of the arena, lay flat on the ground and fell asleep, snoring deeply. He lay there for two hours. Many people could not believe what they were seeing and some could not hold back the tears.

I obviously saw and felt something that other people could not see or feel. What was the most difficult thing for me about doing something like that? Learning? Becoming sensitive? No, the most difficult thing for me was believing in it myself and following this belief, representing it and trusting it, recognising that the symbolic and the mythical actually exist in us and have an effect.

The word myth, derived from the Greek, actually means 'the true word'. The language refers to an inner relationship that people today can no longer or no longer want to recognise, namely that reality, the 'true word' can only be found in myths, in the relation and connection to an often invisible original cause and origin.

When people today turn to certain brand products, is this not the search for a lost myth? Footwear and clothing of certain brands – is the myth that is apparently inherent not transferred to the wearer, giving them something that cannot be expressed in words but that only lives in images and myths? Product pirates — isn't that exactly what they are stealing? Don't they take the myth of a brand and apply it to any other product, for the same effect? Because the brand — the modern myth of our material times — is often more than the actual value of the product.

The paradox: our world of commodities has absolved itself from all of the original myths. It not only questions their inner value, but does away with them completely. But it cannot get by without the new mythical creations. However much we may want to free ourselves from myths and symbols, we cannot, because our inner reality will not allow us to, as long as we exist. That is why I chose the path of remembering the real myths, becoming aware of them again, to stop myself from falling for the replacement myths. And that is how I came to horses.

For me, it was never just about riding a horse.

Suggested reading

Hempfling, Klaus Ferdinand:
Dancing with Horses
J.A. Allen & Co Ltd, 2001;
Trafalgar Square Books, 2001

Hempfling, Klaus Ferdinand:
What Horses Reveal
J.A. Allen & Co Ltd, 200;
Trafalgar Square Books, 2004

Hempfling, Klaus Ferdinand:
Frau und Pferd -
Tanzen zwischen den Welten.
München: Goldmann, 2001

Hempfling, Klaus Ferdinand:
Die Botschaft der Pferde
Stuttgart: Franckh-Kosmos, 1995

www.hempfling.com

For praise or criticism of the new book please visit:
www.the-horse-seeks-me.com

The following video clips, which were mentioned in the book, can be seen at www.youtube.com:

Connecting with shy Arabian Horse • The Art of Lungeing • Art of Riding • Calming Spooky Arabian Horse • Borderline Demonstration • Aggressive Stallion Tamed • Amazing Bridle-less Riding • Dancing with Horses • His Powerful, Gentle Leading • Breeding Stallion Harmón Reborn • Collecting a Stallion at Liberty • Riding in the Herd • Rearing Breeding Stallion at Ease • Bonding With Beautiful Horse • Wounded Horses Can't Cry • Horse Dream